Video Intervention Therapy

This book offers a comprehensive guide to using video intervention in psychotherapy or mental health coaching. A video is made of a patient interacting with someone else. The patient and the therapist then explore it together, profiting from its rich information.

Downing clearly elaborates each step of such an intervention. Numerous possible techniques are described. If and when to bring in more such sessions is explained. How, in couple or family therapy, to use such work is covered as well.

The book is designed so that any therapist or mental health coach can begin with video intervention at once. This is invaluable reading for anyone wanting to start in and build up their expertise with this significant contribution to therapeutic work.

George Downing, PhD, worked for years as a psychologist in Child Psychiatry at Pitié-Salpêtrière University Hospital, Paris. He has taught video intervention therapy for clinical teams at the New School for Social Research, New York; Heidelberg University, Saarland University, and Ludwig Maximilian University of Munich, Germany; the University of Basel, Switzerland; the Universities of Milan and Bologna, Italy; and the University of Girona, Spain.

Video Intervention Therapy

Help in Psychotherapy for Relationships

George Downing

Routledge
Taylor & Francis Group

LONDON AND NEW YORK

Designed cover image: Getty Image © VW Pics

First published 2026
by Routledge
4 Park Square, Milton Park, Abingdon, Oxon OX14 4RN

and by Routledge
605 Third Avenue, New York, NY 10158

Routledge is an imprint of the Taylor & Francis Group, an informa business

British Library Cataloguing-in-Publication Data
A catalogue record for this book is available from the British Library

ISBN: 978-1-041-02972-4 (hbk)
ISBN: 978-1-041-02447-7 (pbk)
ISBN: 978-1-003-62166-9 (ebk)

DOI: 10.4324/9781003621669

Typeset in Optima
by KnowledgeWorks Global Ltd.

To the late Michele Beverina

Contents

Introduction

This book is about the use of video intervention in therapy. A short video is filmed of two or more persons interacting. It might be a parent and child, it might be an adult couple, it might be two child peers or siblings. Both persons, or perhaps one of them, then look at the video together with the therapist. What can be done? There is a lot which can be done, a number of options.

Video intervention is easy to learn, fortunately. This book is designed specifically for that. If you are already a mental health professional, what you will find here will be enough to let you add work with video to what you already do. The book covers the basics. And it gives practical tips on how to get started.

It is divided into four sections: Section 1, comprising Chapters 1–3, spells out overall information. When in a therapy should you first intervene with video? How should the video work be coordinated with the rest of the treatment? How many video sessions will likely be appropriate?

What are the options regarding who films an intervention video, for example, you yourself, the patient themselves, or someone else?

What are the options regarding who the video interaction participants should be? What are the options about what they should do together, and why? How long should the video be? And then what if a patient, hearing the proposal to work with video, feels too uncomfortable and wants to refuse? How should you respond?

Section 2, comprising Chapters 4–11, covers the details of work with a video in a session. A number of techniques are described, and examples given of their use. How to structure such a session is explained, along with what is different when a session is online.

Included too, in Chapter 10, is the important topic of what can be done if a patient has suffered severe trauma in the past, and if this history seems to be having effects on the interaction in the video.

Section 3, in Chapters 12–16, covers how you yourself can get started, should you so wish, with using video intervention in your own work setting. A series of suggestions are given. A practical program, spelling out what to try first and what to go to next, etc. is described. It is a way to begin which a good many persons have tried out, and they report to be helpful and user-friendly. Also in Section 3 is a chapter on other video intervention methods (Chapter 13).

Before closing this introduction, it would be good to explain some background. This concerns my own professional journey and how I came to do video intervention.

The therapy method which initially most appealed to me is what, today, is called body psychotherapy. I practiced it, got to know it, and later down the line began to teach and supervise it. Over time (to make a long story short) I developed my own version, done within a cognitive-behavioral therapy framework.[1] It is a methodology which is now used often in psychiatric contexts, among other settings.

But much as I appreciated this approach, at a certain point I had to confront a limitation. Many patients, along with other goals, want to change how they interact with others. There is a massive problem here, however. It is that we cannot see ourselves from the outside.

We cannot see all the complexities of what we are doing with our bodies in an interaction. True, we hear our words, we hear our voice, we feel some movements and posture shifts. But this is only a part, a limited part.

Body psychotherapy can assist of course. Patients learn better how to sense the body from the inside. A therapist can also give feedback about what they observe a patient doing. Nevertheless, both these aids only go so far. So, what else could be added? How might a patient gain a more fine-grained, detailed understanding of how they shape their body in an interaction, of how they use their body?

It was this issue which pushed me to consider video intervention. I had already encountered a couple of existing forms of it.[2] The idea appealed. I decided to experiment. Since I was working at that point in a special psychiatric service for parent-infant dyads, I had plenty of opportunity to try the notion out.

The results were pleasing, but I soon realized that when it came to observing interaction videos there was so much more I could usefully learn. I was lucky enough to have friends who could help here, by chance. These were researchers (Beatrice Beebe, Howard Steele, Miriam Steele, Ed Tronick) who were using video to study how parents and infants interact with one another. They trained my eyes and ears at a level I would never have thought possible. (About these friends I say more in Acknowledgements.)

The result, over time, was I became hooked. I had already found video intervention productive, but now it became fascinating. And its clinical usefulness remained undeniable. In a strong majority of cases, for a patient to witness themselves with the video lens was an instant help.

Are video intervention and body psychotherapy then two separate methods? For myself, no. They mix impeccably. With a video a patient can see themselves from outside, with body techniques better feel themselves from inside.

Nevertheless, in the practical world of therapy training it turns out easier to teach these two methods separately. Each has its own intricacy, its own details, its own atmosphere. Over time I came to accept this, and, in my professional teaching life, learned to wear two hats.

This book reflects what I teach wearing my video intervention hat. It will not surprise you, however, that echoes of body psychotherapy slip in here and there. You can now understand the reason why.

Notes

1 Downing, 2015a, Heller, 2012, Morlinghus, 2012.
2 See Chapter 15.

Acknowledgments

To form the perspective shared in this book has been a journey. On the way I have had so much input and support from others. Regretfully, here I can mention only a few.

Four close friends, Beatrice Beebe, Howard and Miriam Steele, and Ed Tronick, all researchers using video, have taught me an endless amount: both about how to look at videos and how to think about therapy implications. The late Daniel Stern gave a similar help.

Valuable as well have been exchanges with Maria Aarts, Kristie and John Brandt, Antonella Brighi, Elisabeth Fivaz-Depeursinge, Antoine Guedeney, Alexander Harrison, Michel Heller, Mechthild Papoušek, Philippe Rochat, and Alessandra Sansavini. Thanks as well to Lana Dumas for so much aid with the book preparation.

Numerous video intervention therapy (VIT) colleagues have widened my understanding of this work. Among others, I am grateful to Karen Buckwalter, Laura Caetani, Andrea Dixius, Cristina Riva Crugnola, Sergio Facchini, Terry Falcone, Adelaide Garguito, Margarita Ibanez, Marcello Longo, Eva Möhler, Marc Pérez-Burriel, Marcel Raas, Corinna Reck, Marta Sadurní, and Fernando Lacasa Saludas. Many VIT patients have also made me take in the wide range of what video intervention can bring about.

Above all, I thank the person who has walked with me through the whole forest, my gifted wife Carole Gammer.

1 How and when to begin with video sessions

When to start? At what point in a treatment should you introduce video intervention?

In most therapy contexts this can be quite early, though I will soon mention exceptions. There are several strong reasons to begin soon as possible, moreover, when feasible.

One is that a first clinical video often provides important new information which affects our understanding of a case. Normally the therapist will already have met one or more times with the family or couple. (By "family" here I include the possibility that coming to the therapy is only a parent, e.g., the mother of an infant.) Tentative goals will have been determined. Any more formal assessments will have been carried out, for example, using questionnaires, or tests for a child. An initial case conceptualization will have taken shape.

But a clinical video almost inevitably yields new insights. What are this family's or couple's interactional strengths? What are their weaknesses? The video will reveal the details in a way nothing else can.

Frequently, too, with respect to a child, new clues will become evident concerning his level of development: his social capacities, concentration ability, practical language use, and the like. Obviously, it makes sense to profit from such information as soon as possible, given that nothing stands against an early start.

A second reason is that a clinical video can be highly motivating. When a family or couple first see themselves on video, and when the therapist leads them into this experience in the right supportive manner (about which more later), they typically react with a heightened interest in change.

With the therapist's help they will have identified a number of positive elements in the interaction: they can thus see for themselves that they possess capabilities. If a discussion has also emerged of one or more new behaviors which could be cultivated, these new behaviors will feel to them unmysterious, clearly defined, and concrete. (With a first clinical video the therapeutic conversation may or may not go this far. How this decision is made will be explained soon.)

DOI: 10.4324/9781003621669-1

A third reason, in an institutional setting, concerns team communication and sharing. Teams frequently struggle to coordinate their perspectives: the primary therapist has one way of thinking, and a particular vocabulary for it; the art therapist another way, and so on. Lillas and Turnbull (2009) have described this dilemma well. When a team can, on occasion, look jointly at excerpts from one or more clinical videos (with, of course, the permission of the patient or patients), usually a more coherent shared focus will quickly be found.

Some institutions even use video as one part of the initial assessment itself. For example, an evaluation procedure such as that of Rosanne Clark (1986) includes the filming of parent-child interaction as a standard part. Naturally, in this instance, it is simple enough to use the same video for a first intervention.

I might mention, by the way, that concerning assessment, that is, the original assessment before a first video is made, some teams using video intervention therapy (VIT) find it fruitful to include the Adult Attachment Interview (AAI) among the instruments they use. As Steele and Steele (2008) have pointed out, at a certain level of detail the AAI can highlight potential clinical issues quite useful for the therapist to have in mind. Given the VIT emphasis upon attachment issues, this can serve as a natural complement.

Initial Case Conceptualization and Decisions About the Role of Video

A typical beginning of treatment unfolds as follows:

1 An initial diagnosis and assessment is made.
2 Treatment goals are negotiated, and a tentative case conceptualization formed.
3 Based upon the case conceptualization, the team or therapist plans how intervention with video can best fit into the overall treatment.
4 Decided, too, is when to start with video intervention.

    The usual choice is to begin with right away. But at times a delay is necessary. There may be an immediate crisis, for example, a suicide attempt. Or a patient's motivation for the therapy in general may be so low that this must be addressed before anything else. Factors of this nature may dictate a certain period of prior work before video intervention can be considered.

    A few institutions, due to the nature of treatment they do, regularly postpone a use of video until other goals have been reached. A substance abuse treatment center will wait until detoxification has been accomplished. A program for the parents of premature infants might begin with counseling during the time the infant is in the neonate unit, but then conduct the first video intervention only on the day of discharge (i.e., at corrected age zero), or soon after that.
5 Based as well on the treatment goals, decisions are made about the specifics concerning the first video: what to film, where, and so on. Normally

these choices are made so as to support the highest priority treatment goal or goals.

6 The video is filmed and then subsequently, perhaps one to several days later, used for an intervention.

Making the Video

Video intervention can be done with any grouping: for example, both parents and a child, two siblings with each other, a couple, and so on. However, what serves best for treatment purposes is a video of these persons and them alone. Ideally, neither the therapist nor other staff will be present in the video.

One first explains to a patient (or patients) the rationale for making a video, and wins their agreement. A natural moment to do this immediately after the initial treatment goals have been agreed upon. The therapist now explains how intervention with video can provide a significant help with respect to one or more of these goals.

For many people, this first proposal is sufficient. They hear how video intervention functions, they hear the reasons for it, and they are ready to try. They may express a sense of awkwardness or embarrassment about the prospect of sitting with the therapist and looking at themselves in the video, but their grasp of the advantages outweighs any reluctance. In addition, the younger the patient – an adult or older child patient, I mean – the more at ease they are likely to feel with the idea of other persons seeing filmed images of themselves, this being an everyday part of their social universe.

But it is not that way for everyone. As you can imagine, it can also happen that a patient balks at the notion of using video in the therapy. So, what then? In this case there are a number of steps the therapist can take: ways to discuss and to explain, as well as ways to explore what a patient sees as obstacles. Most of the time an effort of this kind will bring them on board, perhaps at once, perhaps after a waiting period. This important subject will taken up in Chapter 2.

Next, assuming the patient has consented, a series of collaborative decisions are made about the practical details: who will carry out the filming, where it will be done, and such.

Who Will Film, and Where?

A basic choice is whether the video should be filmed in the institution, in the patients' home, or possibly elsewhere.

If it is done in the institution (or in a therapist's or counselor's private office), then the therapist or another staff member arranges everything. Perhaps the camera will be set on a tripod, or is already on a fixed mounting. Perhaps the therapist or staff colleague will shoot by hand. If, on the other hand, the filming is done at home, then typically it is the parent or couple who take it over, with some prior tips from the therapist.

What goes into this decision? In principle there are advantages and disadvantages to either solution.

When filming is done in the institution the biggest advantage is technical control. The therapist, after having done this a few times, will know the best distance at which to set or hold the camera. The lighting will be optimal for a video. There will be no television blaring away in the corner, interfering with audio reception.

The biggest disadvantage in the institution is the limitations regarding what kind of scenario can be filmed. Parent-child play? A couple discussing a theme? No problems here. But, a mother helping her older daughter with school homework? Possible, but harder to arrange. A father and mother trying to get their school-refusing young son out the door in the morning? Not possible at all.

Another obvious disadvantage is the additional cost of time for the therapist or whichever other staff member is responsible.

If filming is done at home, by a parent or couple, the practical arrangements are simple enough. Most often, the camera is placed on a tripod. Or, perhaps the father films the mother (and child) by hand, and then the mother films the father. Or a friend or relative may be recruited. Naturally, in home visiting programs the professional who goes regularly to the home can also be the one who takes over the filming. Generally speaking, with today's current equipment, the use of a camera is preferable, but filming with a phone can be an option when necessary.

The biggest advantage of home filming is the wide choice of scenarios. This is a significant plus. Father giving a bath to the infant? A family meal? Mother and the anorexic daughter in the kitchen preparing a family meal? It can be a definite help in the therapy to have so many options.

Another advantage is naturalness. Not that persons being filmed for a clinical video will ever feel completely natural; they will remain aware of the camera, a factor which will be discussed in a coming chapter.

All the same there are degrees. Many patients report that at home, the familiar setting puts them more at ease. The behaviors which emerge are more likely to be typical as well. Famously, children with behavioral and aggression problems often act sweet in a therapist's office, much to the exasperation of a parent who had counted on a demonstration of what is difficult at home. This is much less often the case when home filming is carried out.

An advantage, too, with some families or couples, is room for spontaneity and creativity. After having already done intervention sessions with one or two videos, some patients like to seize the moment when something they find of interest is happening: out comes the camera or the phone. One of the most interesting couple videos I have ever seen was filmed in a parked car. The couple had gotten into an argument while driving. They decided to pull over, attach the camera to the internal rear view mirror, put themselves into the back seat, and, with the camera now registering, continue the dispute.

This last example brings out another point, incidentally. When I say "at home," what this really means is somewhere in the patient's or patients' everyday world. Parents with a child will sometimes film in a supermarket, or a park, or at the school entrance, for example.

The chief disadvantage to home filming is the occasional loss of technical quality. If this happens, it will usually occur with the initial video. The therapist will have explained, for example, that it is best that the lighting be not too dim; that no source of extremely strong light (sunlight blazing through a window, for example) is just behind someone being filmed, and that any potentially competing audio noise, for example, a television, be shut off. Some patients, however, don't grasp the point of these recommendations at first, and bring in a video which is slightly marred with respect to one of these factors.

All the same, this is no serious obstacle, normally. A VIT therapist becomes adept at working with any sort of video, however flawed. Almost always it can be accomplished. And once a patient has experienced one or two sessions with video, they will better understand how the video can optimally be registered.

A second, small disadvantage is that arrangements must be made, and carried out, such that the therapist obtains a copy of the video sometime prior to the intervention session. The therapist needs to spend a short time alone with the video, planning for the session (as discussed in Chapter 3). The usual solution is that the video is sent electronically. Or a patient can simply drop it by.

Once in a while there can be the difficulty that a patient has no camera, nor a phone which can film. This will require trouble-shooting. Where can they borrow a camera or a phone? Normally an answer will be found, but it can be less than easy. (One team I supervised decided they would keep a camera on premises which could be lent out to patients. They quickly found out that this solution is not a practical one.)

What about filming with a phone? Here, too, there are trade-offs. As of the writing of this book, video cameras give superior quality. The resolution is better, and the image dimensions – the ratio of horizontal to vertical – are better.

On the other hand, using a phone is often more attractive to a patient, since most persons are so used to filming with one. Since a phone is always to hand, nothing special needs to be organized.

So the best thing is for the therapist to discuss these pros and cons with the patient, and to make whatever decision seems best to fit. For some patients, to start out with a phone gives a better chance to get things going. After working in the sessions with one or two videos they may be more ready to take the trouble with a camera (and even to obtain one if they don't already have it).

Spontaneous phone filming, by the way, is quite a different matter. It becomes an especially interesting option later down the line, once a patient has experienced a few intervention sessions and has built up a certain enthusiasm. On the spur of the moment, they may place a phone in a strategic spot, or into someone else's hand, and start the filming. Typically this is a patient who, by this time, has become quite knowing about what could be a useful behavior and/or interaction to capture on video. Incidentally, it is not only adults who might do this. Some adolescents become clever and creative about spontaneous filming.

What if the Therapy is Online?

Little changes in this case. Video intervention is easy to implement online. In some ways it is easier than other therapy modes.

One aspect can be more complicated, however. Special arrangements need to be made if you intend to have several persons present in the video session.

Suppose you are working with a couple. This is not hard to arrange. Either they can both sit together at home, looking a single computer screen. Or they can sit in front of separate computers. (They can even, if necessary, be in separate rooms. For that matter, they can even be in separate physical places – the wife in Paris and the husband in London. That such an arrangement becomes possible is, in fact, one curious advantage of online work.)

But suppose three or more persons will be there, in the session. Usually separate computers are easier in this case.

What about the filming of the video? Obviously, in an online therapy context the choices are reduced. Almost always it will have to be the patient, or patients, who themselves do the filming.

How Long a Video?

The usual recommended length for a clinical video is between 5 and 10 minutes. Many persons are surprised when they first hear how short in duration a typical video is. And in fact, with a therapist familiar with scanning analysis (the observation of the video for clinical purposes), it may even happen that in the session itself a still shorter segment will be viewed and discussed. This selected segment might be 2 or 3 minutes in length, for example.

Why so little? The answer is that an interaction video is usually very rich on a fine-grained level. A little turns out to be a lot. Even in so brief a segment the therapist will typically discover more therapy-relevant material than can reasonably be discussed in a single session.

On occasion a longer video is proposed due to a special context. A child of 2 years is currently eating next to nothing. Mealtimes have become a frightful battle between child and parents. A video of thirty minutes might in this instance be suggested. The greater length will allow the progressive stages of the escalation to be examined, an often-important perspective.

Other decisions include what to film, that is, what kind of scene, and who should be present. These choices depend upon case particulars. A 2-year-old being dressed? Two siblings cooperating on a task? A couple talking about their wishes for leisure time?

Various factors must be taken into account. Obviously desirable, when possible, is that the activity selected be likely to yield a maximum of information about a major problem area and/or symptom – in other words, that it be an activity which lies close to a high-priority treatment goal.

But even more important, for a first video, is that the patient feels comfortable with the scenario selected. What this means in practice is that, though open in principle to video intervention, a patient may be hesitant to accept the filming of a key problem domain.

For an initial video, this may be experienced as too revealing. A parent may be ashamed to show themselves trying to put a crying infant to bed, or show themselves caught in an argument with an adolescent son who denounces them with vicious language, or the like. These are raw slices of family life.

In that case, the solution is simple. An alternative scene is proposed. The first video, and perhaps even a second or third, can be simply of, for example, free play, or a meal, or a short discussion with a child of what took place at school today. These are activities which almost inevitably give information of value for the case.

And, although demanding enough, they will seem less daunting to a patient who feels a threat of embarrassment. Subsequently, after one or two experiences with a video of this nature, such a patient will almost always feel less nervous about allowing a more conflictual moment to be filmed.

Whatever the scene, the usual instructions are: "Do [activity X] just as you normally would do it." Naturally, what will then take place is not quite this. As already mentioned, a parent or couple member will be aware of the camera. They will try to function well, try, perhaps, to do things a little better than usual, despite cooperative intent. How could it be otherwise? In a similar vein a school-age child, or an adolescent, may attempt to act better than habitually.

This tendency creates few problems, fortunately. First, interactional patterns are deeply ingrained. One cannot slip out of them just like that. In by far the majority of videos, little of substance will be different from everyday behavior.

Second, the very fact that one or both parties are attempting to behave well, can itself be of therapeutic interest. To observe what occurs under such a condition is instructive. On the one hand, negative patterns usually show up anyway.

On the other, if one or more persons' behavior is substantially better than usual, then what created the difference? An inquiry can be made. What was it about the fact of being filmed which rendered more skillful action possible? And such questions naturally lead to further ones: what other ways could there be, with no camera around, to mobilize oneself in this more positive manner?

So, to sum up, in one fashion or another, a collaborative plan is formed for a first video. If it is the family or couple who organizes the filming, they will be given a few recommendations about how to go about it.

Arranged, as well, will be how the therapist can receive a copy sufficiently ahead of time, so that they can prepare themselves for the intervention in which the video will be used. In the Chapter 2, I take up how this preparation is undertaken.

2 When a patient is reluctant to work with video

Many patients, first hearing about the idea to make a video, are immediately willing. They find the usefulness apparent, and the therapist can proceed to concrete arrangements right away.

But not all: some patients, at first, have a more negative reaction.

"Thank you but no, not for me," is more or less their answer. So what happens then? How should the therapist respond?

There are number of good options at this point. I will first go over the most typical objections which patients express, and will describe, for each, what in video intervention therapy we call a "counterargument," that is, gentle persuasion from the therapist.

After that, I will explain further steps which can be taken if this initial conversation proves insufficient. More usually the "counterarguments" do the job. But when not, there are additional strategies which can be helpful.

The usual kinds of objection are four in number.

The Artificiality Objection

This is the concern that the filmed behavior in the video is likely to be un-real, unauthentic. As already mentioned, here is a worry shared by many persons, therapists included, when they first hear about the concept of video intervention.

Fortunately, it is easily answered. The basic point the therapist makes is that yes, on the one hand, knowing that the camera is running has an effect on almost everybody. But, on the other, the effect is normally small. More than enough of a person's usual behavior comes through anyway. The exceptions are few.

Here is a typical example of how the therapist can handle this objection. Alison is a 16-year-old girl with anorexia, about to enter a residential unit for eating disorders. Video intervention is regularly used in the program, chiefly during parental visits. At this moment she is meeting alone with a staff therapist.

Alison: Do I have to? Talk with my mom and dad while a video camera is running?

DOI: 10.4324/9781003621669-2

Therapist: It's not a required part of the treatment program, but it's one we have found extremely helpful. With family after family.

Alison: You don't know my mom and dad. They wouldn't be normal for a moment in front of a camera. All you would see is acting. I don't think I would be natural either.

Therapist: I understand what you're concerned about. Many people react this way when they hear about this part of the program. But what you will discover, almost certainly, is that once you and your parents start talking, most of your natural ways to be together will click in. That's just how it goes. We've seen this over and over.

Alison: But I'll be aware of the camera.

Therapist: Of course. And especially at the start. But you'll see. After a little you'll become much more focused on what everybody is saying, and what you think and feel about it, than on the camera.

Alison: Yes?

Therapist: It's what happens. In any case, when we look at the video together, I'll be asking about whether it seems to you typical of what normally goes on. If anything looks to you seriously different from usual, you'll let me know.

Alison: Okay. What's the next part of the program you want to tell me about?

Therapist: First, any other concerns about making a video?

Alison: No, not right now.

The Embarrassment Objection

Here, the patient feels awkward or embarrassed about the prospect of seeing themselves in the video. Note the counterargument the therapist gives. Karen is the mother of an 8-year-old girl referred for anxiety problems. (I will not say more about the girl's difficulties but will go straight to the objection issue.)

Karen: A video? Myself and my daughter in a video? I don't think I want to do that.

Therapist: What seems to you difficult about it?

Karen: The idea of looking at myself. It makes me nervous, and especially if I think of you and I looking together. I hate seeing myself on video.

Therapist: I can understand. For a lot of people it is a little strange in the beginning to see themselves on video. For me too. But what almost always happens is that this goes away in a few minutes once we start looking and talking.

Karen: I don't know.

Therapist: Your choice, of course. But believe me, these kinds of feeling rarely turn out to be a problem.

Karen: Okay, I'll give it a try. We'll see.

Therapist: I'm glad you're willing. It will be a definite help for our work together. Anything else you are uncomfortable about, concerning the video?

Karen: No.

Therapist: Then shall we talk about how the video can be made, the practical details?

Karen: We can do that.

The Criticism Objection

Here the fear is to be criticized by the therapist. Offhand, this might sound similar to the embarrassment objection, but the thoughts driving it are different. Sometimes the tone with which it is expressed will have an aggressive edge as well.

Several kinds of response to this objection are possible. Here is one. Roberta is a single mother whose 3-year-old son, Harry, has behavioral problems.

Roberta: Sorry, no way. No videos please. The other things you say we can do are all right with me, but this one, no.

Therapist: What do you not like about the idea?

Roberta: I don't like the idea of being criticized. Obviously, the point of filming something is so that you can use it to criticize me. Or?

Therapist: I wouldn't want to be criticized either, in your place. Who would? But the purpose is something quite different. It is to let you and me both find out more exactly what is happening with Harry when he interacts with you. We will see all the details, and think about them. This will give us more ideas about what seems to be coming along well in his development, and what we need to help him with. We know some things about all that already, but after the video we will know more.

Roberta: The idea is not so easy for me.

Therapist: Well, how important is it to you that Harry learn to respect boundaries better?

Roberta: I'm going nuts at home with these things.

Therapist: So, important? Very important even?

Roberta: Okay, maybe I need to try this. One time, anyway.

Therapist: Sounds good.

Of course, in the above example the plan will be that in the video session only the parent will be present, and not the child. But what if the video is to be of a parent and an older child, and the child is intended to be present in the session too? Or what if the video is to be of an adult couple?

Another type of response is needed then. For example, Martin and Sally are in couple therapy.

Martin: This I don't like, to tell the truth. Me and Sally in a video. Don't like, don't like. Anyway, you get to see plenty of our nuttiness right here in front of you, without some video.

Therapist: What is it you don't like?

Martin: All of it. I'll sit here, you'll play the thing, and you'll start telling me everything I'm doing wrong. It's like, you'll have the proof right there in the video.

Therapist: Sounds like you're afraid the video will be used to criticize you.

Martin: Exactly. You'll talk about all my errors, and Sally will too.

Therapist: Martin, that's not what will happen. We'll be doing something very different. For example, our first job with the video will be to look in detail at what each of you is doing which is helpful for the interaction. You have plenty of good skills already, skills for interaction and communication. And with the video you'll get a more exact picture of what those skills are. This is something important for our work.

Martin: Well, skills, easy to say, but pardon me if I'm skeptical. And then what about Sally?

Therapist: What about her? Are you nervous she will criticize you while we look at the video?

Martin: Hey, [turning to Sally] excuse me, Sally, if I say so, [turning to therapist] but you've seen already how we start in on each other. Not that I don't do it just as much, of course.

Therapist: Listen, Martin, what you're saying is absolutely right. To get a video in here and then use it as a way for you two to get hard on each other would be a bad idea.

Martin: Yeah.

Therapist: I agree. What you need to know is that sort of thing will be off-limits. For both of you and for me too. I will make sure our exchange stays constructive. This will be one of my responsibilities.

As I say, we'll use the video to focus on positive skills you two already have. That will be the start. And maybe we will do only this. Or, if you both decide you'd like also to look at, say, one thing it might be interesting to learn to do differently, then we can talk about that too. But only if you want to, and only in a constructive way. How does that sound?

Martin: I'm still skeptical. I'll give it a try, I guess, if Sally will. But what can I say, I have my doubts.

Therapist: I appreciate you being willing to give it a try. Sally, how does this all sound to you?

Notice that the therapist here has pointed out two distinctly different options for the session itself. One possibility is that only positive elements of the video will be highlighted. The other is that positive elements will be discussed initially, and then, if both couple members are willing, a negative pattern will be explored too. How one chooses between these options will be discussed at more length in coming chapters.

The Threat Objection

This objection one sees less often, in most treatment contexts anyway. It is the fear that the video will be used against the patient by someone external. One kind of worry is about, for example, child protective services, a judge, a parole officer. Another kind can surface when a couple is in a process of separation or divorce: for example, "My husband's lawyer might demand access to this video." Still another concern can be about social media: for example, "Could this video end up on You Tube?"

A patient showing this reaction may simply have a suspicious nature, but more often than not a degree of reality is involved. Certain patients have been around the bend with respect to social monitoring: three years ago they had one child taken into custody and now they fear losing a second one, for example. From this perspective, their anxiety that the video might circulate in ways they would find threatening is understandable. In addition, legal problems with divorce proceedings, or troubling experiences with social media, are not uncommon.

How should one respond? Before I explain that I need to say a word about the background issue. What if, in fact, there is a possibility that an external agency or legal entity (a judge, a lawyer) could, in principle, have access to your clinical video?

What I recommend in this case is, for this and like patients, not to make videos. Give up video intervention. Don't impose a risk of this nature upon the patient.

Granted, there could be an argument for the opposite choice. For instance, to show child protective services a video with a lot of positive interaction could perhaps be persuasive in allowing the family keep custody. I have known of such occurrences.

Who knows then what the right answer is here. In any case, my own suggestion has the advantage of guaranteeing safety for the patient in this area.

But let's say your situation is different. Let's say in your work context there is no such risk. What then about the treatment objection? Normally, the response can now be simple and straightforward.

For example, Lorraine is the grandmother of Tania, a 2-year-old girl. Lorraine's own daughter, Tania's mother, has been incarcerated and has lost custody. With hard scrapping, Lorraine has succeeded in becoming Tania's foster parent. She is participating in a home visiting program where video intervention is an optional form of support.

Therapist: So what do you think? Doable?
Lorraine: No way. Sorry.
Therapist: I see you don't like this idea. Why not?
Lorraine: Just not possible.
Therapist: Because?
Lorraine: This is the last thing I need. I make a video, and then someone looks at it, and then they get on my back.
Therapist: You mean I would get on your back?
Lorraine: No, not you. But protective services or whoever. I know how the world works.
Therapist: I think you need another piece of information. You and I and my supervisor are the only ones who will see the video. Absolutely. Guaranteed.
Lorraine: How can you guarantee? I don't see that.
Therapist: We have a fixed policy in our agency. Nobody else gets to see any of our clients' videos. Just ourselves.
Lorraine: Well. I believe you when you say you want it that way. But I don't know if I believe you will be able to get it that way.

An easy additional step, if needed as here, is possible.

Therapist: Look, if you're really that worried, here's a solution. You make the video. I'll explain how. Or I film, but with your phone or camera, or with a phone or camera you borrow if you don't have one.
      Then we look at the video together. And then once we are done you keep the video, or even just delete it. No problem.
Lorraine: What about your supervisor?
Therapist: She can skip looking at this video. She'll go along with that.
Lorraine: I think this could work.

Fundamental to these two counterarguments, obviously, is that the institution concerned does in fact have such a policy, and is accustomed to sticking by it; and that the agency is not restricted in doing so by any local legal constraints. This kind of arrangement is quite feasible in most settings.

There do exist exceptions. In some professional contexts the institution is required to save all documentation pertaining to a case, video included. And they must make such documentation available upon request, should, for example, protective services or the court so demand.

If this happens to be the case, a different overall solution is recommended. In the previous chapter I mentioned that some institutions regularly require that any family entering treatment make one or more interaction videos which will be used as a part of the initial assessment. My suggestion then is that this be done on a regular basis. In other words, it will be routinely required of the parents that an interaction video be made at the start.

Of course, the obligation here is only that the video be filmed, and not that the parent or parents look at the video for a session of therapy or coaching. However, once it has been filmed, there is a good chance the parents will accept the idea of looking at it.

This may occur because they sense it will be useful for them. Or they may be merely curious. Or they may be nervous, or even suspicious, and want to know just what these professionals seem to be seeing when they observe the video.

Whatever their motive, the odds are good that therapist will achieve something, however modest, in the session. A quite brief session, needless to say, with an emphasis on positive patterns only, is recommended in these circumstances, at least for their first video intervention experience.

Additional Responses: Strengthening Representations of Change

A therapist who has mastered the above counterarguments, and who feels at home with them, will find that most of the time they solve the problem. However, there are patients for whom still more will be needed. I will go over some further possibilities for how one can continue.

Whatever the type of objection, a good approach is to try, first, to strengthen the patient's representation of desired change; and then, second, to tie the video proposal to this focus.

Imagine that Karen, the mother of the daughter with anxiety problems in the example above, had not been persuaded by the first counterargument.

Therapist: I can understand. For a lot of people it is a little strange in the beginning to see themselves on video. For me, too. But what almost always happens is that this goes away after we have been working for a few minutes.

Karen: I don't know. For me, I don't think it would be like that. I'm sorry, I don't want to be uncooperative, but I just can't imagine doing this.

Therapist: The idea is difficult for you, I see. On the other hand, I know, from all you've told me, that it is important for you that Stacy [the 6-year-old daughter] learn how to be in the world with less fear and anxiety.

Karen: Yes, exactly.

Therapist: But how important? Somewhat? A lot? Very?

Karen: Double very. Really important.

Therapist: Yes, mainly of course for her, but for you too, if I understand. So that there will be less pressure on you.

Karen: Definitely.

Therapist: This will be a real change in your life, when it happens.

Karen: When it happens. If it happens.

Therapist: I see how the video idea is a real dilemma for you. I think you have at least a rough idea about how much it can help us. At the same time, until you get used to it, it may put you through some discomfort, since you don't like looking at yourself on video. So there are advantages to the idea for you, but a disadvantage too.

Karen: I guess. It's true of course, I really want things different at home, and different for Stacy at school.

Therapist: A dilemma. Picture Stacy [now 6 years old] three years from now. Picture her as 9 years old. If she is much freer of her anxiety, what will that mean for nine-year-old Stacy? What will be better in her life?

Karen: Friends. I'm thinking, friends. Not so scared socially.

Therapist: Sounds like something major for a 9-year-old. What else will be better?

[The dialogue continues several steps more along these lines.]

Therapist: So, a choice with pros and cons, this idea of making a video. How does that choice look to you right now as you consider the pros alongside the cons?

Karen: Maybe I need to give it a try. One time at least.

If More is Needed: Inner Strategies for the Patient

Here is another tack to take. It can be especially helpful for the embarrassment and criticism objections. One can try it before, after, or instead of the previous tactic.

Therapist: Karen, here's another thing for us to think about. Suppose, just suppose, that you did decide to try it, despite everything. Suppose that you were here, in this room, looking at that laptop screen over there, checking out Stacy and what she's doing in the interaction and talking with me about what you are noticing.

What could you do to take care of yourself in this situation, sitting there with me? How could you lower your discomfort? What would help you?

Karen: I suppose I could keep thinking about helping Stacy.

Therapist: That's an idea.

Karen: Maybe I could just say, I'm going to do this. It's important, and I'm going to do it.

Therapist: Say to yourself, you mean,

Karen: Yes.

Therapist: Another good idea. Any others?

Karen: Nothing pops up.

Therapist: So, okay, you are finding some practical ways you could handle the situation: thinking about payoffs for Stacy, and also saying encouraging words to yourself. As you consider how these ideas could help, how do the advantages and disadvantages of doing a video seem to you now?

Karen: Maybe I could manage.

If More is Needed: A Plan for What the Therapist Does

A somewhat similar move is for the therapist to inquire as follows.

Therapist: What could I do, on my side, when we look at the video, to make it any easier for you? Is there anything I could do or say, or anything I could not do or say, that would help?

Karen: You could go slow. And you could remind me how it will be useful for Stacy. Maybe we could talk about that once more just before we start.

Therapist: Sure, no problem. Seems to me like a good plan.

Here follows another example of the same idea, this time in response to the criticism objection. Judy, the mother of a 9-month-old infant, has been referred by her pediatrician for parent-infant therapy because of a continuing postpartum depression.

Judy: This video idea, I think it just doesn't fit for me. Sorry, I don't want to do that.

Therapist: What about it seems difficult to you?

Judy: I just don't like it.

Therapist: Because?

Judy: Hear about all my faults, looking at a video? Thanks but no thanks.

Therapist: Sounds like you expect you will be criticized.

Judy: Well, obviously.

Therapist: So you expect that when we look at the video, I will use it to criticize you, to find all your faults.

Judy: Yes.

Therapist: I'm very glad you are speaking about this. Why don't we see if we can think of anything we could do about it, anything which would make you feel more relaxed? For example, how would it be if, at any point, you began to feel criticized by me, you let me know?

And we can talk about it.

Judy: Really?

Therapist:　Really. And on my side, I will try not to do it. But I do get clumsy at times, so if it happens, or if anything you experience as in that direction happens, you just say something about it.

Judy:　Okay. If I let you know, don't run out the door.

Therapist:　I'll manage. Now, let's go back to this idea about a video....

Judy:　Well, I don't know... maybe....

Therapist:　What if we go over the pros and cons again?

Judy:　Sure.

If More is Needed: The Brief Viewing Compromise

Yet another strategy is to propose a compromise regarding the usual arrangements for a session. For example, an agreement can be made that the first time the patient works with a video, only a very short (e.g., half a minute or a minute) segment will be looked at and discussed. Continuing with the example of the patient named Karen, this might go as follows.

Therapist:　You know, here's something else we could do. We could look at only a very short piece of this first video. Like a minute of it, or even a half a minute. What do you think?

Karen:　Would that defeat the purpose?

Therapist:　Even with a short segment we can find something interesting to discuss.

Karen:　In only a minute, even?

Therapist:　Very probably, yes. I can pick out what seems like a good one-minute piece.

Karen:　That might be all right. Maybe I could try.

Therapist:　How does this idea make it easier for you?

Will one minute, or half a minute, be enough for some effective work with interaction patterns? It might be, it might not be. This is no matter.

Our priority at this point is just that a video be filmed and discussed, period. With luck, as long as we can let the patient experience that she can explore the segment with us without, for example, her feeling criticized, likely she will be ready afterwards to plan the making of a new video. Likely, too, she will then feel more open to permitting a longer segment to be investigated.

To put it another way, the brief viewing compromise, as well as the two compromise responses now to follow, are a kind of exposure technique. The patient is being exposed to the making of a video, to the process of sitting with the therapist and observing the images on the screen, and so on. Gradually, she will become more comfortable with these diverse elements. The question of how long or short the segment to be watched should be, will diminish in importance to her.

If More is Needed: The Offstage Compromise

The "offstage" proposal is another solution.

Therapist: Here is an idea. If it would make you feel more comfortable, the video could be filmed so that we only see Stacy. You could be a bit to one side, just out of the view of the camera. That way, you two could talk, but we would visually only see Stacy. Could this work?

Karen: If you can't see me, will the video be less useful?

Therapist: The best thing, for sure, is to be able to see both of you. But this would still give us useful information, especially about Stacy. And if this way of doing things makes it more acceptable to you, then why not try it?

Karen: It does sound easier. I would just hear myself. That's not so bad.

Here too with this solution the therapist is proposing a form of exposure.

If More is Needed: The Child Only Compromise

This strategy tends to be the easiest of all for a patient to accept. Proposed will be that the child alone is filmed, the child just by themselves (e.g., playing). In contrast to the previous strategy there will be no interaction with a parent, not even with the parent out of camera range.

The odds of consent are high, especially if the parent owns a phone which can film. Many parents are already so accustomed to filming their children with a phone that the further step of bringing such a video to the therapy will not seem enormous.

Therapist: There is an alternative. Why don't we just arrange a video of Stacy by herself? Playing, perhaps. Just her alone.

Karen: Sure, that gets me off the hook. But what use would it be for the therapy?

Therapist: A video with interaction would give us the most information. But a video of a child alone can also be useful. You and I can look at it, and use it to talk about Stacy, about aspects of her development we see in the video. It is helpful, you'll see. What do you think?

Karen: Well, why not.

Naturally a video of the child alone is indeed less useful for us. Interaction is absent. Nevertheless, there are things which can be done with such a video, as will be described later in the book (Chapter 4). It can serve as a point of reference for an elaboration of certain wider-ranging topics: for example, aspects of the child's personality, or their developmental history, or some of the hopes which the parent has for the child's future.

The child's presence on the screen serves nicely to guide and anchor such an exchange (Oppenheim & Koren-Karie, 2002). And, as with the other compromise responses, once a patient has consented to try the "child alone" version a time or two, there is every likelihood they will be willing, subsequently, to take on the challenge of an interaction video.

If More Is Needed: The As If Technique

And if none of these maneuvers work? If, at the end, the patient still insists on declining the video invitation – what then?

In this case, first of all, the therapist shifts to the following rather obvious suggestion.

Therapist: Well, it truly is a dilemma for you. I can see that. I suggest you think about it more, and then we can discuss the possibility another time. In any case, the choice is and will be yours. Yours alone.
Patient: All right.

But this in no way means the conversation is over. It has just been suspended; later in the therapy it will be resumed.

Moreover, it can be resumed in not only a direct but also an indirect fashion. Let's look at an example reflecting the indirect fashion.

We are again with the patient Karen. Today she has just been speaking about a recent upsetting interaction with her daughter.

Therapist: This sounds like a difficult moment, what went on yesterday evening between you and Stacy.
Karen: I tried to keep my cool. I kept just saying, "Calm down, Stacy. Calm down." But she wouldn't.
Therapist: Let's go over exactly how it started. The two of you are at the dinner table, you said, just finishing dessert. So can you describe what happens, step by step, as if we were seeing it now in a video? Speak in the present. What would we hear, what would we see?
Karen: Well, first of all....

And so forth. In other words, the therapist uses the opportunity, when discussing a recent interaction, to adopt the language of "as if we were seeing it in a video."

Questions even more specific can be added too.

Therapist: So here we might see Stacy moving her body exactly how...?
Therapist: So here we might hear your voice moving into a tone of...?

The idea is that to intervene in this manner frequently will heighten the patient's appreciation of the objective, outside viewpoint. It will also make her more curious about behavioral details.

We can hope that at the same time she is also building up more overall trust in the therapy. The combined influence of these factors will augment the chances that sooner or later she will warm up to the notion of trying video intervention itself.

We cannot realistically expect that each and every patient will consent to the idea of video intervention. But any therapist who has made themselves at home with these various ways to increase its appeal will be guaranteed a higher rate of acceptance.

3 How the therapist prepares for the session

The video has been filmed. It has been sent or given to you, or perhaps you did the filming yourself. The day after tomorrow is the session. What do you do to get ready?

Alone with the video, the therapist does what in VIT we call a "scanning analysis." A portion of the video is scanned, that is, looked over carefully.

A more detailed account of how to go about it, along with a suggested grid for observation, will be given in Chapters 14–16. What follows here are some beginning points.

For an experienced VIT therapist, the scanning analysis of most videos goes quickly. Fifteen to 20 minutes will often suffice. Videos do vary in their complexity, however, so now and then a little more time will be wanted.

For a therapist just starting out with video intervention, on the contrary, a good idea is to plan on more time. Half an hour might do; 45 minutes could be needed. Once you have intervened with a dozen or so videos you will find the preparation process can go faster. But for now, to set aside a longer period will let you observe and reflect in a more relaxed manner.

Playing the Video Through and Choosing a Segment

To start in, what is the simplest is first just to play the video one time through. Try, as you watch, to get an overall feel for the interaction.

Next, based on this first viewing, you choose a shorter segment. This will be what you actually show to the patient (or patients).

How long should this part be? It is open. Typically the segment we work with is between 1 and 3 minutes in length, as mentioned in Chapter 1.

For example, suppose the video which was filmed is 10 minutes long. Most likely then a shorter piece will have all the clinically relevant information you need. Most likely, it will have more than enough.

The original video which was filmed will usually be longer. Five to 10 minutes is typical. But for the session we often select a smaller piece. This is because in this smaller piece there will normally be plenty of clinically relevant information. Likely, it will be more than enough for what we need.

DOI: 10.4324/9781003621669-3

Suppose, however, that you do in fact choose to work with a short segment. How do you pick it out?

One helpful question is this: as you first glanced through the video as a whole, how repetitive did it seem?

Clinical videos have definite differences in this regard. The majority are fairly repetitive on a certain behavioral level, even if the fine-grained details vary. What can be seen in the early minutes does not differ hugely from the later minutes.

Now, with the video you are scanning today suppose this is the case. In that instance, you could select any portion to show in the session. The choice will be more or less arbitrary.

You might simply pick the first 3 minutes, for example. Or, as often occurs, a slightly better pick might be minutes 2 to 4. Frequently the reason here will be that during minute 1 the participants appear not yet fully engaged. They needed a little time to settle into their interaction.

But now consider the second possibility. As you glanced through the video the interaction did not seem repetitive. Perhaps, for example, some later portion, minutes 4 to 6, felt different from the earlier part, and more interesting somehow. In that case, go look again more carefully through this later block. Try to pin down more exactly what has captured your attention. Likely, it will be this block you will then choose for the session.

A third possibility could also occur: two separate segments both strike you as useful. Both seem of therapeutic interest, yet they seem different from each other. What then about the idea of working with both in the session? Could this be okay?

It could well be quite okay. With some videos it makes sense to work with separate segments, exploring one with the patient and then passing right away to the second. For that matter, you can even show and work with a full video, start to finish, should this seem worth the trouble. The major constraint here, naturally, is the amount of time which will be available during the session. What you intend to accomplish needs to be planned out with a certain economy, a point which will be further discussed below.

Incidentally, once you have built up a little experience working with videos, there is an alternative way to organize the first look-through as you prepare for a session. You start by looking at the first 3 minutes. You get a feel for this portion of the interaction. Then you look at the rest, using fast forward this time, with a flow of images showing. By watching this flow you can gauge with surprising accuracy to what extent the rest of the video is a repetitive continuation.

Does the nonverbal back and forth remain the same, largely? Or does a distinct shift show up – a shift in how the participants are holding themselves, moving themselves, and the like? If a shift occurs, then probably something different will be taking place, too, with the verbal exchange and the interaction atmosphere. It would make sense in this case to rewind to the shift moment and take a closer look at normal speed.

As mentioned in the last chapter, not all VIT videos are short. What if a patient has given you a video of half an hour? Forty-five minutes? An hour?

It happens. Often we want it to happen. The length may have a purpose. Perhaps the intent was to increase the odds of capturing some particular behavior, for example, a child's meltdown in the afternoon, or an especially emotionally laden moment in a couple negotiation.

With such a video the practical possibilities are twofold. One is that the patient (or one of the patients) has already told you roughly when in the video the significant behavior occurs. Now, all you have to do is go straight to that part and find the events you want to focus on.

Or, second possibility, perhaps you don't have this prior information. In that case there is no choice. You will just have to start looking through the video. This might take a while.

You might play it through at normal speed. You might play it through with fast forward. Or you might, another option, just jump about, checking out 3 minutes here, 2 minutes there and the like. Sooner or later this will tell you where in the video you need to concentrate in more detail.

Under some circumstances it can even happen that you find yourself accepting to work in a session with a video which you have had no opportunity to see. "I forgot to send the video, but I have it here on my phone," announces a patient as they walk in that day.

In this instance a seasoned VIT therapist will usually consent to start with the video on the spot, despite the inconvenience. He will play it one time through, with both himself and the patient watching, and go from there. This is not ideal, but it can be managed.

In one interesting use of VIT, to proceed this way is the norm, in fact. My colleague Sergio Facchini (Facchini, Martin & Downing, 2016) has developed an ingenious format for the use of video intervention by pediatricians and pediatric nurses in well-baby visits. The activities filmed are standardized. The length of the video is 5 minutes.

For example, normally during the first few months the infant receives an inoculation. The infant immediately cries; all of them do. The parent then at once holds and consoles him, and it is this which is filmed. And then, right afterwards, the pediatrician and the parent jointly look through the video. They stop it at relevant moments to discuss what they are seeing in the interaction, but they talk, too, about what goes on more generally at home concerning infant crying and how the adults respond to it.

Research conducted at the University of Padua in Italy has shown nice, positive results for this program. So the idea of jumping into intervention work with a video without the therapist having first seen it is not entirely outlandish. Under usual circumstances, however, before having to intervene, the therapist will be able to scan over a video with leisure. And they can carefully organize a plan for the session.

How, then, is such a plan organized, generally speaking? I turn now to that.

Choosing What in the Session to Highlight

Once the segment, or more than one, has been picked out, next to do is to view it another two or more times, at normal speed. Soak in the details. Any time you feel the urge, stop the video, go back a few seconds, and look again at whatever specific event just caught your eye (or ear).

As you observe in this more fine-grained manner keep these questions in mind.

1 What seem to be positive patterns in the interaction?
2 Which positive patterns might best be highlighted in the session?
3 What seem to be negative patterns in the interaction?
4 Should some negative pattern be explored? If yes, then which? And explored how?

By "pattern" what is meant is a brief piece of interaction behavior.

Before I go any further, let me mention a background issue. When we spot a behavior pattern during 3 minutes of a clinical video, do we really know with what overall frequency this person actually so conducts himself in his daily life? Of course we don't.

Here, throughout a video, a father is trying to feed his 14-month-old son, and he, the father, is patently too intrusive. But how often, at home, is he like this during feeding? Most of the time? Only now and then? Or could what we are seeing – not a likely possibility, but not 100 percent to rule it out – be a one-off occurrence, perhaps somehow stimulated by the context of being filmed?

Fortunately, this uncertainly presents no real problem. If the therapist does not already know, then she can simply raise the question in the session, for example, "What we are seeing here, how often is it like this at home?"

Patients can usually come up with an answer right away, and it is seldom inaccurate. They will have a sense of whether it is a highly frequent pattern, or a moderately frequent one, or merely an occasional but largely infrequent one. And if, exceptionally, they don't have a sense of this, then a useful project can be for them to start to give attention to the matter in their everyday lives. They can find out and come back and tell you what they have noticed.

Another more general issue needs to be mentioned too. As you scan the video you are searching out positive and negative moments. But how do we make these judgements? Who is to say what is positive and what negative? According to what criteria? We might call this the dilemma of the normative.

One answer at times, a partial and limited answer, would seem this. In the video there will typically occur some events which almost anyone would call positive, or almost anyone would call negative. Agreement seems to be close to universal, across cultures and across types of observers. John, the 15-year-old son, makes a cute joke, and both Father and Sandra, the 9-year-old sister, openly laugh in response. The moment seems a fine one to almost anyone who sees it.[1]

And then in some instances we can refer to research. We possess plenty of research which is suggestive with respect to normative quality. Mother and 3-month-old Janet are sitting face to face. Obviously positive is that Mother manages to offer a warm face and a sweet voice. However, we notice something particular in the mother-child vocal exchange: although Janet vocalizes often, Mother gives almost no vocalizations directly in response.[2] Almost totally absent is what video microanalytic researchers call vocal matching.[3]

Here there can be little doubt, based on what has been learned in research contexts. The therapist can safely assume that they, the therapist, will need to aid the mother not only with her depression and anxiety, but also with the specific behavior of providing vocal matching (a behavior which, with the help of video intervention, a parent typically can quickly learn, fortunately).

At the end of the day, however, there are plenty of other interactional events which are fraught with ambiguity, normatively speaking. They don't elicit universal agreement: different observers could have different opinions. And there exists no solid research which suggests an answer.

So a good idea when doing scanning is to keep this reality in mind. For reasons which will become apparent throughout the rest of the book, I would suggest the following guidelines.

Concerning patterns which might be positive – you suspect it but feel unsure – be generous. When in doubt, lean towards the label of positive.

Concerning patterns which perhaps are, which might be, negative, be cautious. Reserve this label for patterns where the negative quality is obvious.

Finding Positive Patterns

In a VIT session the therapist always points out to the patient some positive moments in the interaction. Highlighted might be a positive action of either participant (if there are only two). Here, Mother, handing a toy to 3-year-old Ricky, has a warm smile on her face. Ricky, a bit later, displays some, for his age, noticeable creativity in his play.

A good idea is to write down on a piece of paper the exact times of these events. If you later decide to show them in the session, they will be easy for you to find.

Some positive moments can involve mutual actions. At a certain moment, Mother and Ricky both look at each other and break out laughing. Tronick (2007) speaks of occurrences of what he calls "dyadic expansion," a way of connecting together person A with person B. For a moment we see an increased positive complexity in the joint organizing of the two bodies.

Needless to say, when showing such positive events, we would not want it to be the case that the therapist indicates only positive actions of Ricky, and none or hardly any of Mother.

So, they, the therapist, need to make sure that, with regard to any person present in the session, at least a few of the positive moments highlighted consist of acts of that person. If the video was of an interaction involving Mother,

Father, and Ricky, and if both Mother and Father were going to be there in the session, then, while scanning, obviously, it will be important to locate both positive Mother actions and positive Father actions.

But what if this endeavor turns out to be difficult? Suppose we look and look at a parent's behavior, say, and nothing which strikes us as positive stands out. His or her behavior throughout the whole segment seems relentlessly questionable. Most videos are not so bleak as this, but a few are.

In such an instance we are confronted with a paradox. The more relentlessly negative a patient's behavior appears to be, the more necessary that the therapist find one or more positive events to speak about. In a case of this nature there is a high likelihood that merely motivating the patient to change himself is going to be a hard job. So we have a strong reason for wanting to use the video to demonstrate that some part of the patient's behavior is already competent, with the implication that therefore still more of it could become competent.

The practical answer here is just to seize on anything at all which we might label as positive: anything, however brief, even if the prospect of showing it in the session feels artificial. "It is good how at this moment you turn to look at your crying baby. This way you can get more information," the therapist might remark. And they, the therapist, say this without adding that the fact that the mother is sitting some distance away, and in the 10-minute video only looked one time, is less than optimal. Patients almost never object to observations of this kind, luckily, however forced they may seem to us.

Choosing Which Positive Patterns to Highlight

The selection of which positive patterns in a session to speak about is normally easy enough. Make sure, as mentioned above, to find at least two for each person who will be present in the session. Typically, however, we will show more than two – perhaps five or even more.

As already said, while you pick them out, write down the times they occur. An option also is to add a note or two about what you might say.

This is because when you do show such an event, you may choose also to mention why you find it positive. "Good idea here, James, how you tell Teresa [his 14-year-old daughter, not present in the session]. You can understand how she feels that way, even if you don't agree with her. This will give her a sense of what we call being validated" (cf. Chapter 16). And perhaps soon also, "Another good validation, what you say here."

More than this could of course be said. In Chapter 5, some additional possibilities about how to present positive events will be spelled out.

Finding Negative Patterns

Will the therapist actually speak in the session about one or more negative actions? Perhaps yes, perhaps no.

In a majority of VIT sessions a negative behavior is also highlighted, and then explored therapeutically in some detail. But by no means is this always done. An explanation about how to make this decision will be given shortly below.

Nevertheless, as we are preparing for the session, we want to take careful notice of what appears negative in the interaction, even if our intention, for now, is not to bring the patient's attention to it. Often these examples, so specific, will augment our overall grasp of the case.

Negative events therefore get added to the list also, or at least to the therapist's mental list. Plus, of course, if we are planning to work with a negative behavior in the session, then we will be thinking, too, about which events stand out as the best candidates. I will soon say more about how one decides which negative pattern to use for this purpose.

Deciding Whether or Not to Show a Negative Pattern

Should just positive patterns be highlighted in the session? Or should the therapist first show these, and then move to a negative pattern, intending to investigate the latter in more depth?

As mentioned in a previous chapter, when we show positive moments only, and nothing more, this constitutes what in VIT we call an "abbreviated session." For such a decision there can be various possible reasons. Here are four typical ones:

1   The patient is little engaged in the therapy in general.

Tina, 14 years old, is the mother of a 1-month-old infant. She doesn't want for a moment to be here, in this special therapy and support group for adolescent mothers. She participates only because she is forced to, by her own mother, with whom she lives, and by protective services.

She has consented to being filmed for a video, just as she passively consents to whatever is proposed. But her interest is minimal.

How can Tina be lured, so to speak, into an increased commitment to the therapy? Video can be an excellent aid with this problem, given that a patient goes along with the making of a video in the first place. The therapist will show positive events only, at least for the first video.

As Tina watches it, the probability is high that despite herself she will be intrigued. The visually portrayed interaction will draw her in. The therapist's comments about it will interest her. A video of your own self and another person has a magnetic force that is hard to resist.

2   The patient, though engaged enough in the therapy, was strongly ambivalent about making a video.

They consented, in other words, but just barely. Their discomfort with this new step remains obvious.

To present positive patterns only with this patient could, therefore, be a good strategy. It is highly likely their unease will diminish as a result of the experience.

3   The patient suffers from strong all-or-nothing negative beliefs about herself as a parent or couple partner.

Here, to highlight just positive patterns serves a different purpose. Accented above all will be positive behaviors which can serve as proof against one or more negative beliefs.

Note that this is a maneuver akin to the classic cognitive-behavioral therapy technique of creating an experiment for a patient to undertake in his daily life, an experiment which will let him evaluate whether a dysfunctional negative belief is really valid. With the video, however, the experiment takes place in the session itself, so to speak. "Look here, how you do this, and look how warmly your baby right away responds. So let me ask again, when you see this, and take it in, how does it fit or not with your idea that you are an incompetent, terrible mother?"

4   The therapist simply feels unsure about how the patient is going to respond to working with a video. Given this uncertainty, they, the therapist, want to be sure not to unduly stress the patient in this first intervention session.

By highlighting only positive events they can err on the side of caution. Afterwards, having worked now with this first video, they will have a surer sense of what this patient is ready to handle.

Choosing Which Negative Pattern to Highlight

Suppose your decision is indeed to do a full session, not an abbreviated one. You are going to work with a negative pattern also. How do you select it?

As has been said, typically in a VIT session only a single negative pattern is discussed, if any. Or, at times, two such patterns which are closely tied are given attention.

The reason for bringing a focus to only one pattern (or two closely tied) is that time is needed. The ensuing exploration will have as its purpose not just insight but also a bringing about of change. What could be a more constructive behavior which could replace the negative action? Here is where the discussion is headed.

To arrive there, usually the conversation needs to progress in a gradual manner. The therapist and patient will engage in a succession of relevant reflections. The exchange will continue for a while. From that perspective, it makes more sense to do a thorough investigation of one pattern rather than brief explorations of several.

This point will become even more evident when in Chapter 7 I go into how such an investigation can be structured. We want the patient to walk out the door with a clear, detailed idea of what they can change, and also of how they are going to go about it.

How then to decide on which negative moment to focus? Suppose that, while scanning the video segment, you listed a half dozen different negative patterns. Which should be picked? There are several criteria.

1 Which patterns seem most relevant to the highest-priority goals of the therapy?

In a video of a family meal we see Father, Mother, Aron, 5 years old, and Mike, 8 years old. The family has been referred due to Mike's behavioral problems in school and at home. The school is threatening to expel him.

One pattern showing up twice happens when Mike provocatively slips off his chair and begins to stroll around the table. Each time, Father and Mother both begin to lecture. They explain why families should eat together, everyone seated at the table, at the same time, without disruptions, and so forth. The second time this occurs Mike just turns his back and leaves the room.

Another pattern also shows up twice. Mostly Axel, the brother, sits quietly, eating and not speaking. But twice he does hazard a comment about something, once about the food and once about a playdate he apparently had that day with a friend. Each time, neither parent responds to his interactional bid: the first time they clearly are focused entirely on Mike, and the second time they seem as if in a daze.

So arguably, in this example both patterns are significant. The more immediate need, however, the more pressing need, is for the parents to better set effective limits with Mike. The therapist thus would opt for this. The video would be used to help them, the parents, learn how to give more succinct commands, how to follow up on a command, and the like.

But this is not for a minute to say that the issue of the quality of connection between the parents and Axel is any less important. The choice is merely strategic; it concerns what to deal with when in the therapy.

The therapist can take in this valuable piece of information present in the video – that perhaps (further information would be needed to be certain) the relation between Axel and his parents ought also to be thematized. But if it seems it should be, this would be planned for some later point in the therapy.

2 Which patterns are likely to be easier, relatively speaking, for the patient to change?

Mother is sitting on the floor with 4-year-old Jill. The child was placed with a foster family several weeks ago. Mother has the right to supervised visits once a week. The team responsible for these visits frequently uses video to aid parents with their interaction skills.

As Jill plays, Mother simply watches, saying nothing, doing nothing, her face blank, her body hardly moving. She has already commented to a team member, during a previous visit, that she has no idea how to play with a child.

So where to begin with assisting her? With her emotional inexpressivity, for example? Or perhaps with her lack of speaking? Here are two good therapeutic possibilities. So, in getting ready for the intervention with this video, which to pick?

Obviously, both are important for her to change. However, one learns from experience with patients of this type that to open up more expressiveness, although a realistic goal, may well be a slow process.

To get her speaking, and in a way helpful for the interaction, will be a quicker step, on the other hand. For example, we might begin with so-called descriptive language: the mother can describe the objects and actions of the girl's play. ("You're putting the dog inside the house.") I say more about such a possibility in Chapter 10.

3 With most videos, only the first two criteria are relevant. On occasion, however, this third one is helpful.

Are there any significant negative patterns which (a) are clearly illustrated in this video and (b) might well be difficult to find in so readable a form in other videos? Are there any patterns, in other words, which stimulate us to think: here is an excellent, transparent example of negative behavior X, so why not profit from it, since to come across its equivalent in other videos might not be easy?

Mother is helping Jonathon, 10 years old, with his school homework. Jonathon has serious struggles with attention-deficit/hyperactivity disorder (ADHD).

One recurring negative pattern is Mother's overly critical, exasperated manner. Comments like: "No! I told you already! Finish the first problem before going onto the next! Please listen!," sharp in tone, are delivered several times.

Another is how the joint task of tackling the homework is initiated. This occurs at the beginning of the segment. Jonathon plops his books on the kitchen table and sits. Crossing the kitchen, Mother says, "Let's go, start," and sits in turn. Jonathon abruptly stands. As Mother, apparently annoyed, looks up at him, he says, "Paper," and walks out of the kitchen, returning with a tablet of paper in his hand. Then, as he sits, Mother says, "Can we now?"

What is missing in this interaction episode is what in VIT we call "creating a clear frame."[4] Mother, had, here an opportunity to coach Jonathon about how one can prepare for a practical task.

She could have led him through some quick thinking about what was going to be needed in the coming minutes – which books, what items like pencils and paper. She could have helped him think, too, about how to lay everything out in a useful way on the table. All children need to learn about such preparation procedures. And given Jonathon's ADHD tendencies, this is probably an especially critical skill for him to acquire.

So we have here an example of the applicability of the third criterion. Should we use the video to assist Mother in reducing her critical style? Or should we use it to help her learn how to help Jonathon to better organize and orient himself at the start of a task?

Well, how do the two options look according to the relevance to therapy goals criterion? Equal, roughly. Both seem relevant.

How do they look according to probable easiness of effecting change criterion? Also equal, roughly. Both seem, offhand, like they would be at least moderately difficult for Mother to change. It is hard to say, naturally, but this might be a reasonable guess.

Then what about the third criterion? Here on the contrary we find a noticeable difference. One can safely guess it will be easy enough to find examples of Mother's criticizing tendencies in other videos. Whereas to find another sufficiently transparent example of an opportunity to help Jonathon learn about establishing frames could be much more difficult.

4 There exists a fourth criterion I must mention too. It does not yet apply while the therapist is preparing for the session, however. Instead it would come into play, if it does, during the session itself.

Suppose that the patient, watching the video along with the therapist, becomes aware of a significant negative pattern themselves, and expresses a desire to change it. A good idea, then, is to respect this wish, if at all possible.

In other words, the therapist can put aside his planned agenda. And then, at an appropriate moment, (as will be clarified in another chapter), he can make this pattern, which has seized the patient's attention, a principle focus for further exploration. It is worth the trouble for a couple of reasons.

First, it makes sense to profit from the patient's mobilized motivation for change.

Second, to give priority to the patient's preference helps to create a collaborative atmosphere. Here is something desirable both for the video sessions and for the therapy as a whole.

Finally, here is a last point. It is part and parcel of a more general one. During the process of preparation a VIT therapist tries to organize an optimal plan for the session. But the plan is by no means rigid.

Once the session itself is underway it is important that the therapist attempt to remain flexible. The session plan functions as a default roadmap. But it can be altered at any time.

Much here depends upon what comes spontaneously from the side of the patient, a concept which will be further discussed in coming chapters.

Notes

1 Of course, one could argue that, with respect to a specific behavior, the "universal agreement" might still be mistaken. After all, what could rule this out? And a reasonable guess is that once in a while the situation is in fact so. Consider to what extent "universal" beliefs about raising children have changed over the centuries.

2 Concerning vocal matching see Beebe & Lachmann (2014) and Tronick (2007).

3 Needed also in this case example may be accompanying trauma work, an issue taken up in Chapter 11.

4 Aarts (2008) has nicely developed this notion.

4   Procedure step 1: Starting the session

The Standard Procedure

A video intervention therapy (VIT) session has a fairly precise structure. We divide this "procedure" into four steps. Here is an overview.

Step 1. Initial observation. Show a portion of the video. Ask the patient (or patients) to comment on what has been seen.

Step 2. Positive pattern exploration. Go back to the video. Point out a series of positive events in the interaction.

Step 3. Negative pattern exploration. Following an appropriate transition, show a negative pattern. You will have carefully selected this beforehand. Explore it now at some length.

Step 4. Action plan. Help the patient (or patients) form a plan for one or more new actions in the coming days.

In the rest of this chapter, Step 1 will be explained in detail. Steps 2–4 are covered in the chapters which follow.

Beginning with the Video

In walks a patient, for a VIT session.

First any prior matters are taken up, in a customary manner. The therapist will inquire about how the patient's recent days have been. If any tasks for home were planned in the last session, they will ask about that; and so on. As soon as appropriate, the shift to the video is made.

To start out, the therapist shows a portion of the video. This will be a segment they picked out while preparing. As mentioned, likely it will be short, between 1 and 3 minutes perhaps. Now and then it will be longer.

They play it straight through, saying nothing as it runs. Then they stop it, and invite the patient to comment.

Questions like these are typical.

Therapist: What did you find most interesting here?
Therapist: What seemed important to you in what you just saw?
Therapist: What stood out for you? What did you notice?

DOI: 10.4324/9781003621669-4

Once a patient has already experienced a couple of video sessions, and is accustomed to the ritual, this first invitation to comment might be even briefer.

Therapist: What do you think?
Therapist: So?

Now and then a patient will request to see the segment a second time before commenting. Naturally, the therapist complies.

If a patient has arranged the filming at home themselves, it may also be that they, the patient, have already looked it over. In this case it can be good first to ask them what they remember from when they saw the video at home. Then one can play the segment through, and they can see what stands out for them now.

Why start with the patient's reactions?

First, to find out what a patient notices in a video, before they, the patient, have heard anything about it from the therapist, is informative. We learn something about the patient's observational capacities. We learn, too, about how they think about interaction.

Second, this way to begin emphasizes that reflection upon the video is meant to be collaborative. Both parties, therapist and patient, are going to be contributing, or so we hope.

When video intervention becomes overly pedagogic, something is lost. We want the patient to hear our ideas, but we want them also to formulate their own.

Third, on occasion what the patient discovers, and what they talk about, will be so fruitful that it will cause the therapist to alter their, the therapist's, plan for the rest of the session. About this important possibility more will be said in a moment.

The Patient's Observations

It is striking how differently patients tend to respond when asked to comment on the video.

Some have little to say.

Patient: I don't know. There we are, John [2 years old] is playing.

Some are astute observers, even in a first video session.

Patient: I can see we both are having fun. Emma [5 years old] likes the doll house. She turns and smiles at me several times, so she must like it that I'm sitting there beside her, I suppose. I noticed when she tried to get me to take the piece of furniture I didn't pay attention to her, I was too involved with my baby doll.

Some are accusatory, like an attorney in court. They may be pleased if the other party, for example a child, displays problematic behavior.

Now they can share this evidence with the therapist. In the following example the video is of a mother and her 14-year-old son, discussing household chores. The mother is alone with the therapist in the session.

Patient: See how sarcastic he gets the moment I say what I want him to do? That's how it is at home. That's just how it is. You can see it.

Some make attributions about the other person which seem obviously unwarranted.

Patient: What seems important? The way she [3-month-old infant] is crying. That loud, hostile crying. She's criticizing me. She's trying to tell me I'm a bad father.

Some are moved.

Patient: [Husband looking at a video of himself and his wife eating breakfast in their kitchen. As he now, in the session, speaks, he is almost crying.] It's so quiet. A good quiet. I love this moment, in the morning, the two of us there, just eating our breakfast and being with one another.

The range of variation in what people manage to observe, and what they find to say about it, is immense. So as the therapist takes in these remarks, what should they try to notice? And how should they react?

How the Therapist Responds

Step 1 of the standard procedure is normally kept brief. The therapist listens. He empathizes. He displays curiosity. But for the most part he just absorbs what is being said. Of course, inside himself he is registering it, sifting through it.

Among other questions worth having in mind, as one listens, are these. How much does the patient seem to notice? How willingly do they, the patient, reflect on it? Do they seem interested in both persons, if there are two, in the interaction? To all three, if there are three, and so on?

Do they, the patient, display any evident biases, for example, noticing only positive aspects of behavior, or only negative aspects? How skilled do they seem at mentalizing, that is, at guessing about what might be going on inside the other person? What feeling, if any, do they have for "systemic impact" – the moment by moment influence each person has on the other (Fonagy et al., 1991; Steele & Steele, 2008)?

As the therapist takes in the patient's remarks, they, the therapist, will be noting any apparent implications for the therapy overall. But they will be thinking specifically about today's session too. Does anything in the patient's remarks – maybe an insight, maybe an expressed desire for change – warrant a more extensive exploration? Is there anything which perhaps even deserves a central place in today's session?

In such instances, usually the best strategy is not to delve further right now into what the patient has put on the table. Instead, if the therapist thinks a theme merits further exploration, she makes a mental note to address it later in the session.

The rationale for this postponement is simple. In Step 2, the therapist will be showing and commenting upon positive events in the interaction.

This will create for therapist and patient together a wider perspective, one with more understanding of the video interaction, and more language for it. Any exploration at a later point can then profit from this framework.

It is also important to make sure that Step 2 gets done, and done well, for reasons which will be explained in Chapter 5. This is another reason for waiting right now. When the therapist returns to the new theme later on, she can deal with it without worrying about whether Step 2 will have had the time it needs.

But does this mean we should always postpone an unexpected theme which comes up during Step 1? It does not. There can and should be exceptions: about which, more shortly.

Nor does it mean that when the patient shares his observations the therapist remains mute. Some back-and-forth exchange, however short, will normally take place.

For example, the therapist might validate what the patient has said. Or the therapist might encourage the patient to amplify the patient's remarks. Or the therapist might do both. How, more exactly, might this go?

Validation

Almost always, a helpful response from the therapist is a short validation of what the patient has said – given of course that validation is appropriate! Usually it is, luckily.

Simple praise might be given. Here the video is of a family meal, with a mother, a father, a 5-year-old daughter, and an 11-year-old daughter at the table.

Father: I noticed that Vanessa [the 5-year-old] seemed very interested in the conversation. She never said anything, but she kept turning her head to look at whoever was talking.
Therapist: Nice observation.

Or the therapist might just express agreement with the patient's remarks. In the example, a mother is present alone in the session. We see, in the video, her 5-year-old son playing with a 4-year-old cousin.

Patient: Jason [the son] has a hard time sharing his toys.
Therapist: Looks that way to me too.

Some validations will reflect what a patient says about his own state during the interaction. This can be a particularly supportive response when a patient shares difficult feelings, for example, frustration, anger, disappointment.

This video is of a father and his 6-year-old son. The father is trying to get him to put on his shoes and socks. The boy is refusing to do it. Father and son are shouting at each other.

Patient: This is so how it is. This is what happens, often. I just can't stand it.
Therapist: If I were in your place I would have a hard time too. Who wouldn't?
Patient: I get furious.
Therapist: It's difficult, I can really see that. And then you have the other two children to worry about on top of it all.

But, staying with the example, what if there were problematic communications on the father's side too – for example, insults and yelling? Should the therapist now speak about this as well?

Usually not, at that moment, for one of two possible reasons.

Suppose, first case, that the therapist intends, today, to do just an "abbreviated" session. This means, you will recall, that in Step 2 the therapist will show a series of positive events, and then will conclude the video intervention there.

In other words, in this instance, the therapist wants the patient to have only a limited experience with video today, one without any need to confront his own negative actions. The reasons for this could be various, for example, issues relating to motivation, and so on. To highlight the father's shouting now would sabotage this purpose.

Suppose, on the other hand, the plan is for a "full" session today. For example, perhaps the therapist is already intending during Step 3 of the intervention procedure (see the coming chapters) specifically to target the father's own aggressive style.

Here, as well, it will be more productive to leave the issue aside right at the moment. Coming next, in Step 2, is the discussion of positive patterns. Since we want the patient first to give his full attention to this dimension, it is better to postpone the negative behavior topic until later in the session.

Encouragement to Amplify

Frequently, another useful response is to invite the patient further to unpack their, the patient's, initial remarks. Again, short questions can be used.

Therapist: Can you say more?
Therapist: Anything else to add?

Encouragement to amplify might be joined with validation as well.

Therapist: Very nice observation. Can you add anything to it?
Therapist: Well said. Can you say a little more about your idea here?

A particularly helpful form of amplification is as follows. In the video two siblings, 5 and 7 years old, are playing together. Only the mother is present in the session.

Patient: What seems to me important? They are having fun together. That's the most important.
Therapist: What exactly do you see that tells you they are having fun together?

"What exactly do you see that tells you …?" is an intervention we use often in VIT. On the one hand, being a request for observational detail, it will elicit more information about what has given rise to the patient's comment. On the other hand, it helps train the patient more generally to become aware of observed specifics.

Minimal Reactions

What if a patient has almost nothing to say when asked about the video? What if further questions by the therapist continue to elicit nothing? It happens.

Therapist: What seems to you interesting or important in what we just saw?
Patient: I don't know. Sally [3 years old] is eating her food and I'm watching. I don't really find much to say about it.
Therapist: Did anything in particular stand out for you?
Patient: Not really.
Therapist: What seems to you interesting or important in what we just saw?
Patient: Beats me. I sure don't like that sweater I'm wearing, I can say that.
Therapist: Anything else stand out for you?
Patient: No, nothing else.

With this kind of response the best thing normally is just to move forward right away into Step 2.

Therapist: Okay, then. If it is all right with you, I will show you some things I noticed. Shall I do that?
Patient: Sure.
Therapist: Well, will it be all right if now we look at a few things I find interesting?
Patient: Okay, why not.

You might object that a patient who reacts in this manner seems particularly in need of assistance in learning how to observe. And this is exactly right.

But such assistance can be better given during the later steps of the session. Better now just to move on. Were the therapist to shift here to a didactic stance, it could easily cause the patient to feel pressured.

Self-Critical Reactions

Once in a while a patient will notice some shortcomings in her own behavior in the video, and will react with harsh self-critique. Here the patient is looking at herself interacting with her 7-month-old infant.

Patient: I'm so intrusive. I can't believe it. This is a shock.
Therapist: Sounds like you are having a strong reaction to what you saw. Is this right?
Patient: I'm upset. What I'm doing must be really bad for Julia [the infant]. I had no idea.
Therapist: So maybe there is something here you'd like to modify, and certainly I can help with that. But listen, a lot of what is going on in the interaction looks quite good to me. I'd like to show you what I mean by that. May I?
Patient: I guess, sure.

In other words, the therapist responds by shifting at once into Step 2. But notice the nuance of her comment. She underlines that what is immediately coming, what is going to be looked at now, is positive in nature. "A lot of what's going on in the interaction looks good to me."

Based on this self-criticizing reaction of the patient she, the therapist, may also introduce certain modifications into Step 2. This strategy will be spelled out in the next chapter.

Strong Positive Reactions

Plenty of times a patient, while looking at the video segment, will experience pleasurable emotion. It happens frequently. Perhaps they noticed moments of their own skillfulness which surprised them. Perhaps they appreciate how their son is making positive changes.

These are good feelings, but typically low-key in nature. Once in a while a feeling with much more power will be stimulated, however.

Rachel is the mother of Helena, prematurely born at 5 and a half months gestational age. The video has been filmed in the neonatal intensive care unit, around a week after the birth.

Almost every day Rachel spends several hours there. In the video she is holding Helena on her chest, giving kangaroo care.

Therapist: So what stood out for you as you watched this?
Patient: [Crying.] She's a baby. She's a real baby. She's so beautiful.
Therapist: You're having some strong feelings, I see. Is it a good crying?
Patient: Yes. Definitely. There is so much to worry about here, and she is so small, and the tubes [feeding and oxygen] .... I think it is the first time I have felt like she's truly a baby.

When a positive state of such intensity is activated, it makes sense for the therapist to explore it in some depth. The emotions may well be coupled with a significant insight, or clues about resources (Downing, 2000). Since obviously the best moment to find out more is right now, while the feelings are vivid, the therapist will need to put aside her intention to shift quickly into Step 2. Instead she can encourage the patient to linger with what she, the patient, is experiencing.

Therapist: Stay with all this. Take your time.

She can be helped to investigate it, once she appears ready to talk more.

Therapist: What it is like to let yourself feel this?
Therapist: Where in your body are you feeling it?

The related thoughts should be explored too, naturally.

Therapist: A "real baby." What does that mean to you?
Therapist: If she is a "real baby," what does that say about her?

How to proceed further depends on context: the particular video, the particular patient, the particular point in the therapy. The therapist might inquire about potential resources, for example.

Therapist: This new way to see Helena seems so important. How can it help you?
Therapist: As you continue to go through this difficult situation in the coming weeks, how is it going to be useful for you to think of Helena as a "real baby"?

What in VIT we call an "incorporation technique" might be used now. This is a video-based variant of what in cognitive therapy is sometimes called "imagery intervention" (Hackmann et al., 2011).

The therapist will first make sure that the static image on the screen is one which well fits the resonating emotion.

Therapist: Look at her again here. Concentrate on what you are seeing, together with the feelings. Imagine taking this picture inside, in a way that you can keep it. As if you are putting it in a kind of archive. So that you can come back to it, inside yourself, any time you want.

Other options, too, might be called upon. The idea is to go slow, and take time.

This type of event, the emergence of an intense positive state, is of course not the only reason why a therapist might decide to spend more time than usual with the Step 1 exchange. There can be other kinds of exception too. You weigh the pros and cons.

If Two or More Patients are Present

Naturally, Step 1 takes on more complexity when two or more patients are in the session. For example, imagine how it would be if we were to ask person A what stood out for him in the video, and in reply he lists everything he finds at fault in the behavior of person B! It would poison the atmosphere. It might lower person B's motivation for video work overall.

We can minimize such problems. The answer is to structure Step 1 in a different fashion.

Exactly how depends. One factor to consider is just how many people are there to be seen in the video. A second is how many are present in the session itself.

First, suppose the therapist has just showed a video segment to Cindy and Frank, an adult couple. In the video the two of them are speaking about conflicts they have around parenting Tania, their 9-year-old daughter. It is a video of negotiation, in other words.

Suppose also that, in the video, Tania herself is not present. The interaction there is between the two adults, only. Here is how the therapist can provide guidelines for the sharing of observations.

Therapist: So let's talk about what we just saw. Cindy, okay that you begin? [She nods affirmatively.] First, what did you like best about what you saw Frank doing in the video?

Cindy: Well, he seemed to be really thinking over what I was saying. I liked that. He was paying attention.

Therapist: Good.

Cindy: But then he didn't come up with any suggestions, not a single one, and ....

Therapist: [Interrupting.] Wait a minute, Cindy. Stay with what you found positive in what he was doing in the video interaction. For the moment let's just talk about that.

Cindy: All right.

Therapist: Okay, any other comments about what you liked or appreciated in what Frank was doing?

Cindy: That's all that comes to mind.

Therapist: Fine. So, what about yourself? What did you like best about what you yourself were doing?

Cindy: I was paying attention too. Also, I think I stayed with the point. Sometimes I go off on tangents in these discussions, but here not much.

Therapist: Good, thank you. And with regard to yourself, did you also notice anything which you think might be useful to learn to do differently?

Cindy: I see sometimes I start shaking my head "no" while Frank is still in the middle of what he is saying. That seems counterproductive.

Therapist: This is an interesting thing to have observed. We might talk about it later if you want. Okay, Frank, your turn now ....

In this fashion, the therapist sets up some constraints. We can describe the process more abstractly as follows:

1 The therapist first requests person A (it could be either of the two) to share their observations about person B – but positive observations only.
2 Next, the therapist asks person A to share positive observations about themselves.
3 The therapist then asks person A if they have comments about anything more problematic they found in their own behavior.
4 Only after this does the therapist move to person B, guiding person B through the same sequence.

Naturally, it may happen that one person veers off-course, and, despite the instructions, begins to criticize the other one. The therapist simply comes in at once then, blocking the criticism, and encouraging this person to return to sharing observations in the suggested manner.

Note, too, how, in the example, the therapist does not move into a more complex discussion of how each is reacting to what the other is saying about the video; not at this moment anyway.

Granted, it might be therapeutically interesting to inquire about, for example, what Frank thinks about Cindy's remark about shaking her head. Certainly this would be a classic couple therapy move.

Typically, however, during Step 1 the therapist would forego investigating that. Should they feel a definite leaning to go into it, they can come back to it later in the session. Here as usual, in other words, the immediate goal is to shift as soon as possible to Step 2.

When the therapist first asks for comments about the video segment, with which of the two persons should she begin? For an adult couple, either one: normally it doesn't matter. Naturally, over the course of a series of video sessions, a good idea is more or less to alternate.

On the other hand, when, in a session, the two persons to be worked with consist of a parent and a school-age or adolescent child, a good idea can be to find out the child's preference. Usually what one hears is that they, the child, want the parent to speak first. Now and then the child prefers to be first, however.

It can also happen that a child wishes to say nothing at all. The therapist goes along this choice too. There will be better opportunities later in the session to try to draw the child into the exchange.

Consider now a different variation. Suppose that, as before, a couple has just looked at the first playing of a video segment. But in this particular video their child is present as well in the interaction. The child is not there in the session, however. Should the therapist encourage them to comment on the child too?

Yes, and it is easily added. Imagine Cindy and Frank again. This time they are responding to a new video where Tania, the daughter, also has a role. The video might be of a family meal, for example.

The therapist has started with Frank. She has already asked him to share what he found positive in Cindy's behavior, and he has done this. She then continues.

Therapist: And what about Tania? What stood out for you about her?

Notice that, inquiring about the daughter, the therapist this time does not insist on positive remarks only. Since the daughter is not there, they, the therapist, need not worry about how Frank's comments might affect them.

Once Frank has offered any remarks concerning the daughter, the therapist can pass on to asking him to speak about himself – here differentiating once again between what Frank sees as positive about himself and what he sees as negative.

Finally, what if all three, parents and child together, have come for a video session? And what if the video itself is of an interaction with all three involved?

In that case, during Step 1, the therapist has each of the three comment, in turn, on the segment which has been shown. Each is invited first to speak about each of the other two, mentioning positive aspects only; and then to talk about himself or herself, going initially into positive aspects and then subsequently into negative ones.

So as you can see, this sequence unfolds just as it did when the couple was alone, with no child in the video. The only difference is that here three people in turn talk, not just two. Should still more persons be present – for example, both parents and two children – the guidelines can be structured in a like way.

Typicality Check-in

If we have five minutes of video, does it really represent how things go at home? Can we depend on this? In a previous chapter I suggested it would be naive to take such a thing for granted.

Here, to repeat, is my perspective on the issue. It is based upon my own experience, and that of colleagues, in treatment settings where one has plenty of contact with the family or couple members separate from the video sessions themselves. Think, for example, of a mother-infant residential setting.

The first thing to say is that, in most instances, the video will be close enough to the everyday interactional happenings. Whatever discrepancies are present, they will matter little for the clinical work. As I have said, given that everyone, or at least everyone over 4 years old, is aware of being filmed, the tendency is for the interaction to be slightly better than usual – but only slightly. Our habits rule us.

On the other hand, there are exceptions. In a small minority of times, the video interaction looks not just slightly better than usual, but substantially better. In an even smaller minority of times, it can look substantially worse.

How can we find out about these discrepancies? And what should we do about them?

I call this the correlation issue – the question of the degree of correlation between the video and the patients' everyday reality.

My first recommendation is simple. At any time when you feel yourself in the dark about this issue, inquire about it. Just ask. And during Step 1 is a natural moment to ask.

The question might be phrased in an open fashion.

Therapist: How typical is what we have been seeing here?
Therapist: Does what everyone is doing in the video seem to you for the most part like what usually goes on?

Or you might choose to inquire about something more specific.

Therapist: This throwing his food on the floor, how often does Ron [aged twenty months] do that?
Therapist: You two [a couple in a negotiation video] manage to get some laughs in even though you are talking about hard things. Is this something typical?

Yet how reliable will the patient's answer be? Reliable enough, I would suggest, again basing my answer on practical experience. Patients tend to have a fairly accurate sense of how close the correlation is. Normally they are honest, too, in how they respond.

Suppose, then, one day you do hear from a patient that the interaction on the screen is indeed unlike how things typically are. The video interaction is substantially better than the usual, or substantially worse. This does have a consequence: you will now work with the video in a slightly altered manner. Exactly how to do so will be explained in a coming chapter.

Yet another possibility also needs to be mentioned. There can be a few parents or couples who are more deceptive. The video interaction is substantially better than usual, but they claim it is typical. They say this even though they are well aware it is not.

This, when it occurs, will be for rather obvious reasons. Typically these patients will be highly suspicious of the agencies or institutions they have been dealing with. They may fear some practical threat, such as having a child taken into custody, for instance. As a result, they want to sell a polished image. During the video filming they manage deliberately, artificially, to upgrade their interaction style.[1]

So be on the lookout, too, for this last type of situation. But if you suspect it may be going on, how then should you proceed? This matter, too, I take up in a later chapter.

Keep in mind that the spirit of Step 1 is to stimulate the patient's own thinking. Keep in mind that different persons will have different degrees of readiness for this, and different capacities for it.

Note

1 Typically, such a video will also have a stilted, unnatural quality.

5 Procedure step 2: Showing positive patterns

Who doesn't like to hear they are doing something well? During Step 2, patients have their competencies pointed out. They appreciate this, almost universally.

Why take the time? One answer is it stimulates a cooperative atmosphere. If, as is usual, the therapist intends later to move to a negative pattern, then first highlighting positive capacities will be a helpful prelude for engaging the patient.

Second, information is transmitted, information of several kinds.

There is information about specific skills. Thanks to the highlighted video moments, together with the therapist's commentary, the patient can learn in a more precise way what some of the abilities they already possess are.

You might think they would already know this. Surprisingly, however, people in general tend to have only a hazy sense of what they do competently in interactions. With the help of the video the patient can get a better grasp of at least certain competencies already in place. This will also help them to better understand and specify goals for change.

Then there is information about any new behaviors reflecting work in previous sessions. Has the patient managed to implement an action already discussed, already planned for? If yes, showing her this moment will be both instructive and motivating.

Other kinds of information will perhaps be transmitted, if the video is of an interaction between a parent (or more than one) and a child (or more than one). Psychoeducation about development, for example, may be woven into the discussion at an opportune moment. By tying psychoeducation directly to one or more video events, the therapist can render what is being explained much more concrete.

Any positive changes in a child's behavior can also be pointed out. Parents can update their profile of what the child, on their side, is newly learning to do.

In sum, quite a bit of discovery can take place during Step 2.

So exactly how do you show the positive behaviors up on the screen? And what do you say about them? In this chapter I will weave back and forth between these two topics, covering a number of points about each.

DOI: 10.4324/9781003621669-5

The following basic techniques will be described:

- How to show a positive behavior in a brief manner
- What kinds to show
- How many to show
- In what order to show them
- The suspense technique, for showing two or more closely related events
- The acoustics-only technique, for listening more carefully
- The micro-viewing technique, for looking at a more fine-grained level
- When to show child behaviors as well as adult behaviors

Concerning possible ways to discuss whatever has been highlighted, the following points will also be covered:

- Different types of praise the therapist can give
- Different types of mentalization comments
- How to discuss a visible change the patient has succeeded in making
- How to give attention to a patient's emotional response when viewing a positive event
- The image incorporation technique
- How to discuss a positive exception to an otherwise negative behavior tendency in the video

I turn now to the specifics.

Showing During Step 2

How to proceed during Step 2 is straightforward. You show a series of good moments in the video. These events, which you will have picked out beforehand, are quite specific behaviors: a smile, a well-chosen verbal phrase. As already mentioned, useful will be to note on a piece of paper where each can be found – at 0:36, at 0:52, at 1:18, and so on.

Show a mini-segment leading up to a positive moment, and then stop on what seems to you an attractive image of the behavior itself. Let me give an example. Two-year-old Cody, mother sitting beside him, is putting another block on a tower he is building. The tower accidentally crashes.

Cody and mother both spontaneously turn their faces towards each other, laughing. *Click*. The therapist stops on this nice image of the two of them looking at each other.

Here the whole mini-segment shown might have taken around five seconds. This is typical. But, depending on the event, use as short or long a lead-in as seems to you right.

It is fine occasionally to show something a child does too, a positive behavior, even if the child will not be present in the session. This can motivate parents to give more attention to positive elements in a child's behavior – an attention all too often lacking.

Sometimes as well it can permit information about development to be communicated. "This is what we call 'narrative play,'" remarks the therapist. "Jerry is making the puppets act out a story. It is good to see this starting to happen at his age [4 years]."

So, summing up, whenever your show some type of positive action you will end up with a static image on the screen. It will be like a nice photograph of the positive event. It will also, guaranteed, have the patient's full attention. What, then, do you say about it?

Commenting: Forms of Praise

There are a number of useful ways to comment. A good idea is to use a mixture of these choices. You can deliberately vary them.

Why vary them? One reason, as you will see, is that different forms of comment have different advantages.

But another reason concerns the atmosphere. If you start using the same type of comment, over and over, the exchange will take on a stilted quality. Whereas if you draw on different types the dialogue will feel more natural.

One good way to comment is with descriptive praise. Sometimes it is also called labeled praise. There are a number of versions.

An example. The mother of a 14-month-old girl is changing her diaper. At one point the mother leans forward, smiles at the girl, and says "Hi!"

Therapist: This is good, how you here take a moment to make social contact with her.
Patient: Hm, okay.

Descriptive praise explicitly mentions what the praise is about. Sometimes the description will be fairly abstract: "you take a moment to make social contact with her." Sometimes it will be more specific, more detailed. The choice is open.

Staying with the same example, a more specific descriptive praise could be as follows:

Therapist: This is good: you lean forward, you smile, and you say something. You take a moment to make social contact.
Patient: Hm, okay.

Descriptive praise can also include brief psychoeducation. This, in fact, can be a particularly effective way to transmit psychoeducation concepts. Consider again our same example.

Therapist: Here you make a little break in what you are doing, and you give her some social contact. You lean forward and say something, with a nice smile.

Patient: Right. Okay.
Therapist: And when you do this kind of thing you are also teaching her how, when people are doing practical things together, they can have moments of warm contact too.

When psychoeducation commentary is added to descriptive praise, it might be about child development. Or it might be about interaction in general – for example, systemic impact and the like. Or it might address some other topic.

Does praise for positive moments always need to have an accompanying description? No, not at all. What we can call simple praise, which is briefer, can be brought in at times, too.

Be careful, however, about when you use simple praise. I will explain. Let's go back to the previous example, of the mother and her 14-month-old daughter.

The therapist has just played the sequence of the mother leaning forward, smiling, and saying, "Hi!"

Therapist: Fine! Just right!
Patient: Hm, okay.

A tiny remark, but arguably it has therapeutic value. It gives positive reinforcement. It communicates, more or less, "What you just saw yourself doing is a good thing to be doing."

At the same time note that the information transmitted is minimal. Does the patient fully understand what the therapist wishes to imply?

We might wonder. For example, might she, the patient, take the comment as meaning that it was her leaning forward which was positive? Or that it was her smiling, or that it was her saying, "Hi"? Or that all of these are being indicated? A lot of ambiguity remains.

For this reason, non-descriptive praise should be used judiciously. It is best suited to moments when the therapist can be reasonably sure that the patient will grasp what the therapist wants to imply.

For example, suppose that, in the segment being reviewed, this is the third time the therapist has shown the mother leaning forward and smiling. Suppose, as well, that the two times before, the therapist used descriptive praise.

In this case, it is almost sure that, this third time, the therapist's "Fine!" will be enough. The patient will take the remark as meaning: "Here is another positive example of what we were just talking about."

Commenting Using Mentalization

Being an attachment-based method, video intervention therapy (VIT) brings a frequent focus on mentalization. Emphasized especially is what can be called "other-mentalization," that is, thinking about what might be going on inside someone else.

The assumption is that mentalization consists of a set of skills (Downing, 2015b), and that patients can be aided to improve these skills. What could be more important when working with relationships and interaction?

In VIT, techniques designed to enhance mentalization capacities are used often. As remarked, several are used primarily in Step 2. Others, more complex, are used primarily during Step 3.

In Chapter 9, I will give some theoretical background concerning the concept of mentalization. Here I will simply describe the Step 2 techniques.

Let's take an example. Rosa, 15 years old, is the mother of Federico, 11 months old. Rosa is in a special outpatient intensive program for adolescent mothers. The work with the video is taking place in a group setting (Riva Crugnola et al., 2018).

In the video the boy, who just fell down, begins crying loudly. The mother gently guides him into her lap and holds and rocks him. The crying softens, then gradually stops.

Therapist: You did this so well, Rosa. I imagine he is feeling now like he got just what he needed, and in just the moment he needed it.

Notice what is particular about this remark. *"I imagine he is feeling now like …"*: the therapist is not just giving praise, but also speculating about the child's inner state.

Such comments are highly useful. You are not only giving praise but also modeling how to mentalize. You are implicitly communicating, too, that mentalizing is important.

There are other variations. Here is one. Imagine the same therapist responding to the same event.

Therapist: You did this well, Rosa. You were so gentle, and the rocking looked just right. What do you imagine he is experiencing inside? What is he perhaps feeling and thinking – I mean, what might his thoughts be, if he had more language?
Patient: I don't know. He quieted down. I think he liked what happened.
Therapist: Sounds on target to me.

So here the therapist first gives descriptive praise, and then asks the mother to do the speculating. She is being encouraged on the spot to practice a short piece of mentalizing.

Still another version, one in VIT we find particularly effective, I call "giving a voice." It is derived from a technique developed by Sheena Carter and her colleagues (Carter et al., 1991). They called it "speaking for the baby."[1] In VIT we refer to it as "giving a voice," for a reason which will soon be clear.

Again we are with the same example, the therapist having just shown the crying, the holding, and the quieting down.

Therapist: Hey, just what I needed! Thanks!
Patient: [Laughs.]

The therapist "gives a voice" to the child, the "voice" reflecting what might be the child's subjective state.

This version can be done by itself, as a stand-alone remark. Or, still another option, it can be combined with praise, descriptive or non-descriptive. A combined variant might go like this:

Therapist: Hey, just what I needed! Thanks! [Therapist now changes his voice tone a little.] That's sort of what I imagine he is feeling. You responded to him in such a soothing manner, and right at the right moment.
Patient: Hmm.

Finally, the task to "give a voice" can also be turned over to the patient. It is the variation that is perhaps most helpful of all. The patient must practice mentalization on the spot, but in a cognitively more demanding manner. She has not just to reflect about the other, but also to imagine being the other. She puts herself in the other's place.

We are still with the same example.

Therapist: Give him a voice right now.
Patient: I ... I ... I'm calming down. When you hold me like this I calm down, Mom. I'm starting to feel okay again.
Therapist: Good.

"Giving a voice" is an interesting technique in group settings too. Imagine Rosa participating in a group program with several other young mothers.

Therapist: [Nods to the other group members.] Okay now, give him a voice. Valeria, you start.
Valeria: Now I feel better. Thanks, Mom.
Sara [next in the circle]:   I like it when you take care of me like this.
Alessandra: Sorry, I'm not coming up with anything ....
Melissa: I'm relaxing now.
Therapist: And now you, Rosa?
Rosa: Like Valeria said, now I feel better.

Here the group members provide a collective support for the patient. At the same time, they get to practice their own mentalizing abilities. It is a technique which often creates a lively group atmosphere.

With a parental couple, giving a voice can be used in a similar manner, that is, similar to what was just described for a group. Suppose in the video we see a mother, a father, and 6-year-old boy having a meal. The boy is having evident trouble as he attempts to cut up a piece of meat. The mother, with a friendly voice, says, "Shall I cut it for you?" The boy reacts by turning to her and saying, "Yes."

Therapist:	Joel [the father], give him a voice here.
Father:	I like it that you asked first, Mom. You didn't just cut it without asking.
Therapist:	Fine. Kathy [the mother], your turn.
Patient:	Thanks, Mom, this is a good way to help me.
Therapist:	Seems to me like good thinking, both your ideas.

"Giving a voice" can be also used with couples (i.e., the video is of couple interaction only, no children involved). Partner A "gives a voice" to partner B. Next, the therapist can check out with partner B about the extent to which A's comment seems to fit.

You can see why in VIT we call the technique "giving a voice." The original Sheena Carter version, "speaking for the baby," was done with infants. And only the therapist did the "speaking." The VIT version is used for mentalizing about persons of all ages.

Also, patients are often asked to do the mentalizing, with the therapist saying, for example, "give Jack a voice here." The phrase "give a voice" gives a more adept wording for such interventions.

But how far should such discussions go? Be careful here. At this point you are only in Step 2 of the session and there remain other things to accomplish. So it is normally best to keep the exchange fairly brief.

Have in mind this too. An advantage of the VIT model is that themes which emerge in a video session can always be further pursued, if it seems appropriate, in non-video sessions. If you find you really want a lengthier discussion, consider returning to it in a coming non-video session.

More about Showing

How many positive behaviors should one highlight? This is open. Suppose just one patient is present in the session. A rough guideline, then, would be to show between three and 10, if possible.

If more than one patient is present, fewer may be necessary. Step 2 needs to be kept fairly short. Between three and six for each person might be realistic, for instance.

What then should count as a positive behavior in the first place? How stringent should one be?

Try to be generous. Don't set the bar high. Actions which look less than impressive are fine to include.

Be generous especially if, when preparing for the session, you are confronted by a video interaction which seems oppressively negative. Scanning it, you have a hard time locating anything positive.

In that case accept as positive a few actions which appear only minimally good, and/or quite banal. "Here again while Diane is speaking you nod your head. That shows you are listening, and it communicates to Diane you are listening."

What then do you show first, what second, and so on?

Easiest usually is to let the order of showing follow the order of the interaction. Say you are working with the first 4 minutes of the video – that is, the segment you already played through for Step 1. Now you start in with the first positive event on your list which occurs in those 4 minutes. Then you pass to the next, then the next.

However, if for some reason you prefer some other sequence, nothing stands against it. You can shift forwards and backwards in the video, as needed.

For example, perhaps when planning for the session, one positive moment especially stood out for you. It seemed rich. You feel it would be good to have plenty of time to reflect together about this event. However, it occurs late in the segment.

An option would then be to start out with this moment, or in any case show it early on. Afterwards you can go back to earlier events, if you so want.

The Suspense Technique

I have been talking about describing a positive event – an action, a doing, a happening, a behavior. But plenty of times it is coupled events which deserve to be brought into focus. What I mean by this is two or more actions which happen in succession and which appear connected with each other. This can give an opportunity for an interesting technique.

Imagine again the same mother and 14-month-old daughter. Imagine now the following sequence. First, mother leans forward, smiles, and says "Hi!" And then, a couple of seconds after, the infant responds with a smile and a throaty coo. So here are two events which look coupled: what mother does, and the contingent response of the infant.

Clearly, it makes sense to show both together. The mother can observe not only what she does well, but also the response it elicits. To view the reaction of the infant will be additionally reinforcing for the mother. It is as if the infant were adding her own praise alongside the praise of the therapist.

There are several good ways to show coupled events. One is just to play a short sequence which includes both events, and then comment.

Therapist: [Having shown the mother's action followed by the infant's response.] Here you make a little break in what you are doing, and you give her some social contact. And look how she likes it.

Patient: [Laughs.] Right. She did.

But an interesting alternative is to separate the two events. Show them one by one, in a manner which creates a little drama.[2]

Therapist: [Having first shown just the mother leaning forward.] Here you make a little break in what you are doing, and you give her some social contact. Let's see how she responds this time.
Therapist: [Now shows the girl's smile reaction.] Ah, she likes it!

"Let's see how she responds this time" – here is the key remark. Any time you say the equivalent of "Now let's see what comes next," you will have a very attentive patient watching the screen.

Consider another example. In the one just recounted the first event was a parent action, the second a child action. Let's see an instance now of the opposite, first child and then parent.[3]

Jackson, a 4-year-old autistic boy with almost no language, is playing on the floor with his father. Jackson hands the father a toy while at the same time looking at his face. This is a new, unhabitual behavior for the boy, whose usual tendency is to ignore opportunities for eye contact.

Therapist: [Having just stopped the video on an image of the boy handing the father the toy.] Hey. Look at this. He hands you the car. And he's even looking at your face. This is encouraging to see, isn't it?
Patient: Really!
Therapist: Let's see now what you do with it. [Shows the subsequent reaction of the father, who lights up in his own face, takes the toy in his hand, and says enthusiastically, "Thanks!"]
Therapist: Perfect! Just right. This reinforces him, and it models how one person can respond to another.

It can even be of interest, occasionally, to show (1) the child's action, then (2) the parent's response, and then (3) the child's response to the parent's response. All three can be seen in an unbroken flow, if you wish. Or they can be shown separately, with comments in between, as in the following example.

Here are Jackson and his father again, still playing.

Therapist: [Shows the boy banging a spoon on the floor.] He certainly likes his spoon here, doesn't he. Let's see how you react.
Patient: Okay.
Therapist: [Shows the father as he picks up a second spoon, bangs it on the floor in a similar way, saying, "Spoon! Spoon!" The boy looks at him as the father does this.] Clever. You are imitating him. And look how this interests him.
Patient: Hmm.
Therapist: [Now shows the next several seconds, during which Jackson says, "Oooh."] Did you hear? He even imitated your word. His "oooh" is clearly a repeat of your "spoon."
Patient: I thought so too. This is the kind of thing which gives me hope.

A careful showing of coupled events is one of the best ways there is for helping patients learn about interactional impact, the systemic effects of each person on the other.

The Acoustics-Only Technique

Now and then it can be of value to focus more closely on the acoustic output in itself. It can be easily done.

First, show the relevant passage in the ordinary way. Then play it again. But now ask the patient not to look at the screen, and just listen instead to the sounds. Immediately this will render the acoustic dimension more salient.

A mother and father are with their prematurely born infant in a neonate unit, one where VIT is used for support and therapeutic intervention. The couple has just been filmed interacting with their baby. Now they are in a separate room, reviewing the video with the therapist.

Therapist: This is sensitive here, Judith [the mother], how you give little echoes to his sounds. And good too is how you keep your voice so subdued. Your soft tone fits his soft tone. You're managing to stay right within the range of stimulation he can tolerate.

Mother: Okay then.

Father: Right.

Therapist: Just so you both can really take in this fine example, let's go through the segment again. But this time don't look at the screen. Look away, or close your eyes. Just listen to the sounds, to his sounds and to yours. [Plays the fifteen seconds again.] So what did you notice?

Father: I can hear how Judith's echoing fits right in with the sounds Danny [the infant] was making. It is like they are cooing with each other.

Therapist: Exactly.

The acoustics-only technique, as we call it in VIT, can have different functions. Sometimes, like here, it is the quality of the voice tones themselves we want to highlight. Sometimes it is the rhythm of the back-and-forth exchange, that is, the acoustic turn-taking.[4] Sometimes it is the content of the verbal language, the words and phrases used. Sometimes it is all of these.

The Micro-Viewing Technique

Here is another special focus you can bring to an interaction event. It is one of my favorite techniques.

It can especially illuminate what the two (or more) bodies are doing. Adept forms of body-body mutuality, of coordination, can be pointed out in a new manner.

Perhaps one person offers an object and the other reaches out and takes it, for instance. Or perhaps one person leans in their body against the other person's body, and as they do so the second person reshapes themselves to accommodate.

These are fast-occurring events, over in a flash. But the micro-viewing technique can make them much more readable for the patient.

Imagine we see this in a video. A crying infant runs to her mother. Immediately the mother, who is standing, picks him up, and deftly, with a quality of softness, brings him to her, the mother's, chest. In response, the infant at once leans his head in against the mother's body.

You could show this at normal speed, then stop the video and offer praise. You might say something like this, for instance:

Therapist: This was nicely done on your part. On both your parts, really. It is one of those attachment-need moments like we were talking about in the last session. You pick him up right away but in such a calm, soft manner. You're very careful about how you bring his body against your own. And we see this gives him just what he needs now.
Mother: I see he likes it.
Therapist: Look at it again. I'm going to play it in a slow-motion way.

And now you go back to a moment just before the mother picks up the child, and you stop the video there. Then you press the mouse with your finger and next, almost right away, press it a second time – click-click.

The result on the screen will be that a fraction of the ongoing movement is shown, just this fragment. And you continue in the same way – click-click, click-click, click-click. With each click-click the two bodies will continue to move, but a tiny bit each time.

The effect will be amazingly graphic. When you see such interactions at a micro-level, the body-body coordination becomes readable in a totally new way. Patients frequently report that, when they have observed a piece of video this way, it stays with them for days afterwards.

Commenting on Positive Change

As you can see, highlighting the positive comes with many possible variants. Here is still another, one of the most important.

Suppose that, during a previous session (a video or non-video session), an area for change was targeted. The patient and the therapist had agreed on a new action for the patient to try to implement. Now, in today's video, we indeed see one or more behaviors which clearly reflect this plan.

To highlight this visible change moment is then a high priority, obviously. It will be not only informative but encouraging too.

Sometimes, when you show positive change, a more amplified discussion can be worth the trouble. First, you give a brief praise, as usual. Then, if appropriate, you can refer to mentalization implications – for example, you and the patient can jointly speculate about the other person's reaction.

Next, you can steer the conversation in this direction.

Therapist: How did you manage to do it? What helped you to act in this new way?

Therapist: What else may have helped you?

These are classic questions from the solution-oriented therapy tradition (Berg 1994; de Shazer, 1984). A patient may or may not find answers. But even if they do not, no matter. The questions transmit a useful thinking style about change, a thinking style we want the patient to adopt.

Further exploration might go like so:

Therapist: What will help you to continue to change in this way?

Therapist: To do [action X] more fully, what do you need? What will help you?

Here too, the patient may or may not come up with answers. And here too, if they do not, this is okay. The therapist's message is clear. It is that auxiliary strategies can be of help and it is good to be on the lookout for them.

Earlier in this chapter I suggested to be generous rather than stringent when deciding about what to count as a positive behavior. This attitude is all the more important when it comes to finding any examples in the video of positive change.

Treat as a success an action which is only a part of what was wished for. Treat it as a success too even if it occurs only once or twice, despite multiple opportunities when it could have been done. A few solution-oriented interventions are also fine to use in this instance.

Keep in mind, too, that a certain number of patients have a deep pessimism concerning their capacity to change. They are mired in a belief that how they are is how they are, end of story. To highlight a positive action, however small, can help disconfirm this dysfunctional belief.

I now turn to some further points worth having in mind when you discuss a positive change example.

The Patient's Response

Throughout Step 2, give attention to how the patient is reacting to what you show, and to what you say. Watch the nonverbal signs. Listen to the tone of voice.

They are looking at themselves interacting. They are being told what they do well there, and on the screen they see it. This can easily become an experience with an emotional charge.

Typically the feelings are positive. Still, on occasion they may need you to slow down, and to make space for them to absorb what is happening in them. They may also need help finding language for their immediate experience.

These reactions may be to the video image itself. Or they may be to what you say about it, or to both. Sometimes, too, what takes place is a gradual buildup of feeling, an accumulation, as one positive event after another is brought into focus.

Surprise can be a response. Being touched and moved, in a deeper way, can be another. Feelings of relief can come – a sense of "Ah, things are not as bad as I had thought."

When you think something emotional may be stirring in the patient, ask about it. Give support, a kind of holding, for what they are experiencing. Interventions like these can be helpful.

Therapist: How is it for you to see this?
Therapist: What are you feeling as I tell you this?
Therapist: What are you feeling as we look at these things?

An example. The patient appears close to crying. The video is of her and her 5-year-old daughter.

Therapist: I see that what we are looking at here is affecting you a lot. What are you feeling?
Patient: Moved. This is so good to see.
Therapist: What is it which is so good to see?
Patient: That Patty [the daughter] and I really do have some good moments together. It's not just a war.
Therapist: We're watching a lot of good moments here. And in just a short video too.
Patient: Yes.

This is one typical form of stronger emotional response. In the example, the thoughts driving the feelings are not so much, for example, "Oh, I'm glad I'm doing something right here," but more along the lines of "Something between us is still solid, still intact." It is a kind of reaction which counteracts parental burnout and pessimism.

The Image Incorporation Technique

One example of this effective technique was already given in the Chapter 4 discussion of Step 1. The image incorporation technique is more often used in Step 2, however. And frequently, the context is a discussion of positive change.

An easy way to explain it will be if I go straight to an example. Imagine a couple, Harriet and Leonard, in couple therapy. In the previous session, looking at a video, Harriet had observed something about herself. The video had been of a negotiation dialogue. Harriet had caught how, listening to her partner, she tended to respond with scowls and scornful grimaces.

In response to several mentalization questions from the therapist, she realized that for her partner, these facial expressions must be toxic. He confirmed it was so. She then formed a plan to reduce this tendency.

Today the new video is again of a negotiation. The therapist now calls their attention to how, in this interaction, Harriet is listening more respectfully. The negative signals are few. Her face has a more open quality.

Dave, her partner, lets her know he appreciates the shift. Next, the exchange continues as follows:

Therapist: Harriet, what will help you to continue to do this? And how can you maybe bring it even further along, this sitting and listening in such a constructive way? Any ideas?

Patient: I don't know. I'll just have to remind myself, somehow.

Therapist: That sounds sensible. And let me ask you this. Look at this picture on the screen [a carefully selected image of Harriet with a relaxed face]. For a moment try to really take this picture inside. Store it away in yourself.

Patient: Okay.

Therapist: What is this like? What do you feel yourself doing?

Patient: I'm just making room for it in me, sort of.

Therapist: How does doing that seem emotionally for you?

Patient: Good … a warm feeling. Soft almost. It's like, Harriet, you're okay, and you can do this new thing, just look at this picture here.

Therapist: Very nice. And how can it help you when you are at home?

Patient: I'll try to think about that. When David and I are into something hard it could be useful, for sure.

The example shows a typical use of the image incorporation technique.[5] Usually, the image the patient now "takes in" is one of themselves doing a behavior which is positive, but, on the other hand, one they are not able to accomplish often.

The technique is close to what in cognitive-behavioral therapy is sometimes called "imagery rehearsal" (Hackmann et al., 2011). The difference is that with video intervention the image is being directly seen, in the video, as opposed to being just imagined.[6]

To use this technique, however, we don't necessarily need for the patient be experiencing strong feelings. Sufficient will be that they, the patient, seem genuinely to agree that what is visible on the screen represents something worthwhile, and that for them to continue to act this way, or perhaps to act more this way, would indeed be worthwhile.

Using the Video at Home

With VIT we often draw on the image incorporation technique. There is of course a related possibility too. What if the patient would like to take the physical video home? What if they so enjoyed seeing the positive exception event that they have a wish to look at it more at home?

Normally, we comply, given no legal reasons to refuse. There are in fact three possibilities here:

One is that the patient straightforwardly take the video itself. They could write down that the appreciated event takes place at 6:57.

A second is that they take an edited version. You might edit it for them before the next session, preparing a brief clip showing only the positive exception moment. Or the clip might include a few other positive moments too. Or the patient themselves, if they want, could take the original video and then make their own edited version.

A third possibility is a static picture, like a photo, a picture of the positive exception event. This could be made from the video by either you or the patient.

Let me add a remark here. It concerns school age children. In my experience they can get particularly excited about taking home the video, or an edited clip from it. Some of them will look at it over and over.

Of course, an adolescent or an adult will at times become interested in the same idea. But the "look at it at home" possibility seems even more frequently to appeal to younger child patients.

Why should this be? Who knows, but perhaps it has to do with brain development.

As we all know today, the executive function brain areas become fully operative only during adolescence. It could be that for a younger child the very forming of self-change goals is more elusive, is less sharp and compelling. Should this be so, then the video image of oneself successfully performing a new behavior might provide an important aid. It might give the goal more clarity and force.

By the way, just to anticipate, there can be another, entirely different reason for a patient to take home a video or an extracted clip. As we will see in Chapter 10, this has to do with trauma triggers and work with exposure.

Identifying Other Positive Exceptions

Let me first explain what I mean by "other" positive exceptions.

One I already talked about. Let me summarize.

Suppose in a previous session a patient had formed a plan for implementing a new behavior at home. Now, as you prepare for today's session, in the new video you notice that the patient seems to have a hard time doing the planned-for action. Repeatedly, the new behavior fails to appear, despite opportunities.

Yet you do spot an exception. Maybe you spot two or three. They do manage to accomplish it at least once in any case, even if in a rather partial mode.

So, as explained earlier in the chapter, this would be a significant moment to show. Described earlier too was how the therapist could add a few solution-oriented questions, for example, "What will help you do more of this action?"

But there is another kind of positive exception, also quite significant, which you will notice at times. This kind has no tie to any previously agreed-on action plan. Rather, it simply shows up. Nevertheless, it is an exception to what in the video seems a much more predominant negative pattern.

In other words, in this video the patient frequently displays a certain negative behavior which seems to have problematic effects. For example, one couple partner, during a negotiation exchange, repeatedly uses sarcastic humor, mocking the other person's wishes and reflections

Yet an exception to this does appear. Perhaps, in the video of 30 minutes, there is one passage of around 4 minutes where this sarcasm partner acts more receptive. They drop the nasty humor. Their face and voice tones have an "I'm listening, I'm trying to understand" quality.

So likely these 4 minutes would be worth highlighting. You would not have to show all 4 minutes, of course. Around a single minute would be enough. But when and how should this be done?

Generally speaking, with this type of positive exception – an exception to a predominately negative tendency visible in the video – there are two good options for what to do with it.

One is to include it briefly during Step 2. Show it, discuss it a short while. Add one or more solution-oriented questions.

The other option would be to profit more extensively from the positive exception event. In this case you would work with it in Step 3, instead of Step 2.

It would then become the chief theme, in other words. During Step 3 you would investigate it in depth, exploring both the negative behaviors and the exception moment.

So how should one decide? Better to discuss the exception briefly during Step 2, or to investigate it in more depth during Step 3? The major criterion is this: to what extent would a change in such a behavior be useful for the main goals of the therapy?

For instance, consider the couple therapy example just given. Most probably for the sarcastic humor partner to learn how to set aside their nastiness would fit well with the therapy goals.[7]

Let me be clear here, however. To give a discovered positive exception of this nature a central place in Step 3 is only an option. It is not necessary. Should some other theme seems to you more important, then fine, plan on that instead. A discovered positive exception is simply a good candidate for Step 3 work.

Suppose, however, you do in fact decide to give the discovered positive exception a prominent place in Step 3. How would the work with it then be undertaken? This question I take up in detail in Chapter 7.

Summary

Let's review the ground covered in this chapter.

A series of positive actions can be selected while preparing for the session. These can be shown briefly, one after another.

For commenting on any positive action there are a good many possibilities. For instance, you can use non-descriptive praise or descriptive praise. Descriptive praise can be worded at different levels of abstraction. Relevant psychoeducation can be added too.

Brief mentalization techniques are also possible. Four kinds were outlined. Either the therapist or the patient can simply state a guess about what may be going on in another person in the video. Or either therapist or patient can imaginatively "give a voice" to this other person.

Some more special techniques for showing positive behaviors were also explained. These included the suspense technique, the acoustics-only technique, and the micro-viewing technique.

Covered too was how, when discussing a positive pattern up on the screen, to give careful attention to the patient's emotional responses. The technique of image incorporation was explained as well.

Two important forms of positive exception were clarified. One occurs when (1) in a previous session a plan was made for the patient to implement a new behavior. Yet (2) in today's video you see almost no doing of the new action, despite opportunities. Nevertheless (3) one or more times the new action does appear, however minimally.

The other occurs when (1) in the video you see some type of negative behavior being repeatedly done, yet nevertheless (2) one or more times a positive exception to this dominant negative pattern appears.

Emphasized was that with both forms of positive exception the use of solution-oriented interventions can be helpful. Explained, too, were two options concerning the second form. You might choose to discuss it briefly during Step 2, or you might choose to make it a main theme for Step 3.

So what in the session comes next? It depends on the type of session intended for today.

Is it to be an abbreviated session? In that case, just say the video exploration is now over. Ask for feedback about how, for the patient, it was to do it. Ask what were the most useful points the two of you covered. Then shift to your more usual ways of working, without video, for the remaining time.

Or is a full session planned for today? In that instance, now is time to move on to Step 3. The next five chapters will cover what you can do in Step 3.

Notes

1 Carter developed "speaking for the baby" for therapy with live parent-child interaction. Arietta Slade and her colleagues (Slade et al., 2005) have also made it a central technique, in a home visiting context. In *Video Intervention for Positive*

Parenting (Juffer et al., 2007), another home-visiting approach, the technique is regularly combined with video work.

2 Maria Aarts (2008) originally described this clever technique. For teaching purposes I call it the "suspense technique."

3 This is the version of praise favored by Mary Dozier and her colleagues, (Dozier et al., 2005). They use it both in live coaching of parent-child interaction and in video contexts.

4 The exact timing of turn-taking can have definite effects on interaction (Beebe & Lachmann 2014). I return to this point in Chapter 15.

5 Notice that the example in the last chapter, of the mother in the neonate unit looking at her baby in the video, was somewhat different. There the technique was used not to strengthen an overt behavior, but as a help for the mother to incorporate an altered perception of her infant. Of course, one could also argue that this too is a new action, in this instance a mental action.

6 It is close, as well, to a sports coaching use of video which has been around since the 1970s, about which I say a little more in Chapter 14. In sports coaching it has often been called "self-modeling" (e.g., Rothstein & Arnold, 1976).

7 Some of Gottman's research findings (e.g., Gottman, 1979) underline the perniciousness of repetitive sarcasm in couple negotiations.

6 Procedure step 3: Making the transition

Step 3 is the heart of a video intervention therapy session. Sustained attention will now be given to a problematic element in the interaction – a negative behavior, or a missing positive one.

This unhelpful pattern will be observed anew. It will be discussed and reflected upon, likely from several perspectives. Relevant psychoeducation may be brought in too.

Step 3 begins in a simple manner, but soon the road forks. It may fork several times.

The Outer Movie and the Inner Movie

The most important choices concern what I call the "outer movie" and the "inner movie."

The outer movie is everything we see and hear in the video. It is behavior, externally observed.

The inner movie is what is going on within the interaction participants. It is their subjective experience. What they were thinking during the filming? What were they feeling? This we don't see or hear, we can only guess.

VIT prioritizes work with the inner movie. But not exclusively. Behavior is at times examined in depth. Sometimes the entirety of Step 3 is given over to the outer movie, to behavior.

This is one basic decision, in other words. Where is the overall focus going to be, on (predominantly) the outer or the inner movie?

If, as more often is the case, your plan is to give attention to the inner movie, then another choice emerges. Which inner movie, whose inner movie, is this (predominantly) to be? Will the patient be aided (predominantly) to explore their own thoughts, feelings, and intentions, as they took place in the interaction? Or will they be encouraged mainly to speculate about the inside experience of the other person, or persons (i.e., what have I called "other-mentalization")? Here is another possible forking.

DOI: 10.4324/9781003621669-6

Lastly, there is the past, the patient's own childhood past. Might it be a good idea that some element of this history be briefly explored? This might be done in conjunction with either the outer movie or the inner movie. Some specifics of how to go about it will be taken up in Chapter 7. But the choice of whether to include it, or not, is worth considering during session planning.

On what basis can these various decisions be made? This matter I will take up shortly. First let's see how you go about shifting from Step 2 to Step 3.

The Transition

Usually the transition from Step 2 to Step 3 is simple and short.

What needs to take place, basically, is an explicit proposal that a negative pattern be explored now. You propose; the patient accepts.

Suppose it is only the first or second time a full session is being done. Here are examples of the kinds of thing you can say.

Therapist: Okay, we have seen a number of positive things you do in this interaction. Shall we go on to think about something you might want to change, or would you prefer we just stop here for today with the video?

Patient: Sure, let's go on.

Therapist: So is that enough for today with the video? Or shall we look also at something which might be interesting to try to do differently?

Patient: Definitely. Something to do differently. That's what I'm here for.

Therapist: So, is it okay with you if we talk also about something you might do differently in a situation like this?

Patient: Yes, it's fine.

Next the therapist moves to whatever part of the video best illustrates the negative pattern they want to highlight. Step 3 is underway.

But it is not always this easy.

When the Patient Responds with Ambivalence

Most patients make this shift without difficulty. They may feel some discomfort about moving to a negative pattern, but their motivation to do so is strong enough.

Understandably, however, a few patients become more ill at ease than you had expected.

Therapist: So, is it okay with you if we talk also about something you might do differently in a situation like this?

Patient: Well .... I don't know, I guess we should ....

The words might be like this. More tellingly, the nonverbal signals express ambivalence: a fading away, a scowl, a sharp voice tone, or such. When you see and hear this, what is the best way to proceed?

Emphasizing the Patient's Choice

A first good idea is just to slow down, and to emphasize anew the patient's right to decide.

Therapist: Look, let me remind you that, as we just saw, there are a number of positive things you do in the interaction. These are good skills. I'm glad today you are getting a clearer picture of them.

Patient: Thank god I get some things right.

Therapist: You do, definitely. Quite a few things. And for sure you have other skills too for interaction, ones which don't show up in these short 5 minutes.

Patient: Maybe.

Therapist: So now we need to make a choice. About what we do next. Do you remember, the last two times we worked with video, we saw some positive moments, just like now, and then we stopped there?

Today we can do the same thing, if you want. We can end here with the video, and use the rest of our time to talk about other things.

Or we can stay with the video a little longer this time. If you would like. We can use it to think about what might be some new skill you might want to develop, something you could add to what you already know how to do.

Your choice. Let's do what fits for you.

Patient: Well, I am thinking …. Okay, let's do it.

Therapist: You mean, go on with working with the video?

Patient: Yes. Let's do that.

So it might go. Just as possible, the patient might opt not to continue.

Whichever the result, a message of this kind from the therapist is important. It drives home again, and at a critical moment, that, when it comes to work with videos, the patient's autonomy is going to be respected. Either choice the patient makes will be supported by the therapist.

Asking About What Might Help

Another tactic, when a patient is on the fence, is to try problem-solving. It is often effective.

In the example, the patient is the mother of a 5-year-old girl with multiple anxieties.

Patient: Sure, let's go on. I mean, I don't know really. Perhaps we could just talk some more about Darcy [the daughter]'s problems. Well, you can decide ....

Therapist: I get the impression, Connie [the mother], that even though you are interested in our doing more with the video, part of you feels uncomfortable with the idea.

Patient: Well, yes, to be frank. I want to, but it makes me good and nervous.

Therapist: Nervous about? What are you afraid might happen?

Patient: I'll get discouraged. I already criticize myself a lot. You know that. Now I'll just criticize myself even more.

Therapist: I understand. That certainly could be a legitimate reason to stop here.

Patient: But also I want more help with getting myself moving forward. I really do want it.

Therapist: A dilemma.

Patient: A dilemma. So solve it, please. You decide.

Therapist: I think it's better the decision be yours. But listen, here's a thought. If we do continue with the video, is there anything you can do, or that I can, or that we both can, to make it less likely you'll just criticize yourself even more afterwards?

Patient: Well. I don't know. Maybe this. After we talk about what I could do that's different, could we then look again at a couple of those places in the video where Darcy really liked how I responded? They were great to see.

Therapist: Sure. That's easy enough. I'll just make sure we have some time to do that towards the end of the session. It could be a nice way to wind up.

Patient: All right. Then, on with it.

Patients often are creative with finding solutions of this kind.

Ambivalence When Two or More Persons are Present

Be ready for this possibility. The transition to Step 3 can be trickier if you are working with a couple, or with a parent and child, with both present in the session.

Take a couple, for example. The problem you may face is that one may show enthusiasm about shifting to a focus on change, while the other is obviously reluctant. This may well reflect a difference in motivation for the therapy in general.

In this instance, be sure to give an unambiguous message that a move into Step 3 will take place today only if both partners feel ready.

If person A, the enthusiastic one, now also begins to pressure person B – it easily happens – then you need actively to counter this.

Kevin: Here is a chance for us, Daniella. Let's do it. Come on.

Therapist: Easy there, Kevin. We already did some good things with this video and there is no need to do anything more. We could go on with it, but I'm willing to do that only if both of you clearly want to. Please let Daniella decide for herself.

The same can happen if you are working with a parent and a child. One or the other may suddenly want to hold back. Give the necessary support to this more ambivalent person.

Naturally if three or more family members are present the same situation can occur. Support the reluctant person, or persons, right away.

The Positive Exception Technique

Here is an elegant way to make the transition. It can be done with any patient. It is particularly useful when you suspect someone might well be ambivalent about confronting change.

The technique is drawn from the solution-focused therapy tradition (de Shazer, 1984, Berg, 1994).[1] You lay the groundwork while you are alone, scanning the video for what to highlight in the session. First, pick out what strikes you as a significant negative pattern. Next, check the video more thoroughly for a positive exception to this pattern.

For example, suppose a behavior we would like to see present appears, at first glance, to be missing entirely. But is this really so? Let's take another look. Can perhaps one instance of it be found – one instance, however partial, however inadept?

Suppose that in the video we have Emma, a mother, and Will, 9 years old. Emma is in the kitchen helping Will with his homework.

Her manner is harsh. She frowns a lot. Her voice sounds annoyed. When Will gets something right, she voices no praise or confirmation.

But let's have another look. Is it true that every time that the boy gets things right, every last time, no confirming response comes from her? Or, in the 10 minutes of the video, can we find perhaps one moment when she reacts better?

Maybe we discover that at 4:25 she does come up with a brief "Yes," apparently in response to his writing down the correct answer to a math problem. She says it gruffly, but she does say it. Here is a positive exception to the negative pattern. And it is a clear, readable exception.

So the therapist can take advantage of this event. During Step 2, as is usual, the therapist shows a series of positive events. They begin, however, with other positive moments. The 4:25 event they save for last.

They first show and comments on it in the usual fashion, saying what they find good about it. But then they continue a little further, posing one or more questions such as the following:

Therapist: Emma, suppose you were to respond like this more often? What do think might be the effect of that?

Therapist: Emma, when Will does something right, and you give him praise, like here, how do you think that is for him? Imagine you are him. What is it like to hear this from Mother?

Therapist: Suppose you were to give him praise like this more regularly? What might be the effect for him?

Therapist: I know how much you want him to concentrate better when he does his homework. How might hearing praise like this help with that?

Therapist: How could you do this more often? I mean, give him praise, just as you do here?

Therapist: What else could help you do this more often?

Notice what we have here. Merely by posing the solution-oriented questions, the therapist has already created a bridge to the rest of the session. A shift has been made to Step 3. The theme of behavioral change is on the table.

Notice, too, that in this example, the positive behavior, the "Yes," was just a minimal version of what we would prefer to see happen. The praise could be said differently, the tone could be better, and so on.

But for right now the therapist will not go into that. They will focus only on whatever was positive, however limited.

To be sure, a patient may or may not come up with any immediate answers to the solution-oriented questions. If not, this is no matter. All we really want at this point is for the patient to accept that the highlighted event represents something which could be modified. And which it would be desirable to modify. The behavior performed in the video interaction could be done more frequently, and/or more fully, and/or in another manner, and/or with a clearer intent.

The discussion can and should continue, of course. Does Emma have any reservations about accepting this as a target for change, does she see any potential obstacles, for example?

But this is work for Steps 3 and 4. As long as the mother has reacted cooperatively to the therapist's proposal, the transition has been achieved.

Interestingly, a simple version of the positive exception technique, used with video, has been around a long time. Starting back in the 1970s it has been used for sports coaching. The golfer is shown a video moment where he is doing his swing substantially better than usual. Observing the video, he takes this in, and, as research confirms, it helps him improve. "Video self-modeling" this has been called (e.g., Dowrick, 1991).

The positive exception technique as presented here can be thought of as a version of video self-modeling. The visual image the patient sees of themselves doing the better behavior provides new information. The patient can absorb some fine-grained details about their body, and perhaps about speech content too. The image can be motivating as well.

So, one way or another, the transition has been made. Step 3 is underway. Now come more choices.

Note

1 The positive exception technique is used as well in certain other video intervention approaches, as I mention in Chapter 14.

7   Procedure step 3: The outer movie

Transition achieved, you move into Step 3.

You will already have made decisions, tentative ones, about how to structure this step. The most significant choices have to do with what I call the "outer movie" and the "inner movie."

The Outer and Inner Movies

The outer movie is everything we see and hear in the video. It is behavior, externally observed.

The inner movie is what is going on within the interaction participants. It is their subjective experience. What they were thinking when they interacted? What were they feeling? This we don't see or hear.

Naturally, for the patient, as they watch the video, the situation is more mixed. They will likely have memories of what they thought and felt. Certain techniques can also heighten their access to these inner events, as we will see.

As we go about investigating a negative pattern – the goal of Step 3 – several pathways are available.

We might opt to concentrate almost entirely on the outer movie, on behavior.

Or, we might give the majority of our time to the inner movie. Then we will explore the patient's own thoughts, feelings, and intentions in the interaction. Sensed body organizing (how they are composing her body moment by moment) might be investigated too. The patient can discover more about their personal inner movie.

We might also invite the patient to reflect on the experience of someone else. What, perhaps, were the thoughts, feelings, and so on, of this second person in the interaction? What went on in the other's inner movie? Therapeutic attention can be brought to the these mentalization capacities.

Perfectly feasible, as well, is to interweave any of these strands. The therapist might focus first on the inner movie and then the outer; first on the personal inner movie, then on the other's inner movie; and so on.

Let's see what these options look like in more detail.

DOI: 10.4324/9781003621669-7

Showing the Negative Pattern

Step 3 almost always starts the same way. This is independent of any plan to work more with the outer or inner movie.

You now play a selected piece of the video, one where the negative pattern occurs. This might be an action which could have been done differently. It might be an action better not done at all.

It might be an absent positive behavior. In that case, the piece of video you play will be one where an opportunity for the missing action is evident.

You show the chosen segment. It may well have been already seen during Step 2, when positive patterns were pointed out. But the segment must be viewed again, as what will now be discussed is something other.

The typical, and easiest way, to initiate the discussion, is that you now indicate what you have in mind. You point out what you see as a pattern worth exploring.

For example, the video is of a mother trying to spoon-feed her 11-month-old daughter. The mother is both abrupt and intrusive, often trying, with a sudden movement, to force the spoon into the girl's mouth. On her side the girl repeatedly twists away. The case has been referred by a pediatrician who is concerned about the girl's low weight.

Therapist: Can you see the problem here? You are so right to be trying hard. Katie has to eat more, as we both know. But it is difficult to find the right maneuvers. The ones you are using are not getting her to cooperate.
Patient: That's for sure. She sabotages everything I do. I'm at my wit's end, I'll tell you.
Therapist: I would feel upset too. You're in a difficult dilemma.
Patient: Really.
Therapist: Shall we think about what might be other things to try?
Patient: My God, yes.

An alternative is to first ask the patient what she sees as possibilities for change. You play the segment, and then prompt her to speak.

Therapist: What stood out for you? Was there anything here you could imagine doing differently?

A mentalization variant can also be used. In the video, a father is playing on the floor with Tony, 4 years old. Tony has picked out a toy fire engine and is moving it about. Father takes a space cadet into his hand and repeatedly tries to offer it to Tony. On his side the boy just glances at the space cadet and then ignores it.

Therapist: Here is something to try, if you are willing. I'm going to play the video again, the same part we saw before [i.e., in Step 1]. This time, as you watch, imagine you are Tony. See if, as Tony, any ideas come to you, ideas about what Dad might do differently. Something he could do more of, or something he could do less of. Or maybe something completely different he could try.

Patient: Good enough. I'll see if I can do that.

Therapist: Fine.

There is of course a small risk with this option. What if the patient comes up with an idea different than yours?

Usually it is no problem. You can just go along with his idea. You explore it, you work with it; you put your own notion aside.

More complicated is if the patient's choice strikes you as bizarre, unproductive, or even inappropriate. This occurs seldom, fortunately.

Yet it can. For example, in the video segment a 6-year-old girl is having a tantrum, and the father is physically rough with her, pulling her by the arm. His idea now, observing the segment, is he wasn't rough enough.

How can we avoid this kind of awkward situation? My recommendation is to be selective about turning to this open inquiry option. Save it for sessions where you feel fairly certain that (a) what is negative in the video will be obvious to the patient, and (b) his sense of what might be a preferred action will be more or less in accord with yours.

What about with a couple, or any other combinations of two or more persons? Here also the open inquiry option can be used. But structure it carefully.

Suppose it is a couple, for example. You can have both of them review the video segment, each thinking about something they personally might want to change.

But be sure to emphasize that they are to talk, for right now, about their own actions only, not their partner's; they should share what they might change, not their partner. And their partner likewise should focus on their own change possibilities.

In other words, you proceed in a manner similar to how you structure the analogous situation in Step 1. We want to stimulate an atmosphere of creative thinking, not acrimony.

When a Negative Pattern Was Already Identified

It can also occur that, earlier in the session, the patient spontaneously pointed out a negative pattern.

Usually it happens during Step 1, as discussed in Chapter 4. Asked to comment about the video, the patient refers to something problematic in their own behavior. And they also express a wish that they were able to act otherwise.

Of course, what struck them might be the same pattern you had intended to focus on. Or it might be something other. Either way, most likely you would first confirm what they saw, and then propose that further exploration of it be postponed until later in the session. (For possible exceptions to this decision on the therapist's part, see Chapter 4.)

Now, at the start of Step 3, you can mention what the patient earlier saw, and suggest a return to it. You might propose this before you even show the video segment, for instance.

In the example, the video is of an anorexic 15-year-old girl, Francine, eating a meal with her single mother. The girl is in treatment in an in-patient unit, but returns home on weekends.

In the session, taking place in the unit, the girl is alone with the therapist.

Therapist: So, to sum up, there are some good changes here. Including about the eating.
Patient: Yeah, but like I said, I hated every bite.
Therapist: But you ate. Anyway.
Patient: I ate.
Therapist: So listen. When we first looked the video today, you were struck by how short your answers were when your mother was speaking to you.
Patient: I said almost nothing. Each time.
Therapist: True. But, as we saw, you didn't say anything nasty. Not once.
Patient: Right.
Therapist: So, when you talked about this earlier, I promised that later, if you want, we could think about what you might do differently when you reply to her. Shall we go into that?
Patient: Yes.
Therapist: Fine. I will play the part of the video we saw before. Let's both notice what Mom says and exactly how you answer her.

Specifying the Alternative Action

To point out a negative action (or missing positive action) is one thing. To suggest what might replace it is another.

Should it, the new alternative, be a physical action? To use a different voice tone would be an example.

Should it be a mental action? To say something calming to oneself, or reassuring, would be examples. To attempt more helpful mentalization would be another.

How large or minute should the recommended action be? Should it be a package of smaller actions, for example? In the food refusal case above, the therapist proposed both "present the spoon more slowly," and "wait until she opens her mouth." These are closely connected behaviors, yet, if we are being precise, distinct ones. At play can be other types of question too.

Normally, you would have decided ahead of time just what alternative action to propose. You would have thought it through when preparing for the session (See Chapter 3).

A good idea, however, is to keep this choice tentative. New thoughts may come to you as the session moves along. You may end up deciding another propose would better fit.

For example, as Step 3 proceeds you will be learning more about the patient's relationship to the highlighted negative pattern. How entrenched does the pattern seem? As the patient reflects, thinking about different aspects of it, how insightful is she? What emotional responses does she show?

Perhaps you had estimated, while preparing for the session, that the patient's motivation for this change would be modest, limited. But as you move along through Step 3 it becomes clear her motivation is high. So instead of a minimal new action you decide to propose a more complex one, logically enough.

Or the opposite could occur. A patient you were confident would be more than ready shows ambivalence, a strong ambivalence. So, scaling back what you had planned, you suggest a simpler new behavior.

Such modifications are common. Once in a while it can even happen that the patient themselves comes up with an idea for change, an idea entirely different from yours. Given that their idea seems not outlandish you will likely want to shift to their plan.

The patient's response to your suggestion, and the ensuing discussion between the two of you, may also result in a modification.

The Outer Movie: Psychoeducation

Psychoeducation has a frequent role in Step 3.

A short amount is sufficient, normally. Consider again 4-year-old Tony and his father. You will recall the boy was playing with a fire engine, and father was trying instead to bring his attention to a space cadet.

It is a pattern one sees often in parent-child play. Looking at the video, the father might himself have understood that his idea was not working. The negative behavior, in the sense that his space cadet was interfering with the boy's play, would have been clear to him. He would probably be clueless about what might be a replacement behavior, however, such usually being the case with this particular negative pattern.

So, suppose the therapist chooses to recommend so-called "descriptive language" as an alternative. To explain what this means, they would bring in a small psychoeducation package.

For example, they might first sketch out the more general notion of how an adult can "follow the child's lead" in play contexts. They could add that there are several more specific ways a parent can implement this more general action. One of these ways is descriptive language.

He could then tell more about the concept of descriptive language – that is, language for what the child is seeing, or doing, or perhaps feeling. (For a theoretical discussion see Chapter 16.) They could explain why it is thought useful.

Therapist: It will help Tom form inner language for his own actions and perceptions and feelings. Probably it will also make him feel more connected to you, since he will be hearing about how much interest you are having in his world. Anyway, this is what a lot of us in our field think.

At other times, a more sizeable psychoeducation package will be appropriate. On occasion even the entirety of Step 3 may be given over to it.

Take "Time Out." Perhaps, in the video, two parents were confronted by a young child's aggressive behavior. The parents appeared helpless, and did little. So to provide them with more effective skills, the therapist decides to inform them about "Time Out."

This will cost time. "Time Out" needs to be carefully spelled out, in a lot of detail, and with room for parents' questions. Typically this exchange will take up most of today's Step 3, if not all of it. ("Time Out" is not an intrinsic part of video intervention therapy (VIT). Most of us use it, some do not.)

Several other topics typically needing a longer psychoeducation dialogue are attachment needs; rules and limit-setting; child trauma and its effects; adoption; special needs children; and issues about parental separation and divorce.

Where to Next?

You have shown the specific negative moment, or moments, in the video. You have discussed it in a beginning way. Any needed psychoeducation has been brought in. How should you now go on? There are several options.

One is to stop right here with Step 3. You can move immediately to Step 4: the collaborative forming of an action plan for the coming days. The conversation will shift to, for example, what specific new behavior to try, when, how often, and the like.

A second option is to stay longer with the outer movie, exploring it more extensively. In this case additional techniques will be drawn upon, some of which I will describe shortly.

A third possibility is to turn to the inner movie, giving the rest of Step 4 to this. The outer movie will not be entirely abandoned, since attention will continue to be given to the video. But the focus will now be predominantly on inward experience.

For the rest of this chapter I will say more now about the second option, a continuation with the outer movie. Several additional types of technique can here be of interest.

Linking Techniques

When we analyze a video, some of the events observed have significance well beyond the filmed interaction. When a particular behavior stands out – a visible negative behavior or a missing positive one – we can wonder:

- How habitual is it? How often does the patient do it? What are its variations?
- When they, the patient, are with this same other person (i.e., the same as in the video), when else, in what other types of situation, do they do it?

And in what other relationships, and in what ways, might this behavior also be having consequences?

Such questions are often worth raising. To do so is to use what we call in VIT a "linking" technique. You make a link between an event seen in the video and events which occur at other times.

Normally, the use of a linking technique is kept short. Five minutes or less is typical.

Naturally these are subjects which could be discussed at far more length. Suppose we see a father, in a video interaction with his 8-year-old daughter, several times give needlessly devaluing messages. How often does he give devaluing messages during conflict moments with his wife? What impact does this communication style have on that relationship? This is not a small subject.

Typically, however, during a video session we raise such themes only in passing. It is for the usual reason: in order to profit maximally from the video, we want to keep today's work closely tied to it. Should a next-door theme seem to merit a more extensive discussion, this can be taken up in a subsequent non-video session.

Let's see an example of the use of linking techniques. The video is of play between a mother and Petra, 5 years old.

As the girl plays with a doll, the mother nicely follows the girl's agenda. The mother uses good descriptive language, as well as appropriate praise. These are skills she has learned from earlier sessions.

Missing in the interaction is liveliness in the mother's face. Her expression remains stern. Also, her voice tones have little modulation.

The therapist, therefore, has chosen to work today with facial expression. During Step 2, a positive exception technique was used. In the video, 10 minutes long, there were two times the mother's face did break into a smile, fleeting but evident.

The therapist highlighted both these moments. They, the therapist, proposed that in the coming days the mother experiment with showing more facial liveliness in play with Fanny. The mother readily agreed.

So, this exchange having taken place, the therapist could have moved straight into Step 4. Instead, they, the therapist, have decided first to use two linking techniques. In the dialogue below, they wind up a discussion they were having about smiles and artificiality, and then turn to the linking techniques.

Therapist: So is this clear, my answer to your question? In the next days, when you play with Petra, if you bring in more smiles and they sometimes feel artificial, don't worry about that. With time, it will become more natural. Bit by bit.

Patient: All right. Bit by bit.

Now the therapist shifts to the linking techniques.

Therapist: Good. I'm glad to see how you are on board. By the way, a question. As you get more comfortable with this, I mean, with smiling more while you are playing with Petra, what is likely to change between you two during other parts of the day? At times when you are not playing, but doing other activities?

Patient: I suppose maybe I'll smile more often then, too. If I'm in the mood.

Therapist: That makes sense. What will this be like for Petra?

Patient: Positive. How could it not be.

Therapist: How will it be for you? If you experience more smile exchanges with her, what effect might that have on your mood?

Patient: Interesting idea. I don't know.

Therapist: Well, you can find out about it, if you want. And what about with Mary [the 10-year-old sister]? As you get more skilled at engaging in smile exchanges, could this have any effect on your relationship with Mary?

Patient: For sure. As you know, I'm having trouble with her too right now.

Therapist: Well, this will all be interesting to see. Okay then, shall we make a concrete plan about adding more smiles during play times with Fanny?

With this last proposal, about a "concrete plan," the therapist has moved to Step 4. But prior to that, thanks to the linking techniques, they have managed to thematize other areas of possible change: non-play interactions with Petra, and also interactions with Mary, the sister.

On the other hand, notice how, once they turn to the topic of an action plan, they return to the specific video context – mother and Fanny playing – and talk further about this alone. The allusions to the other two contexts have been set aside.

It is deliberate. Frequently we want the plan for change to be as simple as possible, a point which will be taken up in Chapter 11. Nevertheless, these few minutes the therapist has invested in making the linking connections are worth the trouble.

First, they lay a better groundwork for generalization. The immediate plan will be for a small change. But our hope is that once a new behavior is learned, its practical use will be extended to – will be generalized to – as many related contexts as possible.

Second, linking techniques tend to be highly motivating. The patient begins to grasp how much is at play. "Hey, if I start to make this change in how I interact with [person X], I could maybe use what I learn in other areas of my life too," is the thought.

Insertion Techniques

Some videos can be used for practicing new behavior. For this we draw on insertion techniques. The patient tries out a new action, coordinating it with specific moments of the video. He "inserts" it.

Let's return again to 14-month-old Tony, playing with his fire engine, and his father. We already saw how the therapist might bring in psychoeducation about "descriptive language." He would explain how an adult can comment on elements of what the child is doing or perceiving or perhaps feeling. This would be one of several possible ways in which the father could better support the child's initiative.

Suppose now the explanation is over. The father clearly has understood. Should they, the therapist, choose to draw on an insertion technique as well, the exchange might continue as follows:

Therapist: How would it be if we use the video now to let you practice some descriptive language comments?

Patient: What do you mean?

Therapist: I will play a little of the video. A bit of the part we already saw. I will occasionally stop it on a particular image. Each time I stop it, you can make a descriptive language comment.

Patient: Fine.

Therapist: [Plays around ten seconds of the video, showing Tony reaching for the fire engine, and then stops the video on an image of Tony holding it.]

Therapist: So here you could say …?

Patient: Uh … that's a fire engine.

Therapist: Okay, fine. [Plays a few seconds more and stops on another image. Tony has started to roll the fire engine on the floor.]

Patient: See if you can make it go faster. It has to get to the fire.

Therapist: Try for now just to stay with descriptions. Something more about the fire engine, or something about what he is doing with it, or something about how he maybe feels about it.

Patient: Hey, you like this fire engine.

Therapist: Perfect.

Patient: You're making it go somewhere.

Therapist: Good.

You get the idea. The patient "inserts" his remarks, thereby practicing new responses to the other person in the video. It is like a classic role-play technique, but with the helpful difference that the patient is reacting to visual and auditory representations of the other person as they (the other person) actually appear.

To note, by the way, is one last thing. Often it is in procedural Step 3 that an insertion technique is used. But sometimes, instead, it will be done in Step 4.

The reason is simple. During Step 4 a specific homework task is determined. It can easily happen that the therapist and patient first agree on such a task and then, before the session ends, the therapist proposes an insertion technique as a trial run of the homework itself.

Continuation Techniques

Continuation techniques are another way to practice something new. They can be used when two or more persons are present in the session.

They are akin to insertion techniques. But instead of a series of insertion moments, a series of play-stop, play-stop, play-stop, the therapist does something simpler.

A negative pattern has been discussed. The patients appear to have understood what the positive replacement would be.

Now, returning to the video, the therapist shows a part which they and the patients have been reflecting about. At a crucial point the therapist stops the video. They then ask the patients to continue, with each other, here in the session. They are to continue as if they were still in the video interaction, but now using the agreed-upon new behavior.

Imagine Evelyn and Liam, a couple with two small children. The original task for the video was that they were to talk about how they divide up childcare responsibilities on weekends. They were to negotiate these issues, and try to reach one or more decisions. For this purpose they were asked to make a longer video: half an hour, filmed at home, no children present.

Negotiation videos often have several phases (See Chapter 4). Evelyn's and Liam's exchange started well. Clear statements came from both about their respective wishes. Several new ideas emerged, ideas about how to make room next weekend for some of her desires and some of his.

The tone stayed respectful too. Appropriate humor was here and there expressed.

Only, they never moved into making the decision. Ideas floated about like balloons, yet no agreement was reached. Moreover, some brief linking questions from the therapist elicited that this outcome was typical. Their negotiations often failed to end with a decision.

So now the therapist first introduces some psychoeducation about the typical phases of a successful negotiation. They emphasize the need to move, sooner or later, to making choices.

Next, they return to the video segment.

Therapist: I'm going to play a part of what we already saw. Imagine you are right there, in the interaction.

   At a certain point I'm going to stop it. And then you two can continue your discussion. I mean, you can continue in the room here, live, but as if it were just a next step in what was going on in the video.

   And as you do that, try to move forward to a decision. See if you can come to at least the beginnings of an agreement. See if you can get there within 5 to 10 minutes. Clear enough?

Evelyn: You mean, we are going to talk to each other right here?

Therapist: Exactly. Immediately after we revisit the video a little.

Liam:	Okay. A concrete plan. That's what we should try to get to, now.
Therapist:	Exactly. Watch the video, get the feel of what you were saying to each other then, and after I stop the video, see if you can go fairly soon to finding a solution.
Evelyn:	Not our strong point, this.
Therapist:	Do what you can. If you need it, I'll give some help. Shall we start in?
Evelyn:	Let's.
Liam:	Sure.
Therapist:	[Plays several minutes of the video and then stops it.] Okay, take it from there. Turn your chairs and face each other. Go on with the discussion, looking for a solution.

As Evelyn and Liam now bring the exchange farther along, the therapist will follow attentively. Especially, they will watch for any positive attempts, by either party, to shift into firming up an agreement. They might even take a few notes on paper as they speak.

If they succeed in forming an agreement, fine. The therapist can praise them for it, and also mention several of the positive moves, made by either or both, which helped bring them that far. In the event they don't succeed, they can praise any such positive moves all the same.

The therapist can also intervene at any moment with a helpful suggestion, should they find it appropriate.

There also exists an interesting variant of this technique. It is to have a video camera on hand, and actually film the continuation.

This new short video can then be looked at right away by all three, the couple and the therapist. Positive moments in particular can be highlighted. To do it this way, of course, demands a longer session.

Continuation techniques are not just for couples, naturally. We can use a continuation technique with an 8-year-old and his grandmother, a mother and a father and a 16-year-old, or any such combination of persons.

Why at Times Work with The Outer Movie Alone?

What might lead us give the entirety of Step 3 to the outer movie?

One reason may be there is simply a lot to get done.

Psychoeducation could here be the cause, for example. Perhaps the material to transmit requires a thick block of time: for example, issues about attachment needs, or about how to establish appropriate rules and boundaries with a child of age X.

A second reason could be that the patient appears to us not yet ready for a deeper investigation of their inner world. They are uncomfortable delving into inner experience, and resist it.

In this instance it makes sense to focus more on behavior, at least for the moment. We can use video work with the outer movie to stimulate a beginning change process. Small doses of inner experience can be bought in too, obviously, but in a limited way. Such doses can then be progressively lengthened in subsequent sessions.

A third reason could reflect the professional background of the practitioner. Perhaps, whatever his degree or title, they have been trained only in straightforward behavioral coaching. Can they still use VIT effectively?

They definitely can. They can use the full VIT procedure. Each step will then be carried out with coaching techniques. A consequence, however, is that likely the focus of Step 3 will have to stay on behavior alone, that is, on the outer movie.

Lastly, there are sessions where Step 3 has to be made very brief just because the clock is ticking. Time is running out. Consider several examples.

Suppose that, in Step 1, a couple had unusually insightful reflections about the video segment they had just observed. Sharing these observations took a while, but it was an exchange definitely deserving space.

Or perhaps during Step 2 a patient came into contact with a strong emotional state, one which merited a slow investigation, and appropriate support from the therapist. This took a while.

Or suppose that, in the transition from Step 2 to Step 3, a 16-year-old girl was very ready to examine a negative pattern, a joint pattern involving her and her mother. The mother, however, feeling reluctant, was holding back. Eventually the dilemma was resolved and the shift to Step 3 could be made. But the necessary transition discussion required extra time.

Many like examples could be given. The therapist had a good reason to give more space than intended to some earlier part of the session. It seemed the best call.

So then, accepting the trade-off, we scale down Step 3. We confine it to a short discussion of a negative behavior (or absent positive behavior), and shift from there straight to Step 4.

To sum up, normally when Step 3 begins, the therapist and the patient look again at a portion of the video. A negative action, or absent positive one, is pointed out.

Then comes a choice of direction. Shall the focus now stay, largely, with the outer movie? Or shall it be shifted to the inner movie? Or shall a mix of the two perhaps be used?

In this chapter we have gone over the outer movie option, considering different ways it can be carried out.

What if our decision instead is to concentrate on the inner movie? How might that work? I take up this topic in the next four chapters.

8 Procedure step 3: The inner movie

Let's review. At the start of Step 3, the therapist shows a negative pattern in the video. They explain, if the point is not obvious, why to change the pattern could be useful. Should more psychoeducation about the matter be needed, this can be brought in too.

Then comes a major choice. How shall we continue? Shall we stay with the outer movie? Or shall we shift to the inner movie?

The last chapter covered options for work with the outer movie in Step 3. In this chapter, and the three which follow, I turn to what can be done with the inner movie.

Here I will go into a series of cognitive-behavioral ways to explore. As you will see, although for the most part they can be used in a standard cognitive-behavioral therapy mode, certain modifications are necessary because of the video session context.

A Key Intervention

The most common entry into the inner movie is with a specific type of intervention. The therapist is about to play again a small part of the video. This will be the part showing the negative pattern. They now say something like the following:

Therapist: As you watch, imagine you are there in the interaction. Can you imagine this?
Patient: Okay, I'll try.

"Imagine you are there .... " Here is the critical thing to communicate. Now, as the video plays, the therapist can stop on a particular image, and then continue with questions like these:

Therapist: What thoughts are in you now?
Therapist: What are you thinking in this moment? Take time. See what is going on inside you.
Therapist: While Mia [7-month-old infant in a high chair] has been crying so intensely these last 10 seconds or so, what have you been thinking? What have you been feeling?

DOI: 10.4324/9781003621669-8

You can see the point. We are not asking, for example, "What *were* you thinking and feeling back when this interaction took place?" We are having the patient re-immerse themselves in it anew, as if the interaction were occurring here and now. Re-immersion will put the patient more in touch with relevant thoughts and feelings.

This may remind you of a classic CBT (cognitive behavioral therapy) procedure called a "replay." A fine technique, it is often employed when a patient has been talking about a recent interaction. The therapist proposes that the patient tell step by step exactly how the exchange occurred. Related thoughts and feelings can be delved into at any point.

To use a video to explore inner processes is partly similar. But in important ways it is different.

First, for the patient it is usually a more vivid experience. How could it not be? Instead of imagining the scene, they are looking at it. There it is right in front of him, happening on the screen.

Second, the level of detail is incomparably different. A memory of an interaction is mostly murky, and highly selective. A video gives a flood of specifics, visual and acoustic.

Third, the therapist is perceiving the specifics too, and not just hearing about them secondhand. This allows, for them, a much greater comprehension of the scene being talked about. The patient also knows the therapist is perceiving the specifics.

Fourth, both patient and therapist can make reference anytime to what is on the screen – for example, the exact facial expression the patient seems to have, or a particular movement the other person makes. They can even go back and look at something a second or third time, or watch an event in slow motion. With a video many such opportunities are available.

Investigation of Thoughts

Needless to say, when exploring the inner movie in this manner, the thoughts which patients find, and the related feelings, will be mainly about the self or the other or both. Some of these thoughts will be positive, some will be neutral, some will be negative.

Typically it is the negative thoughts we want further to investigate. (Although occasionally it will be a positive thought, as will be seen shortly.)

Imagine, for example, an infant feeding disorder case. The video is of a mother trying, unsuccessfully, to spoon-feed her 13-month-old daughter. Having been asked to notice her thoughts, the mother might share something like any of the following:

Patient: She is eating so little. Again. She has to eat more. If she doesn't eat more, she won't grow. If she doesn't eat more, it will be bad for her health.

Patient: What is going on with her? I don't get it.

Patient: She just wants to frustrate me, I think. It gives her a kind of satisfaction.
Patient: I feel helpless.
Patient: I feel burned out. I feel like I'm useless as a parent.
Patient: Why is she doing this? Doesn't she understand how tired I am?
Patient: If she really loved me, she wouldn't do this.
Patient: I'd like to hit her. But I know that would make things worse. But I'd like to.
Patient: I deserve better than this. I deserve a child who treats me well.

Glancing over these examples, which are typical ones, you will notice that some seem to reflect distorted thinking, and some not. All appear unhelpful for the interaction, however.

Take the belief "If she doesn't eat more, it will be bad for her health." Given a feeding disorder, the belief may reflect a genuine possibility. All the same, if this is the main thought dominating the patient's inner state during the interaction, its effect may be crippling. The thought may be dysfunctional in a practical sense.

How should the therapist proceed, once thoughts like these are on the table? For the most part, one can follow ordinary cognitive-behavioral procedures. Certain modifications can be useful, however, ones which reflect the video intervention context.

Investigation of Emotion

Naturally the therapist asks about emotions also. To observe the interaction usually reignites them in a patient. Even if the patient is someone who overall has poor contact with emotions, during a video session they will likely find them more accessible.

In the example, Daphne, 15 years old, is alone in the session. She and the therapist have been looking at a video of herself in dialogue with her parents. Following her choice, it was planned that she and her parents would work with the video separately. The two parents will be coming for their session the next day.

In the video, all three are sitting at the kitchen table. The exchange is about a punishment. Daphne has been having problems with drugs and with not going to school. The parents, with therapeutic assistance, have been trying to put into place a system of negative consequences for these and some related behaviors.

The particular punishment being discussed concerns her cell phone. Last week the parents took it away, a consequence for her having one day skipped school. In the video she is pleading to have it back. They are refusing, saying she can't have it for several more days.

Is their response excessive? Perhaps, given that adolescents are now so dependent on their phones for maintaining social contact. To continue the punishment for so long could be called harsh.

I want to put this issue aside, however. When parents have previously been too lax about limits, it is not uncommon that, seeking to change this, they overuse negative consequences at first. In any case, the parents can be invited to reflect about the matter in their own session.

In the present session, the therapist has asked Daphne to imagine herself as being in the interaction, and has then played a 5-minute segment. They now inquire about the girl's experience.

Therapist: So there you are, talking about all this with your mom and dad. Inside yourself, what do you find yourself thinking while this is going on? And what do you find yourself feeling, emotionally?
Patient: Desperate. I feel desperate.
Therapist: Desperate. Can you say more about that?
Patient: It's as if I'm trapped.
Therapist: So there's a thought here. I'm trapped. What does that mean to you?
Patient: They have my phone, no one can text me or call me, and they don't care how bad that makes me feel. They'll just keep it as long as they want.
Therapist: And this "desperate" – where in your body do you feel the "desperate"?
Patient: [Sweeping a hand from chest to belly.] Here. And here.
Therapist: Is it more like fear, or more like sadness, or both?
Patient: Both. But I'm very afraid.
Therapist: Any anger in there too?
Patient: Maybe. I don't know. It's so unfair what they are doing. They don't care about me. I'm just a burden to them.
Therapist: [Responding to the patient's nonverbal cues] I can see you are with a lot of sadness. How is it for you to let yourself feel this?
Patient: Hard.
Therapist: I can imagine. But it is very good, the way you are letting yourself right now be in contact with it.

Notice several points about this exchange. First, the feelings are strong. One would expect them to be, given the girl's difficult situation in the interaction. Second, the therapist weaves back and forth between emotion and thoughts, in a usual CBT manner. Third, at one point they inquire about how the feelings are experienced in the body. I will shortly say more about the body.

Fourth, a couple of quite significant dysfunctional thoughts have also emerged. "They don't care about me." "I'm just a burden to them." Probably these are exaggerated negative pictures, and highly so, of both the parents and herself.

Cognitive-behavioral therapists vary with respect to how attention they choose to give to emotion. Some place less emphasis on it, some more (e.g., Leahy et al., 2011; Thoma & Greenberg, 2015).

VIT therapists tend to place more. This reflects a theoretical conviction that emotion, be it conscious or nonconscious, often has a strong influence on interaction.

Investigation of Body Organizing

When uncovering thought-emotion connections, it can be productive to explore, too, what I call body organizing. This is the muscular shaping of one's body, a constantly occurring phenomenon. For the most part it is nonconscious, but aspects of it can be brought into awareness (Downing, 2000, 2008, 2015b).

Note the gerund: body organi*zing*, not body organi*zation*. It is an ongoing flow, shifting second by second, however minutely.

One can inquire about body organizing exactly as one can inquire about thoughts and feelings. I return to an example mentioned above, of 7-month-old Mia and her mother.

Therapist: While Mia has been crying so intensely these last ten seconds or so, what have you been thinking? What have you been feeling?

Patient: Sometimes I'm useless as a parent. Right now I'm useless as a parent.

Therapist: What feelings come with that thought?

Patient: Disappointment. A little sadness.

Therapist: As you feel that disappointment, what do you find yourself doing with your body? How are you shaping your body?

Patient: What do you mean?

Therapist: Well, is your body becoming more like this [demonstrates a slightly exaggerated possible posture], or like this [demonstrates another], or maybe more this [demonstrates another]?

Patient: It's ... let me see ... it's more like this [shows a slightly exaggerated slumping along with a sad face].

Therapist: Okay, clear. How do you experience this? Stay with it a moment.

Here the move was from a feeling to body organizing. One can also move directly from thoughts to body organizing.

Therapist: While Mia has been crying so intensely these last ten seconds or so, what have you been thinking? What have you been feeling?

Patient: Sometimes I'm useless as a parent. Right now I'm useless as a parent.

Therapist: As you think that thought, "Right now I'm useless as a parent," what way of shaping your body seems to fit it? Explore this a little. Stay with the thought, and find out what your body starts to do. It may be something tiny, a little something in your posture or your face or your breathing, whatever. See if you can sense it.

Patient: It's like this [shows a slightly exaggerated slumping along with a sad face].

A good way to conceptualize how such an exploration can proceed is to think of a triangle. Thoughts, emotions, and body organizing are the three points of the triangle.

The therapist can move back and forth between any of these points. They can shift from thoughts to feelings, feelings to thoughts; from thoughts to body organizing, body organizing to thoughts; from feelings to body organizing, body organizing to feelings.

Attention to body organizing takes little additional time, yet it almost always enhances the exploration of an inner state. This is useful in itself. But in the context of working with a video, there is a second advantage too.

Body organizing is a critical dimension of interaction. How person A organizes her body, has a moment-by-moment impact on person B; and vice versa. Once a patient can learn better to track this flow, it becomes an aid to building up new interaction skills.

Interventions like the several above, will help them to discover more about their body organizing as sensed from the inside. As they look at successive videos, they will also make continuing discoveries about their body organizing as seen from outside.

So the two viewpoints nicely complement each other. Self-state investigation gets at body organizing sensed from within. Observation of a video gets at it from the external perspective.

Many VIT therapists use these techniques with the body. They do require some training, however. In that sense, they are an exception to what I have elsewhere proposed with respect to this book: that any reader who is a mental health professional background should feel free to try a beginning mode of VIT work manner at once. I do wish to encourage this. But to bring in an intensified focus on the body deserves more preparation than can be communicated in book form alone.

"Downward Arrow" Thought Investigation

Once a dysfunctional thought has been uncovered, another path of interest can be to find out how it is tied to a more general thought, or to several such. This is an accustomed CBT move, and though not necessary, can be quite appropriate in a video session.

"Downward arrow" questions (Greenberger & Padesky, 1995) are helpful. We can go back to the example of the feeding disorder case, with the mother and 13-month-old daughter.

Therapist: If she wants to frustrate you, what does that mean? What does that say about her or about you?
Patient: It means something basic is missing between us, and probably we are going to have endless trouble with each other.
Therapist: You say you feel useless as a parent. If this is true, what does it say about you?

Patient: I'm lost in this role. I'm the wrong person for my poor daughter.
Therapist: You feel helpless here, you say. What does this imply? What does it mean for you?
Patient: It means that my daughter can't count on me. It means I'm someone who can't be counted on. Something in me is missing.

In work with video, such shifts to more general beliefs tend to go quickly. Elements of what Bowlby (1979) called the "internal working model," a person's cognitive map about relationships, are being accessed. If the video is of a parent-child interaction, fundamental expectancies about parents and children, and/or about development, can easily emerge also. If it is of a couple, fundamental expectancies about couple relations are likely to show up.

At times even more basic beliefs, such as "I am unlovable," or "other people cannot be trusted," will surface too.

Cognitive Restructuring

Suppose the patient has been helped to articulate a significant unhelpful belief, or network of beliefs. How, in a video session, can they now be aided to bring about at least a beginning degree of change at this level?

One way is for the therapist directly to challenge the negative thought, as is usual in CBT. The patient can be encouraged to examine the negative thought (or thoughts) from different perspectives. What speaks for and against its possible truthfulness? What are its benefits and costs? Can forms of maladaptive thinking, such as overgeneralization, or black and white thinking, be identified? Can a more useful possible thought be found?

Most patients can generate a more helpful alternative thought. The classic problem, of course, is that the patient is likely to feel little trust of this new thought. They may see the logic of it, but emotionally they feel ill at ease with it. So what should happen next?

It is at this point that what is done in a VIT session tends to differ from a classic CBT procedure. A typical CBT follow-up is to propose that the patient try a behavioral experiment in their daily life. The experiment will cast light on the validity, or lack of validity, of the negative thought. A social anxiety patient is convinced that, if they initiate a conversation at a party, the other person will reject them. Why not try this out next weekend, as a test?

In VIT, however, cognitive restructuring tends to be approached otherwise. There are several reasons.

One is that the presence of the video opens the door to certain other possibilities. Often, for example, something can be found in the video which speaks directly against the negative belief. A father is convinced he is incapable of emotionally reaching his young child. He is a "loser" as a parent. Yet, with the therapist's help, he can again see moments in the video where the child responds to his, the father's, initiatives. The counter-evidence stands right there in front of him.

Or psychoeducation can have a similar impact, as long as the psychoeducation is directly linked to the video, and as long as its content contradicts the negative belief. This might be a piece of psychoeducation shared earlier in the session, and now revisited. Or it might be a fresh piece brought in now.

For example, a mother is sure that, when her 2-month-old infant glances away from her, this implies he is uninterested in her. The therapist might now pass on the information that such "look-look away" patterns are very common (Beebe 2006); and that, as research has shown (Field, Healy, Goldstein, & Guthertz, 1990), an infant who breaks off for several seconds from contact is, in fact, physiologically regulating himself.

Most of the time (but of course not always!) patients trust such input, given, as I have said, that it is in some way tied to the video.

For those VIT practitioners familiar with the body techniques there is also another option. Can the patient, while entertaining the new positive cognition, find a form of body organizing which for them better fits with it? What, if anything, about this alternative body organizing "clicks" for them, or appeals to them?

This can be explored. The strong advantage is there will be likely an immediate effect. Once the new thought being entertained is aligned with a more supportive body organizing, the thought itself typically takes on increased cognitive cogency. It is as if the patient begins to taste what this different way to be in the world might be really like.

A short look at the childhood past of the patient can also sometimes help them disentangle themselves from a negative thought. Work with the past, typically brief, is frequently used in VIT, and one way it can be done is while exploring a dysfunctional cognition. What happened in the past to create this belief? What feelings and reactions come in the patient when they confront this connection? Do these reactions stimulate any questioning of the belief itself?

In Chapter 11, Step 4, the forming of an action plan will be discussed. At that time we will see some additional reasons why the concept of a behavioral "experiment" is seldom invoked in a VIT session. This exception aside, however, a systematic confrontation with negative cognitions frequently plays a key role in work with the inner movie.

Cognitive Distancing

Cognitive distancing is also a possibility. It can be used instead of trying to replace a negative with a positive thought. In recent years there has been a flourishing of literature on this helpful option.

You help the patient to find ways to simply lessen the inner force of a dysfunctional thought. The thought is allowed to be there, floating about in the mind, unchanged in its content. But the patient discredits and weakens it, using mindfulness and related techniques. A spirit of humor and playfulness often plays a part too.

I will not further discuss cognitive distancing techniques here, other than to say they also are to be recommended. They are easy to introduce into a VIT inner movie exploration.

Insertion Techniques for Cognitions

Suppose you have helped a patient discover a more productive cognition. You have helped her not with cognitive distancing, but with thought replacement.

An insertion technique can sometimes be an additional option. It depends upon whether the video lends itself to it. Should you make this move, it will cost little time.

Insertion techniques are more commonly used for the practice of new behavior, not thoughts. This was covered in Chapter 7. The patient looks again at the video, this time "inserting" the new action at specific moments. We saw the example of a father trying out descriptive language, in coordination with how his young son in the video was playing with toys.

But a variation can indeed be used with cognitions. This variation has a couple of different forms.

Suppose that the patient has found a more productive thought, one which could replace the dysfunctional cognition. Say that they can at least see the reasonableness of the new thought, even if, emotionally, their acceptance is still lukewarm.

Now the therapist can have the patient return to the video. Watching it anew, they, the patient, can now say the thought to themselves at selected moments which the therapist will progressively show.

Or, often a more interesting possibility, they even can say the thought aloud each time. The idea is not that, in a real-life interaction, the patient vocally communicate the thought in this way. In the real situation they would evoke it in themselves silently. But the out-loud version which they do now can sometimes have strong positive effects. It can replace inward hesitancy with inward assertiveness, for example.

For example, Jacob, a father, is regarding a video of himself interacting with his 12-year-old son, Peter. Several downward arrow explorations illuminated strong negative assumptions about both himself and the son. With the help of the therapist he then determined some more productive thoughts which could replace the negative assumptions.

Now, as the therapist stops the video at selected moments, he, the father, speaks aloud several of these more productive thoughts.

Patient: Hey, Jacob, you're doing it fine.
Patient: Peter, sometimes you get nasty with me, like now, but you're a complex person, with wonderful parts too.

Thanks to the video he can practice mobilizing these thoughts during actual interaction moments.

To summarize, covered in this chapter has been a beginning look at how the therapist can explore the inner movie in VIT. Most of what has been described are typical cognitive-behavioral therapy investigative modes, but with frequent indications of what becomes different in a video intervention context. Included were the following:

- The importance of the "Imagine you are there …" intervention
- Using the video to work with dysfunctional thoughts
- Using video to contact and clarify emotions
- Using the video to contact and clarify body organizing
- Further possible exploration of thoughts with the "Downward Arrow" technique
- Using the video for what I have called "cognitive rehearsal"
- Using the video to support cognitive distancing
- Insertion techniques with the video to further reinforce selected more functional thoughts

There is more to say about work with the inner movie. We will go, in Chapter 9, to the topic of mentalization.

9 The inner movie and mentalization

I have already mentioned that VIT, as an attachment-based method, puts a strong emphasis on work with mentalization. Intervention with video offers unique opportunities for helping patients in this area.

Some mentalization techniques we have already seen. I will now describe several others. In this book I cannot discuss the full range of work with mentalization in VIT. But what is covered here should be more than enough to help you get underway.

Let me start with a more general overview. The concept of mentalization was first developed by Peter Fonagy, Howard Steele, Miriam Steele, and Mary Target in the 1990s (Fonagy et al., 1991; Fonagy, 2008). Mentalization was held to have two aspects.

One is my ability to discriminate, and find language for, my own subjective states: my thoughts, feelings, intentions, body sensations, and the like, as well as the links between these and how I act in the world.

The other is my ability to form good hypotheses about the subjective states of someone else: their thoughts, feelings, and so on, as well as probable links between those inner elements and their behavior in the world.

As already said, the first aspect I like to call "self-mentalization," and the second, "other-mentalization."

Fonagy, Steele, Steele, and Target created an elaborate research instrument, Reflective Function, which both amplifies and gives precision to the concept (Fonagy et al., 1991; Steele & Steele, 2008). Reflective Function, or RF, is a system for coding spoken discourse. It has been used extensively for research for several decades now.

RF is inspired by and incorporates elements of the Adult Attachment Interview (AAI; originally developed by Mary Main [1999]). At the same time, RF highlights some quite other dimensions of mentalizing. (I will not go into these differences here.)

The RF coding system, to put it another way, divides up mentalizing into a series of distinct skills. To take an example, my capacity to realize how much another person's subjective experience may be unlike my own, is one such skill. My ability to think in a coherent manner about the other, is another – and so on.

DOI: 10.4324/9781003621669-9

With respect to each skill RF also defines different degrees of competence. As regards any given skill, where do my abilities stand? Perhaps they are very low? Perhaps they are moderately low, or maybe okay, or maybe moderately high, or maybe quite high even? RF provides specific indications.

Taken all together, it is a precious gift for us therapists. We have an elaborate, well worked out, research-based instrument for thinking about this critically important topic.

So what about the practical side? How in therapy should we work with mentalization?

Arguably the more pressing question here is how should we work with other-mentalization. As for self-mentalization, most therapy methods already have means of helping with it. This is what therapy has been about since its Freudian beginnings. It is concerning other-mentalization that one has the impression much remains to be done.

Several valuable contributions have been made, nevertheless.

First, Fonagy and some of his colleagues (e.g., Fonagy, 1991, 2008; Bateman & Fonagy, 2004) have created a burgeoning literature on how to work with mentalization in individual and group psychoanalytic settings. (I will henceforth simply use the word "mentalization" to signify "other-mentalization.")

Second, cognitive-behavioral therapy from the start has sought to aid patients to identify and change dysfunctional modes of thinking about other individuals (Beck et al., 1979; Greenberger & Padesky, 1995; Persons, 1989). Although classic CBT covers less ground than does an RF-informed perspective (i.e., it thematizes fewer skill areas), it does provide useful tools.

Third, in the domain of parent-infant therapy, a seminal article was published in 1991 by Sheena Carter, Joy Osofsky, and Della Hann. Inspired by certain innovations of Selma Fraiberg (e.g., Fraiberg et al., 1975), Carter and her colleagues presented the technique which they called "Speaking for the Baby" (Carter et al., 1991). I already referred to this innovation in Chapter 5. The "speaking for" techniques I proposed are simply an amplified version their idea.

Fourth, in systemic family therapy what is called "circular questioning" has multiple purposes, but one is to enhancing the capacities of family members to think about one another's subjective worlds. The therapist invites one family member to speculate about what another family member is feeling or thinking, or about why another family member has just conducted herself in a particular manner, for example. Asen, following some of Fonagy's ideas, has developed additional such techniques for intervention with families (Asen & Fonagy, 2021).

Fifth, role-plays in therapy can sometimes have a similar function. By playing the role of someone else, for example, a friend or work colleague, the patient can gain new intuitions about how things go on within that person.

Sixth, the more specific psychodrama technique of "doubling," used dur-ing role-plays, is explicitly meant to promote mentalization. As the role-play progresses, the therapist gives words, using the grammar of "I," to what one of the protagonists may be experiencing.

(To note, however, is that this technique tends to be limited to psycho-drama settings only. Although role-play is widely used in diverse treatment methods today, the practice of doubling is rarely included.)

VIT work with mentalization draws, in different degrees, upon all these currents.

Several types of technique have already been seen in Chapter 5. As you will recall, they are brief, cost little time, and can be used often. Each type is introduced in a similar way. The therapist stops the video on a particular im-age and only then brings in the technique.

Here is a summarized list:

- Simple reflection, therapist leading
   (The therapist comments about the other person in the video, making a guess about his or her inside experience.)
- Simple reflection, patient leading
   (The patient is asked to comment about the other person.)
- Giving a voice, therapist leading
   (The therapist "gives a voice" to the other person. "Hey Dad, I like that!" says the therapist, echoing how the 2-year-old in the video is laughing at her father's antics.)
- Giving a voice, the patient leading
   (The patient is asked to "give a voice" to the other person.)
   I turn now to some additional techniques.

Simulation Techniques

A simulation technique has similarities to "giving a voice." But it is more com-plex, and has the potential for deeper emotional impact and more insight.

The patient is requested, for a portion of the video, to imagine that they are the other person. Anywhere from 30 seconds to 10 or so minutes of the video is then shown anew.

As the video plays, the patient's task is to try to put himself in the shoes of the other person. They should to try to think what the other person might be thinking, and try to feel what they might feel.

Here is an example. The video is of Alan, 9 years old, and his mother, Elena. Only Elena is present in the session.

Therapist: So the idea is clear? You are going to imagine you are Alan. Watch what happens in the video, and notice what thoughts and feelings come to you, as Alan.

Patient: Okay.

The therapist lets the video run. Eventually they stop it, and inquire about what has been going on in the patient – that is, about what she has been experiencing "as" the other person.

Therapist: [*In the video Alan has been sitting at the kitchen table, preparing to do his homework. The therapist stops on an image of Alan placing books and papers on the table.*] So what's going on inside of you here, as Alan.

Patient: "I'm nervous. Homework is hard for me. A lot of the time anyway."

Therapist: Fine. Anything else?

Patient: Frustrated. Annoyed. "I don't want to do this."

Therapist: Okay.

Therapist: [*Plays the video again, then stops on an image around 20 seconds later with Alan now sitting and mother standing beside him. In the video mother has just asked, in a curt, somewhat harsh voice, "Are you sure now you have everything you need?"*] And now? As Alan what have you been experiencing in this last exchange?

Patient: Kind of, "Why does Mom have to talk like that? Why can't she just say it nicely?"

Therapist: What are the feelings with that?

Patient: Tense.

Therapist: What else? I mean, as Alan, are you noticing a touch of anger, or fear, or shame, anything like that?

Patient: A touch of anger, actually.

Therapist: So something is starting to cook up in you, as Alan.

Patient: Yes. I – I mean myself, Elena – didn't really need to say it that way to him, I see. It's as if I'm already criticizing him.

Therapist: Good observation, we'll come back to that in a bit. For now, if it's ok, just continue to be Alan. Is that all right?

Patient: Sure.

[*Therapist continues with the video.*]

As you can see, extended simulation, in one sense, is simply a more elaborate version of "giving a voice." But it produces another kind of atmosphere. To do it feels quite different for patients, and its effects are usually deeper.

You will recall that the techniques of simple reflection, and of giving a voice, can easily be used in either procedure Step 2 (where we highlight positive patterns) or Step 3 (where we work with a negative pattern). These techniques are brief, and easy to fit in. And if they are used also during Step 3, this might be during an exploration of either the outer or inner movie.

An extended simulation, on the other hand, is normally brought in only during Step 3, not Step 2. And it will be more likely combined with a focus on the inner movie. Indeed, it is intrinsically a form of inner movie work, we might say – but in this case with the other person's inner movie.

It is more strenuous technique too. Concentration is required. So is an acceptance of inner experiences. At times also, as in the above example, the technique can mobilize a degree of self-confrontation on the patient's part. The therapist must judge when the time for it feels ripe.

Evaluation of Mentalization Competencies

An excellent therapeutic step is, sooner or later, to thematize the topic of mentalization. This requires a move to a meta-cognitive level.

The basic idea is that you want to the patient to think about his thinking, and you want him specifically to wonder about questions like these. When I reflect about the inside world of someone else, in what ways am I good at it? In what ways am I not so good? And as for the not so good ways, might change be possible? How would I go about making changes? What would I gain if I could do that?

Note the assumptions implied.

One (to say it again) is that mentalization is comprised of a series of distinct mental skills.

Another is that these skills can be noticed on a meta level. They can be monitored, they can be evaluated, they can be talked about, they can be reflected upon.

Another is that where such skills are weak they can be improved.

Yet another is that any improvements along such lines will have strong positive consequences for the patient's life.

So how can you help the patient on this explicit, thematized level?

A first step is simply to gather information. Use the various mentalization techniques often. Use, especially, the briefer ones: they are so easy to add, they usually cost no time. Make joint reflecting about what happens inside other humans an ongoing conversation.

This in turn will let you pay attention to the patient's apparent strengths and weaknesses. You can begin to evaluate specific skills. For example, is the patient's thinking coherent, without excessive contradictions?

Are they overly sure they just "know" what is happening in the other? Or are they aware that other-mentalization produces only hypotheses, hopefully true but maybe not?

Can they recognize both the positives and the faults in others, and in a balanced way?

Do they understand that how the other sees things, and thinks about things, may be quite different from their own way?

Can they keep their thinking focused on the other, without constantly jumping to thoughts about themselves?

As they mentalizes, is their thinking rigid and fixed, or are they open to new ideas?

Can they make good connections between the actions they see the other person doing, and the likely related thoughts and feelings this person is having?

Does their thinking stay relevant, without getting lost in tangents or cliches?

If they are mentalizing about a child, can they take into account their developmental level?

If they are mentalizing about a person with neurological disorder (e.g., autistic spectrum), can they take this into account?

Every patient has their own profile here. With respect to each such ability, what appears to be their level of competency? Which abilities, if any, seem very low? Which seem moderately low, which moderately good, which very good?

RF, by the way, provides detailed criteria for these multiple aspects (save for the last one – mentalizing when the other has a neurological disorder – which I have added).

In VIT trainings these criteria are taught. But there is plenty you can do without this. Merely by inviting your patients to mentalize, and paying attention to how they respond, you will start to find your way around in the territory.

Helpful, also, would be to familiarize yourself with the writings of Fonagy and his colleagues. Of the skills mentioned above, Fonagy especially emphasizes three:

One is the ability to make good connections between outer behavior and probable inside experience. Someone low in this area is operating in what Fonagy names "teleological mode." They overly depend on physical acts and cues when reading others. Simplistic, shallow readings of the other become frequent.

"Psychic equivalence mode" is Fonagy's term for mentalizing with a low awareness that what the other thinks and feels may be different, and may even be very different, from what I am thinking and feeling. I unwarrantably assume that the other's psychic state is "equivalent" to my own.

"Pretend mode," as Fonagy calls it, concerns the skill area of relevance. A patient with deficits here, when trying to reflect about the other, will easily veer into thinking which is artificial, with a "pseudo" quality.

What you will find particularly helpful, if you spend some time with Fonagy's writings, are the many case examples. They will give you a more concrete sense of what poor mentalization skills can look like in clinical contexts.

Thematizing a Specific Ability

"We all have our difficulties with thinking about what is going on inside someone else. Each of us is better at some aspects of this, and less good at other aspects." This is the fundamental message we want to transmit to our patients.

And there is more. We want to transmit as well: "If you, patient, could become more aware of which aspects you have the most trouble with;

and if you could begin to make progress with those skills; then you would see some clear positive consequences in how you live and manage your relationships."

But how, in practice, can we best communicate such notions? How can we shift the therapeutic dialogue in this way?

In my experience the easiest time to introduce the subject is when a patient has just performed a moment of competent mentalizing.

There are two possibilities here. This, the competent moment, might be in a mentalizing skill area where the patient has already struck you as fairly adept. Or it might be in an area where they tend to do poorly.

When you talk about all this, by the way, there is no need to use the word "mentalization." You can speak about it in a more everyday manner, as in the examples to come.

Let's take a first example. Imagine a video of a father playing with his 3-year-old son. The father has been given a "put away toys" task – that is, at a certain point he is supposed to organize that he and the child place the toys, that are out, back into a big box where they originally were found.

The therapist is using a simple mentalization reflection technique. They are stopping the video on certain images, and asking the father what he thinks is going on in the boy.

At one point the boy picks up a small car, walks to the box, and with an aggressive looking movement throws it noisily in. The therapist stops the video on an image of the boy just after this movement.

Therapist: And now? What you think is happening in him now?
Patient: He's getting rebellious for a moment, it looks like. He's been co-operating, I think he wants to cooperate. But another part of him is angry we are ending the play, and he needs to act up a little.
Therapist: Makes sense to me.

So far the exchange is simple enough. But now the therapist brings in something more.

Therapist: You know, Roger, what I like particularly about what you are saying is that you are talking about two different parts of him, his cooperative part and his oppositional part. This is something I have noticed before, that you have a good capacity to consider both positive and negative things which might be going on in him.

With this remark the therapist has shifted their discourse. At first they were talking on the basic level – "What is perhaps happening here within person X?" Now they have just moved to the thematization level – "What does it mean, in general, to think skillfully about what might be happening inside another person?" The topic has been introduced.

Or, better said, it has been half-introduced, if this is the first time the therapist has intervened in such a manner. In that case an additional comment would amplify what they are getting at.

Therapist: After all, to think well about what is happening inside someone else, to make good guesses about it, is not so easy. Every one of us is better at some aspects of this kind of thinking and less good at other aspects.
          And one aspect is the ability to reflect about both positive and negative elements of another person's inner world. Some people have trouble with this. But you are capable here, quite capable. I have seen it a number of times.

Patient: You mean, for some people this is hard in what way?

Therapist: Some persons tend to jump regularly to just the negative. Or they jump to just the positive. Not all the time, but too often. But you manage to have a good balance between the two in your thinking.

Patient: I see what you mean, I think. Interesting.

A next step can be to focus on a moment when a patient (1) has just performed a moment of competent mentalizing, but (2) in a skill area where they are usually less able. In other words, here you are going to talk about a positive exception.

This is a more complicated move, naturally. Just to praise what the patient said would be easy enough. But now your intent is, first, to clarify that the exception is indeed an exception; and, second, to motivate the patient to better develop the relevant mentalizing ability.

Exactly what to say, and how much to say, depends on the patient. Let's take one example.

Let me say something first about the treatment setting. Helen is the mother of Sabine, 14 years old. Sabine, who has anorexia, is currently in a residential eating disorder clinic.

On weekends Sabine returns home. She and Helen, who is a single mother, are together Friday evening until Monday morning.

The video, arranged by the two of them, was filmed at home. In the video they are discussing Sabine's current experience in the treatment unit. Today, in the session, only Helen is present, Sabine having preferred that each of them work separately with the video.

In previous sessions, ones with and without video, the therapist has already noticed that Helen appears regularly to be overly certain that she, Helen, knows what Sabine underneath the surface is thinking and feeling.

She stays too much in what Fonagy calls "psychic equivalence mode," in other words. She is quite low in the skill of "tentativeness," to use Reflective Function coding language.

Sabine, in the non-video sessions with mother and daughter both present, has, a couple of times, complained about this attitude. Up to now Helen has brushed the issue aside.

In today's video session, however, something different occurs. In the video interaction itself, mother and daughter slip into a sharp-tongued argument about Sabine's dislike of the unit's breakfast, and her occasional refusal to eat it. Helen makes some critical, rather demeaning comments. Sabine rolls her eyes and grunts, saying little.

The therapist stops the video just after one such comment and eye rolling exchange.

Therapist: So what do you think is going on in her now?

Patient: She ... she just .... You know, I'm not so sure. She doesn't like what I am saying. That's obvious. But what else she is feeling, it's hard for me to say.

Therapist: Helen, I really like what I hear you telling me right now.

Patient: Huh?

Therapist: What I really like is this. You are feeling puzzled, clearly. And you know it, you are aware of it. You know that you don't know.

Patient: What good is that?

Therapist: It's a form of inner clarity, to know that you don't know. An important form of inner clarity.

After all, at the end of the day we can only make guesses about what is happening inside someone else. And it is very important to be aware of that. It keeps our minds more open to the situation.

Patient: Okay. I guess that makes sense.

So far, the patient is on board. The therapist can now move to another step.

Therapist: I have a question here, if that's okay.

Patient: [Nods.]

Therapist: Could it be useful for you to get aware of this more often, to make yourself conscious that your guesses are only guesses? I mean, when you are thinking about Sabine's inner world, or about anyone else's for that matter? Many people do find it a help to make themselves more aware of this.

Patient: Maybe. It's sort of a new idea to me, to tell the truth. I don't know, I'll have to turn it over inside myself some.

Therapist: Well, you certainly got yourself nicely aware of this important idea just now.

This might well be enough for now. The subject has been raised.

Indeed, several aspects have been raised. The notion itself of mentalization – "making guesses about what is happening inside someone else" – has been thematized. Added too has been the idea of being conscious of "not knowing." The proposal that the patient might profit from change in this area has been mentioned also, if fleetingly.

Note, as well, that although a reference to change was brought in, the therapist then said nothing further about it.

Why did the therapist not pursue the topic of change? Was it necessary to say so little?

Who knows. Again, it depends on the patient. With someone else, the therapist might well have entered into more discussion of change.

Perhaps, with this patient too, more discussion might have been fine – but perhaps not. The "not-knowing" theme is tricky. Someone who displays this type of exaggerated certainty, can easily become resistant when the problem is pointed out. [Exaggerated mentalization certainty typically has defensive functions, I would suggest. I will not pursue this topic further here, other than to say that for some patients the potential shift to a world where other persons are often opaque is a shift which provokes anxiety.]

More generally speaking, a good idea, after having taken steps like those just recounted, is to carefully watch the patient's nonverbal signals and not try to go too far. Just to have brought into the open the idea of mentalization, along with the hint that the patient might want to improve her abilities, can be enough for today.

In later sessions, both video and non-video, the topic can be elaborated. The therapist can continue with a frequent use of mentalization techniques. This will create plenty of further opportunities to discuss strengths and weakness.

Furthermore, after one such skill area has first been thematized, it will become progressively easier to talk about other skill areas too. The patient will be acquiring a wider picture of how things stand with their capacities. Hopefully they will also become more motivated to seek the changes which will best serve them.

Plenty of additional ways to work with mentalization are possible. This has been only a first look. One more quite useful technique will be covered in Chapter 10, for example.

10 Procedure step 3: Working with the relational effects of trauma

Some patients have suffered severe trauma in their childhoods – for example, sexual abuse, physical violence, extreme neglect, the loss of an important parenting figure.

Such a history is quite likely to influence their present-day relationships. The effects may be strong and obvious, or they may be subtle. They may be pervasive, or they may be only occasional.

Other patients have gone through significant trauma as adults – violence, loss, or the like. Beebe (Beebe et al., 2012) did a microanalytic study of mother-infant dyads whose lives were upended by the New York September 11 terrorist attacks. All the mothers were pregnant at the time of the attacks; all lost their partners. Videos of the mother-infant exchange at infant age 4 months showed significant differences from normative population studies. One such result I will mention shortly.

Even less dramatic adult trauma can have its effects. A mother or father whose premature infant was in a neonate unit, especially if the birth was very early, may have undergone experiences they felt to be overwhelming. This, too, can have consequences.

Bonding may be felt as difficult. And/or, an intense need to give to the infant, a need to heal and nurture, can spin out of control. The adult's overdone giving can then seriously mismatch the infant's limited tolerance for strong signals.

Attention to such consequences, whatever the trauma type and whenever it occurred, has a critical place in VIT.

What type of help does a traumatized patient need? A good hypothesis, in my opinion, is that for many such patients – not all, but many – two distinct kinds are recommended.

One is direct work with the trauma memories. This will be carried out using exposure, and/or some type of emotional processing of the memories. The other is help for an improvement of interaction capacities. I will explain.

For aid with trauma memories, there are available today a number of useful approaches: straightforward exposure procedures (e.g., Foa et al., 2007); hypnosis procedures (e.g., Hunter, 2007); cognitive-behavioral procedures (e.g., Zayfert & Becker, 2007); eye movement desensitization and reprocessing (EMDR); Shapiro, 2018); and body psychotherapy procedures (e.g., Levine,

DOI: 10.4324/9781003621669-10

1997; Ogden et al., 2006), for example. (The body techniques I myself teach include ones especially for work with trauma.)

Yet with all these methodologies there exists a basic limitation. Usually they are quite effective for reducing symptoms such as flashbacks, hyperarousal, and states of numbness. But they tend to be less effective with respect to trauma-affected relational abilities. I have seen this in case after case, as have many of my VIT colleagues.

Perhaps, thanks to some such processing procedure, a patient has gained more distance from the trauma memories. They have achieved an important reduction of hyperarousal, flashbacks, and numbness states.

Certainly this will be a gain for interaction contexts too. For instance, this patient might now seem more present, with less dissociative tendencies.

But what do they do with this heightened presence? What do they say? How do they shape their ongoing posture, gestures, facial expressions? And how well do they decipher what is going on in others?

Quite frequently, they will need further therapeutic aid with much of all this – which, if you think about it, seems hardly surprising, as we are talking now about more complex levels of behavior.[1]

For this second level of help video intervention can be an optimal choice. Observing the videos, the patient can see, with precision, exactly when they are more present, and when less. They can see exactly what they do when they are less present, and what not. And then once they start to change more specific behaviors, they can see what this looks like in an interaction, and what the effects are on the other person.

So if we accept this perspective, this idea of adding a second type of help, just what does it mean on a practical level?

Such will be our topic for the rest of the chapter. To anticipate, I will be going over several main points.

First, I describe some of the more typical trauma-influenced behaviors which might be seen in a video. Preparing for a session, looking over a video segment, what might you notice?

After that I talk about specific techniques. What should you do about behaviors in a video session? What might you explore, and how? And then, if the behavior you have pinpointed turns out indeed to be trauma-based, what comes next? How should the session continue?

Finally, I take up the important topic of overall case conceptualization. Once you have learned that a patient does in fact have a severe trauma history, what is implied for the continuation of the therapy? This question has its own complexities, as we will see.

Let's turn to the first of these themes.

Typical Triggered Reactions

If past trauma is influencing how a patient interacts, what type of behavior might be the effect? Specifically, what might we see on the video screen?

I will now describe nine kinds of interactional pattern which often prove to have a severe trauma background.

"Often," I am saying, let us note. Because it would be a serious mistake to assume, automatically, that if we find one of these patterns in a video then for sure it is tied to past trauma. At times these patterns can have other causes.

I will return to this point later on. First, let's look at the types themselves.

1 One is *passive dissociation*. At a certain moment the person simply fades. They are present but not present.

Their movement and facial expressions decrease, in either quantity or amplitude (i.e., how large or small the movement is) or both. Their body appears perhaps more rigid, perhaps limper. If they speak, their tone sounds flatter.

It is a surprisingly frequent phenomenon. With time, you will become more adept at spotting it in videos.

When it occurs, it may last only a few seconds, or it may last for minutes. With a few patients you even have the impression they live more of the time in this state than in more activated states.

2 *Oversexualized contact* is another behavior which can show up. This will usually concern an adult with a child.

Perhaps the adult fondles the child's buttocks, or even the child's genitals (rare, at least in a video, but I have seen it). Or the adult demands that the child kiss them, on the lips, in a manner which seems eroticized (See Sroufe & Ward, 1980).[2]

Or it is the child who seems to cross the line. They open the mother's blouse and stroke a breast, with the mother seeming oblivious.

Oversexualized behaviors can occasionally be found in a child-child interaction. One child is excessively sexual, and quite a bit, with the other. Or perhaps both act this way. You get the impression of something well beyond "normal" sex play.

3 *Sudden fear signals* can be sometimes be apparent. Here in the video is a parent playing with a child. In response, say, to a close-quarters abrupt movement of the child, the parent's face breaks into a strong fear expression (See Lyons-Ruth et al., 1999).

Or, in a couple video, you might see similar expressions in reaction to the other partner suddenly raising their voice, or shifting into an aggressive posture.

Be aware, by the way, that a fear signal is not the same as passive dissociation. It can be combined with dissociation, but plenty of times it is not.

4 *Eruption* takes place when a parent, or a couple partner, quickly and strongly escalates his anger. The key indicator here is the suddenness. They zoom in an instant from neutral to menacing aggressiveness.

A trauma history – for example, war trauma, or experiencing and/ or witnessing family violence – may stand behind what you are seeing.

Something has triggered an activation of the sympathetic nervous system, that is, the flight-fight response, here being the fight version.[3]

What if you see such a sudden and intense outburst on the part of a child or adolescent? Here, too, a trauma history may be at play. But know that the likelihood is lower. Prefrontal cortex control over strong emotion develops fully in the brain only late in adolescence. For plenty of children and adolescents with problems with behavior of this kind the causes are other.

5 *Extremely invasive physical handling* is to watch out for. This, too, normally concerns an adult with a child. The adult is unusually rough and intrusive while, for example, dressing or bathing or spoon-feeding a child. Research shows high amounts of this behavior are correlated with a likelihood of disorganized attachment on the part of the child (Lyons-Ruth et al., 1999).

6 *Autonomy restriction* can occur between an adult with a child. The adult repeatedly blocks what, given the child's developmental level, would be a normal autonomous behavior.

Most of the time, when you see this, it will not at all look like the "invasive handling" type just described (although it can). The adult's manner may be friendly and nice, for example. Nevertheless, autonomy blocking is taking place.

Interestingly, this interaction phenomenon can occur even at child age 2 months, as I have seen a good number of times. The child engages with the adult in a face-to-face exchange. But, as is normal, every so often the child starts to turn away, presumably seeking a short pause. However, the father or mother blocks the turning away, using a finger or some such means to prompt the child to re-engage in direct contact.

To take a fascinating research example, I already mentioned the study of Beebe and her colleagues with mothers who had lost their partners in New York September 11. Among other things, Beebe analyzed the look-look away patterns in face-to-face interaction. The infants were aged 4 months. Compared to normative dyads, these mothers looked at their infants for (statistically speaking) longer periods, and they looked away less frequently. In addition, *the infants too* looked for longer periods, and looked away less frequently.

These September 11 results are quite typical, by the way, in this sense: when systematic autonomy restriction is trauma-based, the underlying trauma is often one of loss.[4]

Needless to say, there can be numerous other reasons why an adult might have trouble tolerating a child's autonomy. But it is important to be aware that an underlying trauma history can at times be the principle cause.

7 *Excessive disgust signals* are another type. This, for example, you will sometimes see in a video of a parent giving an infant or young child a bath, or changing a diaper; or a mother breastfeeding an infant. When an underlying trauma history is here at play, it will likely be one of past sexual abuse.

8 *Play theme interference* is also something which can be seen when an adult is interacting with a child.

The child might be playing with toys, for instance. Something in the child's play theme inwardly upsets the adult – it reminds him, consciously or unconsciously, of his own earlier experience of, for example, sexual abuse, physical violence, or a serious loss. The adult then all at once pressures the child to change the play theme, or to quit playing and do something else.

A variation concerns secondary trauma on the part of the adult. It was the child who had the principal trauma. And now – this is the most typical version – the child, with toys on floor, is starting to recreate the trauma scenario. Some months ago the child was seriously injured, and subsequently underwent painful surgery; now a doll on the floor looks headed for a similar fate. Unable to tolerate this play scene, the parent breaks it off, for example, insisting the child switch to a different activity.

Needless to say a parent who blocks play might have other motivations, ones not tied to trauma. But the possibility of a triggered trauma history is definitely worth exploring.

9 A last example is *physical submissiveness*. In a video, this will be an adult – almost always a mother – submitting to sustained physical aggression on the part of a child.

These are difficult videos to watch. They are not all that uncommon. The child will be, typically, anywhere from 2 to 10 years old. A rain of hitting, kicking, and sometimes even biting takes place, for a number of minutes.

The mother is passive, and just submits. She may remain more or less silent. Or, in some instances, she will be doing an activity with the child, usually play. Then it is as if two incongruous interactions are taking place at the same time.

Here is a subtype of dissociation, to be sure. But being so different from the more usual forms of dissociation it deserves mention in its own right.[5]

Two Caveats

Do learn to look for patterns similar to the nine types just discussed. And do learn how to explore them, using some of the techniques I will describe in a moment. But first let me make a general comment.

When you investigate patterns like those just listed, keep your mind open. You need to be ready for different possibilities.

One important alternative, for example, is that the behaviors in the video may turn out not to be trauma-based. Some other influence, or influences, may be the explanation.

The mother playing with her 5-year-old seems repeatedly to fade away. But is this in fact a dissociated state triggered by a trauma history? Perhaps you explore, and you find out that earlier in the morning she had an upsetting exchange on the phone with a friend. Later, playing with her child, she is continually distracted inside by a buzz of thoughts about the phone conversation. As a result she acts present yet not present. But the cause has nothing to do with trauma.

A husband negotiating with his partner erupts aggressively and very quickly, zero to high in an instant. But has he been severely traumatized in the past by, for example, experiencing or witnessing violence? As you explore, it turns out that both his childhood and adult past were relatively free of such factors. On the other hand, you find out he suffers from severe attention-deficit/hyperactivity disorder (ADHD), and since forever he has tended too easily to explode in this way. So you have now something important to work with, but it is quite other than a trauma background.

Examples of this nature can be found for all the nine types of behavior.[6] When causes other than trauma are involved, the most frequent you will discover are these: (1) One or more family members from the past served as a model for the patient's actions. Social learning through imitation took place. (2) And/or, some kind of significant reinforcement from the present social environment is operative. Perhaps a patient's aggressive eruptions create submissiveness on the part of a partner or child, and this result rewards him or her (the patient).

Still other causes are possible too, naturally – for example, the phone conversation from the morning.

A second possibility to have in mind, equally important, is overdetermination. It is in fact quite common. Many of the negative patterns we choose to focus on, when working with video, have multiple underlying causes.

One cause may well be severe past trauma. Yet it is a mistake to assume, without further investigation, that this history is "the" reason, end of story.

Instead, the reasons may be multiple. You need to find out. For example, perhaps past trauma is at play – but it turns out past social learning is at play too, and in itself a significant cause.

In addition, for some patients more than one type of trauma can be exerting an influence.[7] Here is another form of overdetermination.

So do take the time to inquire, sooner or later, about other possible causes. It is a general recommendation.

I go now to suggestions about what to do with a video where you suspect one or more actions may be tied to a trauma history.

Choosing What To Show

As always, preparing for the session, you need to pick out which segment of the video to investigate with the patient during Step 3. How should this choice be made when a behavior looks to you like it might be trauma-triggered?

Basically the segment you select will have two short parts. One will be the relevant behavior you have found – for example, a parent disassociating, or a parent cutting off a play activity. Often this part will be especially brief.

The second part will consist of some piece of the interaction just prior to the relevant behavior, a piece leading up to it. To pick out this part may be easy and quick. Or it may be a little more complicated, as I will explain.

Just what was the trigger which stimulated the patient's reaction? Do you have a guess? Perhaps, when first observing the video, you already noticed what seemed a likely trigger. It might be something the other person did, for example, or something they said. Nothing is certain, of course, but what you observed seems a good tentative first guess.

Suppose however you haven't yet noticed a likely trigger. In that case what to do is to go carefully again through what happens in the video just prior the patient's (perhaps) trauma-linked action. A good idea can be to look through a piece of around three minutes, for example.

Check out what you visually see; give attention to what you acoustically hear. More often than not something will now stand out. At 2:31 the child, suddenly solemn, announces that the baby doll is going to the hospital, for instance. At 2:39 the mother, proclaiming that the doll instead wants to have fun, snatches it and bounces it up and down playfully in her lap.

Next, supposing you have located a likely such trigger, comes the question of what to show in the session. How should this be organized? (But if you couldn't find one? What to do in that case I will explain in a moment.)

Plan to use a sequence composed of two parts. One part, the first of the two, will show the probable trigger. Start with a prior 20 or 30 seconds of interaction leading up to it, and then of course include the trigger moment itself. The second part, immediately following, should simply show the patient's reaction behavior itself.

This entire two-part segment will be likely quite brief, in other words. But don't worry about that. These two events, the trigger moment followed by the reaction moment, are all you need. As we will soon see, plenty is going to happen when you work with this segment.

On the other hand, what if you failed to find a probable trigger? You looked and listened carefully, nothing stood out.

Why might this be? There can be three possible reasons.

A first is that the trigger event was so fleeting and minute that you simply missed it.

A second is more complex. Trauma memories, over time, can become overgeneralized. As a result, what stimulates a sense of threat for the patient is sometimes highly idiosyncratic. In the filmed interaction perhaps it was a smell which activated her response, or a color, or a (to us) seemingly banal gesture the other person has made.

Even a word can cause a reaction. In the video his daughter says "junk," and the patient, a combat veteran, unconsciously associating it with "jungle," responds with a dissociative reaction (See McNally, 1987). With instances of this kind, there is next to no chance you will have pinpointed the trigger event just by scanning the video. (With a smell of course there is no chance at all.)

A third possibility is that trigger is not a specific event. Instead it is something about the overall context of the interaction. Perhaps spoon-feeding the infant elicits, unconsciously, a childhood sexual intrusion scenario, for example.

And finally a fourth possibility is that there is in fact no trigger at all. The patient's behavior had nothing to do with a trauma history. It had instead some quite other cause or causes.

So, to return to the practical issue, suppose no trigger caught your eye. How then should you prepare what to show in the session?

This is not hard. What will happen in the session, concerning triggers, is that you will aid the patient to search for one. And for that purpose you can organize the overall segment as follows.

For a first block, simply take around three minutes of whatever is happening prior to the patient's (perhaps) trauma-linked reaction. And next, let the second block be the one where the reaction itself is seen. (Of course, if the reaction already occurs at, say, time 1:27 in the video, then naturally take this one minute and twenty-seven seconds as the initial part.) As we will soon see, in the session this prior three-minute (or less) block will be used to assist the patient themselves to search for a trigger.

So, one way or another then, you are prepared. The video segment is ready. It is ready to help explore whether or not an underlying trauma history is indeed playing a role. It is ready, as well, to help locate the specific trigger for the patient's reaction. How in the session should you go about all this? I turn now to the practical side.

Techniques for Exploring Possible Trauma-based Behavior

Imagine yourself in the session. You have just arrived at Step 3. It is time for the video segment you have readied.

There exist a good many techniques which can now be helpful. I here illustrate several.

Suppose that, back during Step 2, the video piece you then showed was a lengthier one. This is indeed typical. And suppose that your briefer arranged segment, the one with the (perhaps) trauma-linked behavior, was a part of the longer piece, though only a part.

This means, of course, that during Step 2 the briefer segment was already seen. Presumably, however, during Step 2 nothing was said about the (perhaps) trauma-based behavior, nor about any possible trigger. Since in Step 2 we highlight just positive events, the discussion will have gone down other paths.

So here in Step 3 you can now return to the briefer segment. You will try to get the patient to regard it using a different lens.

Of course the briefer segment might be instead from some other portion of the video not even seen yet. Either way, what comes next is alike.

You can start by proposing something like the following:

Therapist: [When in fact the briefer segment was contained in a longer part shown in Step 2.] If it's all right, let's see again a part of what we saw before. A shorter part.

Patient: Sure.

Therapist: Fine. Just pay attention to anything which stands out for you, looking at it this second time.

What you are hoping for, naturally, is that the patient will now spot, and get curious about, the behavior you suspect may be trauma-influenced.

They might even have already made a remark about it during Steps 1 or 2. All the same, in that instance as well, play the segment again and see what else, if anything, captures her attention.

So let's continue with an example. I will go into it at some length, in order to illustrate a series of technique options.

Ann is a young mother, 16 years old. She and her son Cory, now aged 2 years, are in a special residential center for adolescent mothers. They have been there for two weeks.

Video is used in the center for individual sessions. What will now be described concerns the second such session.

In the video Cory has been playing on the floor, with Ann sitting beside him. The video includes both five minutes of play and five minutes of a subsequent "pick up toys" task. (The parent has to organize that the child help put the toys away.)

In the filmed interaction, one can see some problems (these need not concern us at the moment) with how Ann plays with the boy. On the other hand, her expressive manner is lively and warm.

Responding to a signal from the person filming, Ann now tells Cory that their play is finished, and that he should help collect the toys and put them in the box. Cory at once breaks into loud, angry crying. In response, Ann seems to collapse into a dissociated state, her body moving little, her face expressionless. She remains this way for around half a minute.

The therapist, preparing for the session, found this moment quite significant. She wondered whether past trauma was playing a role. Up to now in her treatment, Ann had not spoken about anything of such a nature.

She had, however, said that her father, years ago, had moved to another part of the country, and she had had little communication with him since. Her mother, with whom she currently has been living, she described as helpful with the boy – but only erratically so, as she, the mother, has serious problems with alcohol.

Apparently, their recent life together had become rather chaotic, leading to Ann dropping out of school. A social worker visiting the family had recommended that Ann spend several months in the residential treatment center.

So, returning to the video, the therapist next plays the segment she has prepared for this moment: the last fifteen seconds of play, followed by Ann's "put away" message, and then about 20 seconds of the boy's angry crying. The therapist then asks Ann for comments. How will Ann reply?

Perhaps, possibility one, she will have now noticed the relevant (i.e., her own) behavior. This occurs often enough. By the time we have arrived at Step 3, the video has become more familiar to a patient, which may allow him or her to discriminate details not caught earlier.

Patient: I suddenly got more still there. As if I were half-asleep.
Therapist: Yes. That's right. Good observation. Let's try to find out more about this moment, is that okay?

Or, possibility two, she might still have missed the special behavior (i.e., her own). In this instance, the therapist will need actively to aid her to become more aware of it.

Patient: He's crying and whining. He thinks he should be able to keep playing. That's still what grabs me. Just that.
Therapist: Cory is being difficult, for sure. Is it okay then if I point out something else I also saw?
Patient: Sure.
Therapist: All right, watch.

The therapist can now directly highlight the triggered behavior. For example, they, the therapist, might wind the video to a few seconds before Ann's dissociative state shift. They could then show these prior seconds followed by some seconds of the dissociation itself.

Therapist: Did you see? Suddenly your body goes still, and your face loses the expressiveness you usually have.
Patient: Interesting.
Therapist: I think it would be helpful for us to try and understand this moment better. You all right with that?
Patient: Sure. How?

In either case, that is, whether the patient herself noticed the behavior or the therapist had to point it out, how to continue is the same. We can now move to an investigation of her inward experience – that is, to an "inner movie" focus. The "inner tracking technique," described in Chapter 8, can be utilized, for instance.

Therapist: Would it be okay that we explore some of what was happening inside you right here? This could give us some more information.
Patient: All right, but why I got still like that, I don't know really.

Therapist: Don't worry, that's typical. To understand these kinds of thing is hard for all of us. But there is a good way we can start finding out about it.

I'm going to play a part of the video again. As you watch and listen, imagine you are there now, with Cory, in the interaction. Notice what kind of thoughts come up in you, and what feelings, and anything else in your body.

Patient: Okay, I'll try.

This shift to inner tracking might be enough, in itself. As the patient follows her inward experience, she might discover a trauma memory coming up.

It might be a specific image from whatever happened back then. Or it might be a more diffuse association, a sense of, "Maybe it has to do with all that [i.e., the trauma experience], there are things going on here a little like all that .... "

Either way, the connection will have been made. Ann, for example, might respond so:

Therapist: [Having stopped the video.] Okay, well?
Patient: I just had a bad memory. It's hard to talk about it.
Therapist: Take your time.
Patient: My parents fought a lot when I was a young kid, when my dad was still living with us. It could get out of control. It was physical. A lot of screaming ....

Or, as might happen, it could be that the inner tracking technique, used by itself, fails to illuminate any such connection. This then means either (1) that in fact no such connection exists – perfectly possible – or simply (2) that more will be needed to find it.

Best to do in such an instance is to keep trying, assuming the patient is willing.

For example, you might just show the segment one or several times more, with the patient in the same way tracking her inner experience.

But, if this still yields nothing, a good idea is to bring in additional techniques. (Or you could even have begun with one of these.) I will go over several.

The *visual channel technique* and the *auditory channel technique,* already described in Chapter 5, will very often be productive. You show the video piece again, but with the patient now giving attention only to the visual channel, or only to the auditory.

For example, you can show the segment again with the sound turned off. This will permit the patient to give his full attention to the visual input. The instruction could be like this:

Therapist: So, we'll go through it again, if that's okay. This time I'm going to put the sound off. You can give all your attention now just to what you see on the screen.

Or, for the auditory channel technique, you can have the patient turn her chair so that she can't see the screen, or else close her eyes. She can concentrate on just what she hears.

Therapist: We'll go through it again. But this time, don't look at the screen, just listen to what you can hear. Give all your attention to that. Turn your chair a little, to make it easier not to look.

In our case example, once or twice through with a focus on the auditory channel would be especially recommended. It might well be the sounds themselves, Cory's angry crying, which are functioning as the threat trigger.

Persons traumatized as children by physical violence between parents, often report specific memories of the adults' terrible cries. (The child typically will run to his or her own room, or to a sibling's room, but there is no getting away from what they have to hear.)

With other cases it can be the visual sensory channel technique which elicits a connection. Perhaps a facial expression, or a movement, is serving as trigger.

Another way to explore can be to focus on thoughts. If you unfold some of the thought network, this may bring contact with a memory.

Therapist: [Having stopped the video.] So? What did you find going on inside?
Patient: I just couldn't stand it, like before. I wanted this all to be over. Even though I knew what we were looking at would be short.
Therapist: Can you say more about that reaction? About your "I want this all to be over"? Say it to yourself again. See what other thoughts come with it.
Patient: [Closes her eyes, sits silently again, then opens her eyes.] It's like, "I can't take it. Someone do something. This is too much for me."
Therapist: Very good, what you're getting at sounds important.
        Listen, ask yourself this. When in your life have you gone through something where you probably had thoughts of that kind? Thoughts like, "It's too much, I can't take it," and so on?
Patient: I don't know ….
Therapist: Think about yourself as a kid, over the years. See if anything stands out for you.
Patient: [Again closes her eyes, sits silently, then opens her eyes.] I just had a bad memory ….

A similar technique is to emphasize emotion and ask for associations. This can be of interest especially when an emotion has a certain strength.

For example, the last exchange, about thoughts, could instead have been steered as follows:

Therapist: [Having stopped the video.] So? What did you find going on inside?

Patient: I just couldn't stand it, like before. I wanted this to be all over. Even though I knew what we were looking at would be short.

Therapist: Can you say more about that reaction? This "very uncomfortable"? What emotional feeling, or feelings, are in that? Like, frustration, or fear, or anger? Panic even? Or maybe something else?

Patient: Fear, yes. A crazy panic almost. Well, I'm angry at him too.

Here we notice the patient has spoken about two emotions, fear and anger. Either or both can be explored further, for instance as follows:

Therapist: Close your eyes again. [The patient does.] Stay in contact with that fear part of it, with that panic. See if any images come up, as if you could see something, or hear something. Or if anything else comes up.

Patient: [After a little.] I just had a bad memory ....

Had nothing emerged from the fear, then the anger could have been explored in the same way.

Other kinds of investigation can be done with the body. A number of techniques are possible; I will describe two.

One goes like this. You focus on something the patient is doing with the body, in the video, at the relevant moment (i.e., the moment of the possibly trauma-induced action). You point it out clearly. You might even show it twice, the second time using a micro-viewing technique (see Chapter 5).

Then you ask the patient to reproduce a version of this movement; to reproduce it live, right now; but in a much slowed down fashion. And while doing it they should carefully notice if any associations emerge.

"As if you were doing Tai Chi," can be one way to describe the needed slowness. A father whose movements suddenly became aggressive and intrusive can now move his arms through space in a similar trajectory, but extremely slowly.

In our case example, however, the patient in the video goes into frozen stillness, without movement. In that instance a similar body technique, slightly more complex, could be recommended. It would go so:

Therapist: [Having stopped the video.] Well? What did you find going on inside?

Patient: I just couldn't stand it, like before. I wanted this all to be over. Even though I knew what we were looking at would be short.

Therapist: Okay, clear. So there's all this "I can't stand it" inside. And then, what we see in the video, your body gets very still.

Patient: Yes.

Therapist: Perhaps the getting still is a way of managing the "I can't stand this"? A way of getting through it, if you see what I mean?

Patient: It could be. That sounds sort of right, actually.

Therapist: But this makes perfect sense. Something is so very unpleasant, just awful, when you see Cory acting this way, and hearing him. So to pull away from it somehow is natural.[8]

Patient: Really?

Therapist: Really. Let's explore it some more, okay?

Patient: Sure.

Therapist: Good. Can you still feel some of the "I can't stand this"?

Patient: A little. Ugh.

Therapist: Now stay with it, but at the same time let your body get very still, just like you saw yourself doing in the video.

Patient: Okay, but it won't be the same, to make it happen that way.

Therapist: Don't worry. If it seems a little artificial, no problem. Just bring yourself into being still. You might want to close your eyes, that can make it easier.

Patient: [Gradually becomes more immobile, with her eyes closed.]

Therapist: [Softly.] Right. Good. Just stay with this a moment more. [Waits a few seconds.] What is it all like now?

Patient: I feel bad again. But also sort of dreamy.

Therapist: Fine. Where in your body do you feel the "bad"?

Patient: Hard to tell. Maybe all over. I don't know.

Therapist: Just stay with it, and now try to find out this. If your body could move, instead of staying all still, how would it like to move? Can you let your body tell you about this? Or show you a tiny bit? What would it like to do?

Maybe it would like to run away, for example? Or to protest somehow? Or maybe curl up in a little ball?

You don't have to actually do any of these. Just try to find out what would like to happen. Try to notice the tiniest beginning of a movement, or a getting ready for a movement.

Patient: [After a few seconds.] Maybe run? Or kick? No, run. Get away somewhere.

Therapist: Very good. Do you sense this more in your legs and feet?

Patient: Yes.

Therapist: So stay with it, feeling how your legs and feet would like to move.

At the same time think about this too. Have there been any occasions in the past, when you were a younger kid or older kid or whatever, when you felt this way? As if something was going on, and you just couldn't take it, and you would have liked so much to just run, to get away from it, but you couldn't?

Do any pictures or memories come as I say this?

Patient: [In tense, frightened voice.] Oh no. I don't like what I'm remembering now .... It's hard to talk. I'll tell you in a minute.

Therapist: Take all the time you want. I'm here. I'll wait.

There is an important sense in which serious trauma tends to be embedded in the body (e.g., von der Kolk, 2014). This is what can make body techniques especially productive when exploring facets of a trauma history.

What If No Trigger Was Evident When Preparing for the Session?

In the case example just given, the therapist was able, before the session, to spot a probable trigger: the noncompliant, aggressive sounds and actions of the child Cory. Various techniques were then used to explore the mother's response to his provocation.

But suppose no such likely trigger stands out. Scanning the video, you first found what might well be a trauma-based behavior on the part of the patient. And next, pouring over the events leading up to it, you searched for a possible cause. But nothing at all stood out. How does this alter what to do in the session?

Basically, how to proceed remains the same, but with one important difference.

First, as usual, help the patient explore what looked like a trauma-based behavior. See if they can find a link to trauma events in the past.

But after that, and here is the difference, shift to a new investigation. Returning to the video, try to find out if the patient themselves, with your help, can succeed in pinpointing a specific trigger. This takes only a few minutes, and is definitely worth the trouble to try.

Three techniques can be useful here. All three were described above: inner tracking, the visual channel technique, and the audio channel technique.

Inner tracking, for example, can be a good place to start. The intervention could be as follows.

Therapist: If it's all right, let's move now to an interesting question. You say you don't know why you end up reacting in this special way [e.g., dissociating, erupting, etc.]. Let's look at the video again. Let's explore what's going on in the interaction a little bit before you [fade away, explode, etc.]. Maybe we'll discover something.

I'll play around three minutes of what happens before your reaction. Watch it carefully. Imagine you are in the interaction, and notice what you experience inside. But at the same time, look for anything in what you see, or anything in what you hear, which seems to have some effect on you.

The *visual channel technique*, should inner tracking have failed to illuminate a trigger, might come next. The therapist's intervention would be almost the same.

Therapist: I'll play the same piece again, the three minutes of what happens before your reaction. But this time I'll turn the sound off. You can focus just on the visual images themselves.

Watch them carefully, imagining you are there in the interaction. And notice all your reactions inside.

The *acoustic channel technique*, should more be needed, can also be tried. The intervention could go so:

Therapist: I'll play the same piece again, the three minutes of what happens before your reaction. But this time, turn away from the video. Don't look at it, and instead just listen to the sounds. See if anything about the sounds, at any point, brings up some kind of reaction in you.

To proceed in this manner, using such techniques, costs little time. Yet it frequently will produce a result. It is quite common for a patient to be able to pinpoint something specific which is serving as a trigger.

Let me add two comments before moving on.

First, suppose that earlier, when the patient was investigating the behavior which you suspected might be trauma-based, nothing came of it. No connection emerged with anything in his past. Does that mean that to return now to the video, and to search for a trigger, is not worth pursuing?

Oddly enough, it does not mean this. Assist them to look for a trigger anyway.

If they find one, this is still informative. Moreover, as they give attention to their inner reactions, they might at this point get in touch with a tie to past trauma. Or they might get in touch with something else significant in their past – for example, not severe trauma, but repetitive problematic family dynamics.[9]

And even if they find a trigger, yet no link emerges to the past, this result is nevertheless helpful. Later on I am going to be describing some additional therapeutic work ("video-based exposure," I call it) which can be done with the trigger moment. As we will see, these techniques can be employed even if no tie to a trauma history has emerged.

Secondly, suppose on the other hand you have gone through the segment several times, and nothing in particular emerged. The patient, as well, was unable to locate a trigger.

In that instance I recommend you put the search aside. When such looking for a trigger is successful in a session, it tends to achieve its result quite quickly. If this hasn't occurred after three or so times going through the segment, it makes more sense just to move on.

Following the Discovery

Suppose you have succeeded in finding a link to past trauma. The patient has connected the dots. They see that what they do in the video is tied to past traumatic events. Perhaps they also have found, with your help, the specific trigger.

Emotionally this may well have a strong effect, on both the patient and yourself. On the patient's side several things will be happening simultaneously. First, they are now in touch with the trauma memories. This in itself generates feelings. Second, they are absorbing how the trauma history can affect their present interactions, absorbing a concrete example. This too can be a shock. Third, they are sharing the history with yourself, which can bring its own reactions.

So on your side the primary task for the moment is to give emotional support. Discuss the past but discuss too what they are experiencing now. As you inquire about their immediate feelings, it can be helpful to keep in mind the three points just mentioned. How do they feel as they contact the memories? How do they feel also about seeing the tie between past history and their present behavior? And what is it like for them to share all this with you?

Of course, an influencing factor will be whether or not you and they have already discussed the past trauma. Have you talked together about it in one or more previous sessions, video or non-video sessions? If it is a theme which has already been taken up, that may make it easier for them to speak about it again today. (Or it may not.)

As well, have they done any therapy trauma work – that is, a processing of trauma memories – with either yourself or someone else? If yes, this too may make discussion of the issue easier today. (Or it may not.)

Separate from providing emotional containment, to what extent should you inquire about the details of the past events? Typically, in this session, it is better to limit the discussion of details. What is needed is enough exchange such that you and they can make sense of the trigger in the video. But then how and when should the trauma details be taken up further? I come to this in a moment.

Also to Discuss

When a trauma trigger has been identified, and its tie to a specific trauma history established, you need to organize well what you further talk about. On the one hand, some things are necessary to go into at this point. On the other, there may not be much time remaining. A good solution then, if needed, can be to plan with the patient that today's discussion will continue in the next session, and if necessary even in the one after that. This is in fact typical when working with such a video. As for the discussion itself, there are several topics which need to be taken up, if not today then next time.

One is what to do about the trigger. How can the patient begin to free herself, and free her interaction behavior, from its effects?

There are some highly practical things which can be undertaken in this regard. Especially valuable are what I call video exposure techniques. I will be describing them in Chapter 11.

A use of the video exposure techniques does require some time, however, so it may well be that you will have to wait for this until the next session. But, as you might imagine, these techniques will require a return to the video – exposure is going to be done with the trigger itself. What then about my recommendation in an earlier chapter that, with VIT, one not work with the same video in more than a single session?

The answer is we have to allow exceptions to this idea, as I also remarked then. And indeed, when a trauma history linked to the video interaction has emerged in a session, this is one of the most important exceptions. You just get the patient's agreement that next time more can be done with the video observed today.

Another topic may need to be this. Suppose today is the first time you have been told about the particular trauma history in question.

In that case important to inquire about is the following. What else is going on in the patient's current life which reflects the trauma event, or events? Are they experiencing flashbacks, hyperarousal states, troubling dreams? And do they have ideas about other probable effects (i.e., other than the one seen in the video) upon their interaction patterns?

And then a further topic concerns case conceptualization and planning. What does today's discovery imply concerning in-depth therapeutic work with the trauma?

Recall that earlier in the chapter I emphasized the distinction between video work with trauma triggers, on the one hand, and a therapeutic processing of trauma memories, on the other. They are separate endeavors.

And as mentioned, with regard to processing there exist today a number of good approaches, for example, EMDR. So a question now to confront is whether the patient should sooner or later engage themselves in some such processing work.

Perhaps, of course, they have already done so. Perhaps they have done this with yourself or with someone else. But if they haven't, then almost certainly it should be recommended to them.

And then, if the patient agrees with the idea, further questions arise. Just when should the patient begin the processing work, and with whom? Some hard thinking may be required here.

One possibility, for example, is that the patient (1) continue for now with the video intervention work, but (2) plan at some point later on to undertake some form of trauma processing therapy.

Frequently, this turns out a good solution. A continuation of slow, carefully dosed video exploration can, in fact, be an excellent preparation for later undertaking more intensive work with a trauma past. Gradually, in both video and non-video sessions, the patient can learn to make better contact with themselves. They can become more ready to experience a variety of feelings.

On the other hand, an alternative is that the patient for now put video intervention work aside, and instead undertake a trauma processing therapy. This could be a better answer if you find out that in their current life they are so overwhelmed by the trauma symptoms that they can barely function, and/or that they get pushed into critically dangerous actions. In that instance, video intervention can wait. It can be resumed again at some later point.

Finally, what about the notion of them doing both at once? Could video intervention and trauma processing work be done as two parallel paths?

I suggest to be cautious about this recommendation. Too much can be too much.

In principle it is possible, however. For instance, I have seen it function quite successfully in psychiatric settings where both video intervention and trauma processing are treatment possibilities.

To give one example, I have already recounted how at the University of Heidelberg I once helped a psychiatric team put together a special residential unit where highly disturbed mothers and their infants (0–2 years) could be hospitalized together. We built in video intervention from the beginning.

But we were soon confronted by a hard reality. Most of these mothers were (along with other diagnoses) suffering from severe trauma histories. We decided, therefore, to add a trauma processing treatment option – a body-based mode – to be carried out by a separate therapist. The resulting combination functioned quite well. (See Downing, 2010 for a description of the trauma approach and Morlinghaus, 2012 for an account of its Heidelberg implementation.)

To note, however, is that built into such a treatment context are certain special advantages. On the one hand, an ongoing information exchange between the two separate team members (the one doing video intervention and the one doing trauma treatment) is pretty much guaranteed. This is highly useful. And on the other hand, the patient's evolving condition and reactions are going to be monitored by additional staff as well, and all the more so if the setting is a residential unit.

To sum up, this chapter has been about a special therapeutic situation. Preparing for a session, certain events in the video have caught your eye. There were behaviors on the patient's part which struck you as perhaps trauma-based. Some typical examples are as follows:

- passive dissociation
- oversexualized contact
- sudden fear signals
- eruption
- extremely invasive physical handling
- autonomy restriction

- excessive disgust signals
- play theme interference
- physical submissiveness

You might also even have noticed something the other person did too, something which might have functioned as a trigger.

These possibilities can be important to investigate, and there are multiple ways to go about it.

While preparing, you pick out a short video segment, as short as possible, where these events can be seen. Should no trigger seem evident, a part can be included where the patient can search for one.

In the session you and the patient can then explore this segment repeatedly. A number of techniques can be useful. They include:

- simple inner tracking
- the "audio only" sensory channel technique
- the "visual only" sensory channel technique
- inner tracking focused specifically on thoughts
- inner tracking focused specifically on emotion
- the "slow imitation" body technique
- the "what does the body want to do" body technique
- video-based exposure techniques

These lattermost techniques will be described in the chapter to follow.

Notes

1 Similar reflections can be found, occasionally, in the clinical literature on trauma. At times the notion of an "integration stage," done subsequent to a period of direct processing, includes some of what I am talking about (e.g., Murphy & Eckhardt, 2005). The proposals tend to remain vague, however.

2 Are such occurrences also a red flag for current sexual abuse? The possibility should not be ignored. Such a correlation is infrequent, but the therapist should look hard at the case from this perspective nevertheless.

A closely related question is this. Is the behavior in the video representative of a more general lack of boundaries, and in particular a lack with regard to eroticism, in the wider family system? If yes, are there any hints of possible abuse on the part of another family member?

Moreover, even if no abuse has occurred, this kind of boundaries problem in a family can be a risk factor for abuse at some later point. It deserves, therefore, to be addressed in some manner.

3 Possible, too, is to call eruptions of this kind another form of dissociation (e.g., Porges, 2011).

4 Beebe and her colleagues also did interesting video feedback therapy with some of these mothers (Beebe et al., 2012).

5 Based on their own accounts in therapy, some women enter a similar state during adult couple violence. One never sees open couple violence – physical violence – in a video, or at least I haven't. However, if you work with domestic violence

cases you will often see verbal hostility escalate almost to the point of becoming physical. But at the last moment the clients put on the brakes, being aware of being filmed.

6 Or anyway, they can be found for eight of them. Perhaps an exception is the last type, passive submissiveness. I can only say that in every one of the cases where I have had to do with this phenomenon a trauma history stood right at the center.

7 A still further complication is that plenty of persons have experienced trauma, or traumas, during the first three years of life, but for this have no explicit memories. I am putting aside the interesting question of what this reality might mean for the doing of therapy – that is, any kind of therapy, not just video intervention.

8 Worth mentioning is that a dissociative withdrawal of this kind will at times have a second aspect: it may also be a repetition of a like defensive withdrawal at the time of the trauma itself. This possibility, too, can be explored. Typically, however, an easier time and place to do so is in the context of processing work with the traumatic memories. More will be said later in the chapter about such processing work.

9 Or, should the patient make a tie to something of this nature, should we call the repetitive family dynamics themselves a trauma, one of a long, ongoing sort? I will step aside from the semantic question of what and what not to label as a trauma.

11 Procedure step 4: Planning for change

Procedure Step 4 winds up the session. You and the patient will agree on a homework plan. Arrangements might be made for the filming of a new video too.

Most of what happens in Step 4 is typical for cognitive behavioral therapy (CBT) in general. A few things are more specific to video intervention therapy (VIT) however, as we will see.

We can consider two overall principles to be guidelines for Step 4.

One we might call the early success principle. In a first video session, and sometimes for one or more after, our main hope is that when the patient tries, in their daily life, to implement a new action, they will experience at least a partial success. For us this goal takes precedence over everything else.

The other principle is the opposite. Call it the maximal effect principle. As the therapy progresses, our intent is that the patient will realize as much change in their interpersonal life, as much generalization across contexts, as possible. Fine they start small, but our hope is for much more.

Both these are familiar CBT notions. But with video intervention, as we will see, they have a few different implications.

Step 4 varies a lot in length. One factor here is how much you want to do, but another, often, is simply how much time is left once you end Step 3.

Does this mean that the full procedure, all four steps, has to be finished up in today's session no matter what? Couldn't it be possible to do only a part today, and then continue with the same video in the session next to come?

This is, in fact, possible. But as said in previous chapters, I do recommend you complete the work with today's video before the end of today's session. I think it is better the patient leave the session with the full package, so to speak. Yet there is room for exceptions. If you really need the extra time you can divide up the work with the video, accomplishing a part today and postponing a part until the next session. Later in this chapter we will, in fact, see an example.

In what follows I speak about "homework," about an "assignment," about a "task." But, just to mention it, personally I avoid those words with patients.

DOI: 10.4324/9781003621669-11

We talk about "an action," "a new step," "something to try at home." We say "to strengthen this skill," "to develop this ability," "to start using this new capacity."

Like a certain number of therapists, my observation is that for some patients the language of homework and assignments and tasks too easily evokes toxic school memories.

Defining the Principal Task

By "principal task" we mean the chief goal, the chief target, a main thing for the patient to attempt to accomplish in the coming days. Of course, once you arrive at Step 4, both you and the patient will already have a beginning picture of what this might be.

This is because during Step 3 a negative pattern has been explored. And almost inevitably to talk about what is negative involves talk, too, about what would have been more positive.

Nevertheless, in Step 4 there is typically more to specify. This possible new, more useful behavior, how small or large a version should the patient try to implement? And when should they try, and in what settings, what contexts?

Furthermore, should the task be a "behavior," narrowly speaking, in the first place – an action which is overtly physical, like bringing more expressiveness to the face, or using language which validates a child's feelings? Or should the task be inner in nature, like a use of self-speech, or trying to mentalize more productively? Or should the task be a combination, a mix of outer and inner? Plenty of times a combination is in fact the most helpful thing to propose.

Let's turn to a couple of case examples and see how such decisions can be made.

A First Example

Suppose that the video, in this instance a first video, is of a mother, Jill, playing with her 2-year-old child, Mary. Suppose too, as we see so often, the mother seems clueless about how to support the child's play.

Instead, she turns didactic, trying to teach about colors and objects. Light criticisms are frequent too. The child should hold the doll differently, the child should repeat a color-word with better pronunciation. The mother fails to encourage what the child is doing.

Suppose some more. Today's video is the first one in the therapy. So, once having arrived at Step 4, this will be the first time we will have proposed a homework assignment. Assume, too, that in any previous non-video sessions little was said about homework.

This means we don't know yet how well she will manage with a task at home. Imagine, as well, that our impression of her is of someone who might find it difficult to implement new steps. Given all these factors, how should we think about the task to propose?

To start with, let's note that this negative pattern, the one seen in the video, represents a dynamic all too familiar for anyone who works with parents and small children. And as for what to do about it, there exists a standard recommendation used across many approaches and in VIT. The parent needs to learn how to "follow the child's lead."

So already right here, with the "follow the child's lead" concept, we have an initial description of a new behavior to suggest. But as it stands this description is too abstract. It must be narrowed down. "Follow the child's lead" has different components, for instance. Which component, or which combination of them, should we suggest?

One such is restraint, a conscious waiting, with the adult from their side not trying to impose an agenda. As the adult first watches how the child acts on his play impulses, the adult can then respond in a manner which encourages the child to continue what they are doing.

Other components are forms of so-called descriptive language. Different therapy approaches have different ideas here, but more or less universal is the advice that the parent name what the child is doing ("You're building a tower with the blocks"), and/or name what they might be feeling ("You like this doll"). Some approaches, VIT too, would add more. For instance, what the child sees or hears ("Oh, here comes Tizzy!" as the cat crawls up close) can be labeled.[1]

Still another component is praise. And another, for some approaches, VIT too, is what is can be called language echoing: when the child speaks, the parent replies with a somewhat similar phrasing (e.g., McNeil & Hembree-Kigin, 2010). (The parent might then say more, elaborating, but they start in with the echoing.)

Yet two further components are negative ones, behaviors to eschew. Don't bring in didactic teaching. And don't make criticisms.

So this is quite a bundle so far and there is still more. Up to now I have been speaking just about language choice and have said nothing about the body. If an adult is playing with a child, what would we hope to see in their (the adult's) use of the body? Three obvious elements here are, first, that they show an attentive manner with posture and gaze; and second, that they bring in warm, playful tones; and third, that their face is expressive.

Important, as well, is the level of bodily expressiveness. In this context, which is play with toys, a joint attention context, the expressiveness level should be not too high. A moderate tone will function better. If the adult's signals become overly intense, it can distract the child from his play focus.

How then do we choose? Which of these verbal components, and/or which body elements, should we propose to the patient as a task? A good idea, naturally, is to solicit the patient's ideas also, and to negotiate the matter. In the early video sessions, however, patients have a tendency to feel quite unsure what might work best. Frequently they want a recommendation.

For this case example, as the therapist thinks over what to suggest, to keep in mind before all else would be the early success principle. It would be particularly important given our premonition that this patient might find it hard to implement new behavior. What we want her to experience, whatever the task, is "Yes, I did it, I actually got something new going in my personal life." We want her to experience this at least to a certain degree.

A good idea, therefore, would be to pick a goal as small as possible. It should be not so small she would find it meaningless, but small enough that the likelihood of her accomplishing it, or accomplishing at least a degree of it, is high.

One logical choice, therefore, would be to select just one of the forms of descriptive language, and propose that as an assignment. For instance, it could be descriptive language for what the child is doing, this being a form parents tend to find relatively easy.[2]

What about the body elements – voice tones, facial expressions, leanings of the torso, and the like? Important as they are, better to leave them out for now. The reason is that, generally speaking, patients tend to find verbal tasks easier to implement than nonverbal ones.

Imagine, then, this becomes the suggestion made to her – descriptive language for what the child is doing. Presumably, during Step 3 she will already have heard some psychoeducation about descriptive language, so she will know what is meant. And imagine she accepts the suggestion.

Next, a when and where plan should be agreed upon. For instance, a recommendation could be made, one typical in some child therapy methods, that she make time for a daily "structured play" period.

This could be done for 20 minutes each time, for example. Several toys would be put on the floor. She, the mother, would then let the girl initiate the play direction. And then she, the mother, would try to "follow the child's lead." She would attempt to make frequent descriptive comments about the child's actions and doings. And apart from that she would do nothing to interfere (no criticisms, no unnecessary instruction or teaching, etc.).

Such then might be the proposal. But next it must be negotiated. A typical problem which might emerge at this point, for instance, could be as follows:

Therapist: So I see you understand this new way to play with Mary. It's going to be very helpful for her, I think, as I already said. Let's talk now about exactly when you are going to do it, and for how long. Okay?

Patient: Okay.

Therapist: How about this as a plan. That you get on the floor with her, for structured play, once each day. And that you do it each time for 20 minutes. Could that be all right?

Patient: For 20 minutes? Every single day?

Therapist: If possible. Does it seem difficult to do?

Patient: I have so much I have to get done at home. I've already told you about that. There's all the practical things, and then Peter [an 8-year-old brother] comes home from school, and there's everything with him. I don't know if I can always find 20 minutes free.

Therapist: So 20 minutes seems long.

Patient: Yes. I mean, maybe now and then, some days.

Therapist: But this is good, that you are realizing ahead of time what could be difficult for you. What if we continued to say every day, but made the amount of time shorter?

Patient: That might work. How short?

Therapist: Perhaps 10 minutes a day?

Patient: I don't know. It still feels long.

Therapist: Could you manage 5 minutes day?

Patient: That sounds better.

Therapist: Good, let's plan on that, for now. So just when during the day will it be best for you to do this?

Patient: Afternoons, during the week. After Peter has settled in a little ....

On our side this agreement is fine. We just want that the implementation process, the implementation of the new behavior, gets underway.[3] Based on this last dialogue the probability looks good that there will be at least one or more days when she will get on the floor with the girl and the toys, and that once the play starts she will try at least a few descriptive comments. The problem of how to get change moving along more quickly can be confronted later on.

Another point will be made later in the chapter about this case example. We will be discussing the possible role of insertion techniques in Step 4, and we will see how they might be brought to bear with this patient.

A General Comment

Notice one point about the previous case example. A new behavior was proposed, it was accepted, a plan was made, but there was no talk about trying out the behavior as an "experiment." Instead the talk was only about how to change, for the better, the mother-daughter interaction.

This is usual. In VIT we seldom frame a suggested new action as a type of experiment. As explained in Chapter 8, dysfunctional negative beliefs are frequently worked with in VIT. For example, the patient may be helped to weigh arguments for and against the belief, or to distance, with the aid of body techniques, from the belief (Chapter 8), or to reflect differently using mentalization techniques (Chapter 9). But normally this is not coupled with a recommendation to try new actions merely to "test" the belief and its implicit predictions.

In standard cognitive-behavioral therapy, on the contrary, the concept of testing is often invoked. The new behavior is framed as an experiment. And certainly there can be a logic to this. A patient is petrified of public speaking, convinced that half the audience will march out when they talk. Fine, have the patient give it a try, they can see, in reality, how many people leave the room.

But a VIT session by its very nature creates a different kind of context. Normally, once we have arrived at Step 4, the eventual value of the proposed new behavior already makes sense to the patient. They have seen themselves in the video doing the negative behavior. They have seen or heard explained its probable negative consequences. After all that, to jump to "why not test your negative belief" would feel peculiar, like losing the thread.

Nothing prevents a VIT therapist from using the "test your belief" strategy in a non-video session. But usually they would not do so the day they work with a video.

A Second Example

Now let's turn a case example of a contrasting nature. Consider Jason and his son Stephan, aged 15 years.

The video is the fourth one in the therapy, V-4. The family came for help with Stephan's behavioral problems, which include sometimes not going to school, staying out too late, and too much alcohol and marijuana use with friends. Two previous videos were of Mother, Father, and Stephan together, discussing assigned topics. One previous video was of a family meal, with a second younger son also present.

V-4, the video being explored today, is of a negotiation, between Father and Stephan, concerning at what time this coming Friday night Stephan will need to return home. The idea to have a video of Father and Stephan alone was father's suggestion, and Stephan agreed. Both feel their exchanges around such matters too often turn explosive.

The therapy has been moving forward, everything considered. All three seem to have profited from the previous video explorations. Stephan's choice from the start was to have divided video sessions, that is, each video to be explored once with Stephan alone, parents absent, and a second time with Mother and Father, Stephan absent (see Chapter 1). Several non-video sessions have also taken place, and to these all three have come.

In today's session, as usual, Stephan is not present. Exceptionally, Mother is also absent, due to a professional obligation. Jason is here alone.

In the video itself we see that the interaction starts out smoothly enough. Quickly it emerges that Stephan and Father's opinions are different, and their wishes different. All the same the tone on both sides stays respectful, at least for the first 5 minutes. At two different, separate moments Father also manages, twice, to validate something Stephan has just said (cf. Chapter 16), despite his, Father's, disagreement.

Then, as if out of nowhere, the escalation begins. Stephan's comments turn nasty. Father responds with his own disparaging remarks. The voices become louder, within 3 minutes both are yelling. Stephan announces that this is all a waste of time and he is going to his room and he stomps off. Planned for 15 minutes, the video ends after 11.

During Step 3, working with this video, the therapist brought a focus to Jason's side of the escalation. The concept of self-regulation was shortly discussed. Some linking techniques were used for a brief look at when and where Jason encounters similar self-regulation problems.

Next the therapist helped Jason explore in detail a few exaggerated negative thoughts, ones which had sprung up in him in reaction to the son's hostile remarks. ("He'll never change." "I can't tolerate this." "Our relationship is so hopeless it's no use my even trying.") The therapist also helped him sense the body organizing shifts which had taken over (Chapter 8). Several more productive thoughts were then found, and also some alternative body organizing which could support these thoughts.[4]

So now comes the shift to Step 4, and the question of homework. What task might be proposed for Jason to carry out at home?

Here too, like with our first case example, the Step 3 investigations already point the way. Jason needs to put the brakes on his anger. He needs to regulate himself down. He needs, as well, to minimize aggressive body signals and to minimize aggressive language. Some possible helpful means of going about this were also discovered in Step 3. Jason then found several more useful self-speech thoughts. He came into touch, too, with some uses of the body which could support these more positive thoughts (cf. Chapter 8).

So the general contours of a recommendation are clear enough here. What, however, should be the details? What should a more specific proposal look like?

Should he be encouraged, perhaps, to concentrate on just his language, on the words themselves, for example? Or would it be better he give his attention to just his voice tones maybe, or just his facial expressions, or just his gestures and movements? What seems most feasible?

To make this choice we must take a step back. We must consider the case context. Jason is a highly motivated patient, the therapist has already learned. He can implement new actions. The change process in the therapy is nicely underway. So all in all, we have here a situation which is rather the opposite of the first case example.

A good idea, therefore, would be to suggest he try a fairly full package. It could include both attention to language and attention to the body. With the help of the video, the various body elements could also be clearly spelled out for him. Additionally, insertion techniques could be used at some point. This would clarify both the language and body dimensions all the more.

The therapist might even want to add what can be called a secondary task. This is not necessary but it could be done. Jason's primary task would be to be as attentive as possible during his interactions with Stephan, and, when needed, to mobilize the various new strategies to hold his anger in check. But a secondary task, presented as simply an option, might be proposed too. Typically this secondary task would reflect the goal of generalization.

For instance, the therapist might continue as follows:

Therapist: I have a question. It's about you and this kind of anger, this getting hot and angry, and where it shows up in the rest of your life. I mean, how often does it cause trouble between you and Sandra [the wife], for example?

Patient: There are times. Maybe once or twice a week I lose it. Sandra has her own problems here, but for sure I have mine. I never get physically violent, that idea horrifies me, but I get too up there sometimes, loud, and not listening anymore.

Therapist: What might be the effect on your relationship if you were more on top of this?

Patient: A good effect, I'm sure. Exactly what, I don't know. But positive.

Therapist: And between you and Harry [the 9-year-old younger brother]?

Patient: We don't get into tiffs like Stephan and I do. I think maybe he's a little scared about that idea. He hears what goes on between me and Stephan, and I know it upsets him.

Therapist: Clear enough. And then at work? You're overseeing what a lot of people do. There must be times when things go on which make you angry.

Patient: Well, actually … well, I have my problems with all this there too. I rarely blow up like I do with Stephan. But I can easily get too … huffy, let's say, and cold. Sometimes I even say something sarcastic I'm sorry about afterwards.

Therapist: So if you do manage to build up more skills to settle yourself down inside, settle down in a way that anger is a lot less driving what you do, how will this be useful at work?

Patient: It could be useful. For sure. With some of my reports I have a decent relationship, but with some I could have a better one. That would be good. And I'm thinking now, if I could calm down faster, I could get my mind focused back faster on what counts.

Therapist: I like how you're thinking about this. What you're saying makes a lot of sense.

Patient: To me too, I have to say.

Therapist: Well look, here's an idea. We already agreed you will this week try regularly to be more careful when you interact with Stephan. So that will be the main new thing.

But here could be a second idea. With Sandra and Harry this next week, and also when you are at work, you could just pay attention to this issue, to what happens with anger in you, and what effects that has. You could just track this, observe it. It would give us more detailed information, for sure. What do you think?

Patient: Why just track? I think I need to change things with Sandra and at work, not just track.

Therapist: Of course, fine. Anytime you want you can not just observe, but also try something new, inside or outside. Why not? All the same it could be good to make our plan like this. With Stephan you will definitely, regularly, try to act differently. That will be the main thing on the menu for this week.

And then about Sandra and Harry and your colleagues, we can leave everything open. Just see what feels best to you. It might be only doing some tracking and noticing, only that. But anytime you feel also like acting in some way new, then fine. All this would be an open option.

Patient: Sure. Let's leave it like that.

Therapist: Good.

Given this patient's readiness, such an exchange at this point between therapist and patient would be typical.

Also, as you can imagine, in his enthusiasm the patient might wish to contract for all kinds of additional new behaviors. But here it is better we keep a balance. We want the patient to continue to have some success experiences too.

For that reason it is important here, in the dialogue, that the therapist use terms like "an open option." Should Jason indeed start to act differently with Sandra or Harry or his colleagues, then in the next session he can be congratulated all the more. But if he doesn't, or even if in these other contexts he forgets to do straightforward observing and tracking, this is no failure. All those things were an option.

Exposure Homework

In Chapter 10 we saw how video-based exposure techniques can be used. In the video the patient displays a peculiar behavior, such as dissociation, which seems poorly to fit what is actually happening in the interaction. Discussed in Chapter 10 was how the patient can be helped to find and identify such a trigger in the video, and how they can be helped to get in touch, also, with its connection to the past trauma.

Discussed, too, was how the video itself can now serve as a platform for exposure techniques. A segment showing the trigger, perhaps only several seconds in length, is played and replayed a number of times. During each showing, as they look and/or listen, the patient attempts to habituate to this trigger. If the process goes well, and it usually does, bit by bit the trigger's aversive effects are reduced.

But, in addition, this exposition work can be continued at home, should the patient be willing. A plan can be arranged. They will need to take a copy of the video with them, of course, or least a copy of the relevant segment (e.g., on a computer key, or on her phone).

Then at home, ideally once a day, they can spend around 20 minutes with it. They can look at (or listen to) the trigger moment a half a dozen times or so, and progressively build up their tolerance of what they see and/or hear.[5] A written record of their SUD's scores can be kept as well, along with any accompanying comments they choose to add.

So if the patient is willing to commit to such a project, then you need carefully to explain once more how the procedure is to be done. As for the basic points to communicate, these are covered in Chapter 10.

All of this will require a substantial block of time, needless to say. But as you may recall, I have already recommended (see Chapter 10) that if video-based exposure is to be done, then a better moment to turn to it is in the subsequent session, and in not the same one during which you and the patient first searched for the trauma trigger.

Exposure work at home can prove quite helpful. Regretfully it is possible only for certain cases, however. The reason has to do with the other person in the video interaction. Is this other an infant, or a small child? There is no problem here. But what if this other person is an older child, or an adult?

You can see the problem. It concerns how this person would feel about being the figure on the screen which the patient is focusing on for their exposure work. They will likely feel extremely uncomfortable with the notion that the patient is going to be, once a day, off in a room by themselves and focusing on a video image of this other, an image which they, the patient, find so aversive they almost can't tolerate it. Think for a moment. How would you feel? Realistically, this likelihood limits the use of the exposure technique at home.

Homework Records

Should a patient keep a daily record about what happens with a homework assignment? Should this be part of the task? It depends.

It depends on the therapist. It depends on the patient. It depends on the therapy context.

Most therapists using VIT are integrating it with one or another variant of cognitive-behavioral therapy. They are used to asking for a written record.[6] For them, it is natural to ask for it in a video session too. Personally, I also feel comfortable proposing this as part of a task.

Some therapists however, coming from another background, for example, psychodynamic or gestalt therapy, find the idea of record-keeping foreign and strongly want to leave it out. My own response here, when teaching or supervising, has become to go along with this preference. Over the years, I have seen many such therapists carry out excellent work with video. I now think record-keeping does indeed have a few advantages (e.g., more accurate reporting) but they are unessential ones.

Separate from the leanings of the therapist, some patients have little tolerance for record-keeping. In this instance, to push hard for record-keeping I find a mistake. It runs a risk of reducing the chances of a successful experience with the new action itself.

So the long and short of it is, for VIT, record-keeping is fine to add if you, the therapist, are at ease with it and the patient is at ease with it. Use any type of handout forms which fit the assigned task.[7]

Before I close with this topic, allow me one remark of a different kind. Do you, the reader, find yourself, also, among those for whom the idea of assigning homework goes against the grain?

In that case, let me suggest something interesting to try. In supervision settings I have seen its usefulness.

Pick a small something, any something, which you know you would like to change in your own life. Pick a something having to do with your own behaviors, physical and/or mental, in other words.

Then, assign yourself a homework task. Think of an action (physical and/or mental) which could implement a first part of this change, however minute. And then, work out a record method.

And give it all a try. Be your own patient. Observe, carefully, your implementation efforts. Find out, for instance, what piece of the new action turns out easier than you expected, what piece turns out harder, and the like.

And along with this, notice your reactions to the record-keeping too. Day by day, what annoys you about it, and/or what pleases you? How regularly to you do it? Are there days you forget it, or turn your back on it, for example? And to the extent you actually do it, what does it give you, if anything?

These small experiences, the behavior attempts and the meta-monitoring of the record-keeping, can be interesting in their own right. But they will also give you a better feel for what this area is like for patients themselves.

Homework Follow-Up

Be diligent about this. Whenever a patient takes on a homework assignment, be sure in the next session, the very next, to inquire about it. When doing supervision I am often surprised by the number of therapists who too easily put this to one side. Unfortunately, to be inconsistent about asking sends a mixed message about the value of homework.

Inquire early in the session. If a written record has been kept, have the patient bring it out.

How long should this inquiry go on? Short is naturally preferable. On the other hand, themes will, at times, pop up which are hard to ignore. You have to see what fits.

In any case, during the homework review a number of topics can be of interest. How much of the task was the patient able to accomplish? Were the planned actions, when executed, done in a full or partial way? What was it like for the patient to do it – what thoughts and feelings did they have? Assuming it was an interaction behavior, what seemed to be the reactions of the other person?

Did they, the patient, change or modify the task in any way? (Patients often do.) If they had difficulties with the task, what might help them continue with less trouble? If they didn't try it at all, what might help now to get it going?

Listen with an attitude of curiosity. Praise any partial results, however small.

If nothing was carried out, zero, frame this as a learning opportunity, not a failure. For example, it can be a chance to find out now, in more detail, if the instructions were unclear, or if a serious obstacle came up that neither of you had anticipated. Barriers can perhaps be identified and the two of you can brainstorm about getting past them. Once in a while you will even discover that the patient has something against this change in the first place, something not yet discussed, and this topic can be addressed.

Of interest, as well, can be to ask about any unplanned new actions, ones not planned in the last session but carried out anyway. These might be straightforward extensions of a planned task. Perhaps the plan was for the patient was to use descriptive language during structured play, but they began using it in other contexts too, for example, while they and the child were setting the lunch table.

Or, there might have been unplanned new actions of an entirely different nature. They, this same patient, found herself listening better to their partner, or found themselves more adeptly setting limits with another of their children.

A final matter is even more specific to video therapy. Be on the alert for it, since it frequently occurs. The patient announces that they tried to do the new behavior, but they didn't succeed. It was beyond their abilities, they flatly failed.

Yet you have already seen the new video, the one on the menu for today's session, and you happen to know that what they are saying is wrong. They believe it, of course. But visible in today's video are one or more small instances of the wished-for behavior.

One would wish for fuller, better versions, naturally. One would wish for more frequent occurrences. Nevertheless, a certain minimal amount is there to be seen on the screen.

Two technical options are now of interest. One is simply to tell the patient about it right away, for example, "I hear that your sense is that you weren't able to do it all, but I had another impression when I looked yesterday at the new video. First, let's see if there is anything else it would be good that we discuss about this last week's task, and then we can go take a look at the video."

Or you can not tell the patient right away, a second option. "I hear that your sense is that you weren't able to do it all. But when we look at the new video we can check out carefully whether that's true. First, let's see if there is anything else it would be good we discuss about this last week's task, and next we can go look at the video."

One critical part of this session will then take place during Step 2. You will show a piece of the video, one in which, for sure, the new behavior can be seen. And should the patient themselves not catch these small occurrences, you will point them out. The patient will be surprised, and almost certainly pleased.

Next, of course, you might continue with an exploration of this kind.

Therapist: What do you think helped you do this? What will help you now [e.g., do it in a fuller way, do it more often, do it with better timing, etc.]?

In other words, what you now do is draw on the positive exception technique, as described in Chapter 2.

Typically, this exploration can be kept brief, however. And once you move on into Step 3 it can be put aside. Some other negative behavior, and its potential positive replacement, will then be the main focus for investigation.

However, when you arrive at Step 4, and you discuss homework options, a good idea can be to return to this positive exception example, elaborated during Step 2. The eventual homework assignment settled upon can then consist of two (or perhaps more) parts.

One will concern the positive exception behavior. The patient can plan to try to implement it further. They can do it hopefully more often, and/or in a fuller form.

The second part will be a new task, a doing of some other action. This new action will be a specific change of the negative behavior investigated during Step 3.

To take an example, perhaps last week's task was (a) to spoon-feed more slowly, and (b) without criticizing infant Joelle's eating. The mother thought she made no progress, but, in fact, in today's video, one again of feeding, there were definite positive moments. So, a first continuing task for the coming week can be to try to keep moving forward with this.

And besides, perhaps today, during Step 3, you did some work with how the mother uses her voice. You and she explored how she can bring more expressiveness into her voice. So a second task could be to implement this better vocal action. Perhaps you even had her practice it today with an insertion technique. In sum, the plan is that the patient will do what they can to implement both tasks.

In fact, this occurs often in VIT: that the homework eventually agreed on contains two or more parts. On the one side, a new behavior is to be implemented. On the other side, a behavior already worked with, and which, as today's video reveals, is already beginning to change, is planned for too. The hope is that this behavior which is already changing can now change further.

More generally speaking, it is safe to say that what has just been described is one of the most significant benefits of working with video. The precise degree of new behavior implementation can be tracked so carefully. Each successive video gives us detailed information about this. Frequently, in a video, we even see multiple change processes occurring. It is like listening to a piece of music with several joined melodies playing simultaneously.

Notes

1 In VIT, still more is possible to add. If a third person is present, a descriptive comment about this person, addressed to the child, might be made ("David [a second child, who just smiled] liked it that you gave him the ball"). Or the adult, where appropriate, can give descriptive language for themselves: for what they are doing, or about to do, or for what they are feeling. This more expanded version of descriptive language first originated, as far as I know, with Maria Arts (2008). What then might argue for a widened use along these lines? The topic is significant but I will not take it up here.

2 A second form parents tend to find relatively easy is descriptive language for what the child is seeing or hearing. Whereas once we move to, for example, language for what the child is feeling, some parents can encounter difficulties.

3 Perhaps worth adding is that in the world of treatment of parents and small children a 5-minutes-a-day play task is not at all unusual. For example, in Parent-Infant Intervention Therapy, a widely used model, 5 minutes as day is the standard homework recommendation (McNeil & Hembree-Kigin, 2010).

4 Another assumption, in this example, is that Jason's anger escalations, although unhelpful and clearly warranting change, don't have the more intense flavor of trauma-based outbreaks, as described in Chapter 10. If, on the contrary, they did have this flavor, then at some point the therapist would be inquiring about that possibility.

5 Some therapists, who do classic exposure work with trauma reminders, add a homework task of a very similar nature. In the session itself use will have made of a movie – a movie with a battle scene, or a car accident scene, or the like. The patient is then encouraged to take a copy of the movie home, and continue with self-guided exposure with the same scene (Abramowitz et al., 2011; Zayfert & Becker, 2007). The video-based technique, of course, allows a focus using a more precise trauma-related stimulus.

6 A few patients prefer to do record-keeping by registering vocal comments on their phone. Although this is possible, accessing these comments in the next session tends to be more tedious than with a written record.

7 If you are unfamiliar with such forms Tompkins (2004) has literally dozens of examples. There also exist an ever-growing number of apps for therapy record-keeping.

12 Getting started

If you would like to try working with video, by all means begin. There is no need to wait. Described here is one reliable way to get underway. A number of persons have had success with it, and report they find it user-friendly.

Some professional background is necessary, of course. You need to be already trained in, or be currently learning, some form of psychotherapy or counseling or mental health coaching.

As for professional orientation, if you are already at home with a cognitive behavioral therapy (CBT) format, you will find video intervention therapy (VIT) a reasonably seamless fit. But if you identify more with another framework, for example, psychodynamic or gestalt therapy, to bring in VIT will not be difficult. You work during non-video sessions in your usual mode. And then during a video session you simply put on two hats, your usual plus a CBT one. You can draw on the techniques described here in the book and you can find room for your accustomed orientation too. Likely, especially during Step 3, when doing "inner movie work," you will see opportunities to interweave your familiar perspective.

Whatever your prior professional experience, to start in with VIT it is best to immerse yourself gradually. Ease into this new modality with progressive steps. Video intervention is hardly difficult, but there are things to get accustomed to. The basic setting will seem novel. To talk with someone, yet both be intermittently looking at a screen – it is an altered therapeutic framework.

What follows is a series of suggestions. I have divided my recommendations into three successive stages. Linger with each stage as long as you want. Spend two months with it, spend six months, spend longer, do whatever works best. Then once you feel ready, pass on to the next stage.

Feel no need either to follow the exact steps I recommend. Move along in whatever order best suits you.

The guidelines proposed here will be briefly stated. For this reason I often add a comment to the effect of "concerning this matter, review chapter X." Since specifically what to do in sessions has been covered earlier, and in detail, it would be pointless to repeat all that now. So as you work through the stages, you will want to go back to previous book sections and review whatever is useful for you there.

DOI: 10.4324/9781003621669-12

A First Stage

For this initial period, try, with one or more patients, to do the following. Pick someone you are already seeing. Propose a session with video. Explain how, in your opinion, looking together at a video of interaction could be useful for the goals of the therapy.

Sensible, for now, will be to choose one or more patients you have already found easy enough to work with. A good idea, also, can be to limit yourself to working with one person in the room only. It is easier. Discuss the video with just one parent, not both; with a parent alone, or an older child alone, not parent and child together. To have just a single person present will create fewer demands on your attention.

An exception, naturally, is if you are a couple therapist, or anyway see couples, and you want to try out using video in this context. To have both parties present should, in that instance, feel quite manageable. Of course, for the time being do pick couples who, in sessions already done, proved fairly cooperative, at least with yourself.

The Video

Speak with the patient, acquire consent, and then arrange for the filming of a video. I suggest the video be short, 5 or 10 minutes. Decide on an activity to be filmed. In principle this activity could be anything, but for this first stage you will likely find certain scenarios easier to deal with than others.

For example, does the parent have an infant of between 0 and 6 months? Then you might suggest a simple face to face exchange, the child lying or in an infant seat (e.g., a car seat). Other possibilities are dressing the child or a bath. Is the child between 6 months and 6 years? Here the easiest option is parent-child play, on the floor, with toys.

What about a parent and an older child? Dialogue videos, that is, a discussion to be filmed, are recommended. Good themes are, for example, what the child experienced that day at school, or planning for a coming event, or some area of mild conflict.

Of course, a strong conflict is also a possible theme, and clinically speaking an excellent one, but before tackling this you might want to build up more familiarity with intervening with video.

Similarly for couples: a planning theme, a moderate conflict theme, or the like, is a good pick. If you are a seasoned couple therapist, accustomed to having partners discuss one designated topic or another, to have this unfold now in a video will not seem extremely different. With a couple, make the video perhaps 15 minutes in length.

As for the how, when, and where of filming, review Chapter 1. The patient can film at home. Or you or a team colleague can do the filming, assuming that the therapy is not online.

If the patient is to take care of it, then organize for the video to be sent or brought to you ahead of the session, so you can spend a little time with it prior to intervening.

Preparation for the Session

The type of session I recommend during this first stage is what in previously in the book has been called an abbreviated session. This means that only Steps 1 and 2 of the standard procedure will be carried out. During Step 1 you will ask for the patient's comments on the video, and then during Step 2 you will show a series of positive moments in the interaction.

So how do you prepare yourself for such a session? It is simple enough. Decide which part of the video to show in the session. Remember that 1 or 2 minutes works usually fine. Once this choice has been made, select some positive moments it could be helpful to show.

These can be actions the patient does, or actions the other person does, or mutual, joint actions. Of course, make sure that at least two or three are the patient's actions or else joint ones. We don't want to show just what the other person does positively.

Chapter 3 has lengthy advice about how to do this type of preparation, so to skim through it again would be worthwhile. I will, however, repeat here a couple of points.

First, as you glance through the video don't worry about catching every little detail. Stay with the obvious, with what stands out for you right away. See what events catch your attention, and notice, as well, the general atmosphere of the interaction.

That will do. It will be sufficient and probably more than enough for a useful intervention. With time, as you continue working in this mode, your eyes and ears will get sharper just from reviewing a number of videos. A more fine-grained kind of analysis is described in Chapters 14–16, so later down the line, if you wish, you can familiarize yourself with what is covered there. But there is no need to occupy yourself with a fine-grained level for now.

Second, when choosing positive moments don't set the bar too high. You can include events which appear only barely positive, for example. There will even be videos where barely positive is all there is.

During the Session: Hearing the Patient's Initial Reactions

In the session, to start out, first just play the segment through, the segment you picked when preparing. Then ask the patient for comments. What have they found interesting, or important?

In other words, here you will be doing Step 1 of the standard procedure. Do review Chapter 5, which covers Step 1. I will revisit here only a couple of points.

One is this. Remember, as stressed in Chapter 5, that patients vary immensely in what they see or don't see when you first show a video. And they vary immensely in what they say or don't say. So be ready for anything – including nothing at all. Discussed in Chapter 5 are some options of how to reply to these different possibilities.

Do also give attention to one small but important technical matter. Whenever the video is playing, during those moments don't talk to the patient. And whenever you have anything you wish to say, first stop the video, leaving a static image on the screen, and then say it.

Begin, from the start, to cultivate this habit. Do it whether the session itself is live or online.

Likewise, if the patient begins to talk while the video is running, then stop the video. Hear the patient's comment, respond, and only after that put the video back into motion.

The reason, as previously explained, is a good one. Whenever you and the patient are exchanging remarks, even if briefly, it is better that you give your full attention to the patient. If the session is live this can include attention to their nonverbal signals. Even if the session is online, and at this moment the video clip fills the screen, you can still give attention to the patient's voice quality and to what they say. Likewise, it is better in these moments that the patient, as well, gives their full attention to you.

Showing Positive Moments

Next, move into Step 2. Review Chapter 6 for details.

Now, you show some of the positive events you located while preparing. You let the video run a little, you stop it on a relevant image, and then you briefly say what in the interaction you here find positive.

Inquire now and then too about how the patient is responding to seeing these positive moments, and to hearing your remarks. Patients almost always have appreciative reactions.

And this is enough. You show as a minimum three positive events, if possible, between five and ten. And then you can end the session. Or, if sufficient time is remaining, you can put the video to one side, and then for the rest of the session return to what you more typically do with patients.

As for how to conclude, that is, how to conclude with today's work with the video, there are two options. One is just to end, period, nothing more. The other is to propose homework. What has already been done with the video can now be used as a springboard for determining an at-home task, if you so wish. In Chapter 5 are explained some ways in which an at-home task can be added to an abbreviated session.

To give attention to what patients can implement at home is a basic component of VIT. So much can be learned from a video about new skills which can be developed.

But here too there is no hurry. If you wish add this component now, then fine, but let it wait if you prefer. More important for the moment are the other fundamentals – proposing work with a video, arranging a video be made, exploring the video with the patient in a simple fashion. These are the basics which will get you underway.

Perhaps Add Also

Finally, what more during this first stage might be done?

One obvious continuation is to do further sessions with the same patient. Arrange for new videos. Explore them in the same abbreviated mode. See how these successive experiences help with respect to the goals of the therapy.

Second, consider going down the same road with one or more other patients. You will find it quite interesting to discover what is similar and what different when bringing in video with diverse cases. A good idea, of course, would be to continue to choose patients who are largely cooperative ones.

And then once you feel curious about trying still more, and feel ready, move on. Go to the next stage.

A Second Stage

Here, you will considerably widen what you are doing. First of all, add to your sessions Step 3 of the standard procedure. Or rather, add a simple version of it, as I will explain.

And second, wind up each session with a brief Step 4, a discussion of a practical change at home. You may have been doing this already, or at least some of the time. Now, do it systematically.

It is in Step 3, you will recall, that the therapist begins to focus on a negative pattern in the video. A single negative pattern is picked out, one which seems significant with respect to the goals of the therapy. Should the patient make a change here, it would represent definite progress.

As covered in Chapters 7–10, there are different possibilities for how to organize Step 3. The easiest is to stay focused on the "outer movie," that is, the outwardly visible behavior in the video. Try doing this, for now, in your sessions. Help the patient understand how changing the negative behavior could be useful. Help them plan how to go about it.

The inner movie, in contrast, is what is taking place inside the persons in the interaction – their thoughts, feelings, body sensations, and the like. To explore these elements, too, can give a lot. However, inner movie investigation tends to be more complicated. So it makes sense during this stage to limit yourself, for the most part at least, to a focus on the outer movie. Inner movie investigation can then be taken up in the next, the third stage.

Selecting and Exploring a Negative Pattern

When preparing for the session, decide which negative pattern, which negative behavior, you will want to explore with the patient. And remember that when we say "negative behavior" this can also mean simply the lack of a positive behavior – here at minute 3:05 was an opportunity where the patient could have done X, an action which would have been productive, but the opportunity was missed.

Glance again through Chapter 7, where this decision, the selection of a negative pattern, is explained. Glance, as well, through the discussion of how to work with such a pattern. Review, too, Chapter 11 for tips about how to help the patient to form a homework plan.

Sometimes Two or More Patients in a Video Session

Perhaps up to now, as I have suggested, you have limited yourself to sessions where one patient only is present. If so, now could be a good moment to expand this. Try, at times, to work with two or more patients. Review Chapters 4, 5, and 6 for suggestions.

Pay attention, especially, to what, in Chapter 4, I call traffic control. Don't let one person use the video to criticize the other. The atmosphere will quickly become toxic if this impulse is given free rein.

Keep in mind, as well, finding ways to balance out who receives what degree of attention in a video session. This topic too is covered in Chapters 4, 5 & 6.

Widen the Range of Types of Patient

I counseled that during the first stage, in order to get yourself underway, you limit yourself to trying video intervention with patients who are more or less easy to work with. Consider now taking on one or more patients who are more difficult, less cooperative. Try to get them on board for work with video. Do what you can in the sessions. See Chapter 2 for tips.

A good idea with these patients will be, for the first one or two or even three times, to do only abbreviated sessions, with discussions of positive patterns alone. It will be easier. Get a little bit of movement going. Then move to adding procedure Step 3, once you think the patient can handle a longer, more complex work.

Add Linking Techniques

So far what I have described here is a pruned-down version of external movie exploration. Once this pruned-down version is beginning to seem familiar, you might feel ready to add more.

Linking techniques, for example, can be brought in too. They are simple enough. At a moment which fits you raise some questions about the extent to which the negative behavior seen in the video shows up in other interaction contexts. What are other situations when, in an interaction with person B, the other person in the video, the patient at times does the same action, or some variant of it? And when and where does the same pattern occur in interactions with other people? Chapter 8 has suggestions for such a discussion.

These two topics – variants of the behavior with person B and variants with other persons – are highly significant. With VIT we take care to emphasize them. As you thematize them, first gather relevant information – when, where, how often, with what likely consequences, and so on. And in subsequent sessions, inquire at times about whether and how the patient is starting to change in these other contexts too. The goal here is as much generalization as possible.

In a video session, try to keep these discussions fairly short, nevertheless. Should more discussion seem warranted, and often it does, then take up the issue also in non-video sessions.

Add Insertion Techniques

At some point also, begin bringing in insertion techniques. These are technically a touch more difficult than linking techniques. They require a more precise use of the video itself. They are only possible in some sessions too, not others. It depends upon the nature of the negative behavior being challenged.

Insertion techniques, you will recall, permit the patient to practice a new behavior. You have been exploring a negative pattern. You and the patient have succeeded in defining what could be a more productive behavior, one to replace the negative one.

Now the patient can practice this new behavior, in co-ordination with the video itself. You play a short bit of the video. Just before the patient's negative action is about to take place (that is, to take place in the interaction on the screen) you stop the video. The patient then tries out the new action.

For instance, if the new action is a form of speech, the patient can now say something, as if they were speaking in the interaction itself. Or if the new action is a mental action, a form of more productive self-speech, this, as well, the patient can say out loud. Of course, if they were really in the interaction they would just think it, not pronounce it openly. But for them, here in the session, to say it out loud, and right at the opportune moment, is an excellent form of practice. For more details see Chapter 8.

Add Continuation Techniques

These, too, you can begin to try. Although akin to insertion techniques they are easier technically to implement.

You can use them when two or more persons are present in the session. The technique is also a form of practice. You play a piece of the video, and at a certain point you stop it. The two (or more) persons continue, live, from there. They face each other and speak to each other, but as if they were in the original interaction and now are continuing it.

They try now to move the discussion forward in a more skillful fashion. They try to use more helpful verbal statements, and/or a more helpful nonverbal, body-organizing manner. For more, see Chapter 8.

As with the first stage, stay with the second for as long as suits you – two months, six months, whatever.

A Third Stage: To the Inner Movie

For this final stage, the goal is to turn to the inner movie. Give time to it in some sessions. Expand your ways to explore it.

Choose patients who appear ready for this. Also, choose sessions where it is appropriate – that is, ones with no pressing need to devote a lot of time instead to the outer movie. Let's look at some examples of what you can try.

Exploration of Inner States

Quite useful is a key intervention described in Chapter 8: "Imagine you are there, in the interaction." As they, the patient, are imagining this you can explore their thoughts, feelings, and the like. It is an intervention which typically brings a patient much more in touch with their inner experience than if you had asked, "What *were* you feeling then in the interaction?"

One way to do this is to stop the video on a specific image and next go to, "Imagine you are there .... " A second way, slightly more complicated but very effective, is to tell the patient you are going again to play a segment of the video, and that, as they watch it, they should "imagine" they are there, step by step, tracking what occurs inside them as the interaction proceeds.

Explore their thoughts. Explore their feelings. Explore too, if you like, their body experience, as suggested in Chapter 8.

Then naturally, in most instances at least, help them find more productive thoughts to replace dysfunctional ones. And/or, depending on your working style, help them to mindfully distance themselves from the dysfunctional thoughts.

And should you happen to have some familiarity with body techniques (e.g., as described in Chapter 8), help them replace dysfunctional bits of body organizing with more functional ones. This is a good thing to add in any therapy context, but as an amplification of work with a video it can be particularly effective. (Dysfunctional body organizing can so easily have a negative impact on an interaction.)

Mentalization Techniques

A next option, when you feel ready, could be to take up mentalization techniques. Now you will help the patient hypothesize about the other person's inner movie.

Review Chapter 9 for a detailed discussion. As you may recall, some of the briefer mentalization techniques can be also drawn upon during either Step 2 or Step 3. Most, however, are best used during Step 3.

For example, one such brief technique, as you may remember, is "simple reflection, therapist leading." You stop the video on a particular image, and then you yourself comment about the other person, making a guess about his or her inside experience. "Danny [a 3-month-old infant] seems to really like exchanging these vocal tones with you."

This technique is easy to use either during Step 2 or Step 3 or both. Try it for several sessions. Then you might progressively add the three related brief techniques – "simple reflection, patient leading," "giving a voice, therapist leading," and "giving a voice, patient leading."

Among the complex techniques, the simulation technique is especially recommended for Step 3. It is effective and it will widen your own grasp of the potentialities of video work.

As you may remember, with this technique we ask the patient to look again at a more extended part of the video. And we ask them to imagine as they do so that they are the other person in the interaction. Watching the screen, they are to notice what they, as the other person, thinks and feels. It can be done with a short piece of video, that is, 30 seconds, or with a longer piece, that is, 5 or so minutes. It is a VIT technique of particular importance. (Patients almost always gain new insight.)

In Chapter 9, other mentalization techniques are to be found as well.

Investigate the Past

Something else worth getting yourself used to is, on occasions where it is suitable, a turning to the past. Help the patient to connect the here-and-now video interaction with their childhood history. A short exchange in this area can quickly deepen an inner movie exploration.

The simplest way to execute this move is with a direct question, for example, "How is what we have been seeing like or unlike what went on in your family when you were a child?" Covered in Chapter 8 is how such an inquiry can be expanded. Try it out with several patients.

Another stepping stone to the past can be a dysfunctional belief. Experiment with this, too, when you feel ready. Exploring the inner movie, you have helped the patient arrive at a formulation of an unhelpful belief (e.g., "When someone is so angry at me it means I'm hopeless as a person"). Continuing, you next inquire about how and when the patient first came to believe this, or to believe something of this nature.

Videos and Trauma

Finally, a more challenging way to move to the past – highly complex, and frequently evoking strong countertransference as well – is when you suspect a background of severe trauma is having effects upon the interaction seen on the screen. You will have noticed one or more specific behaviors, such as dissociation, which may well have trauma roots.

Highly useful now can be an exploration having two parts. What was the specific trigger (or triggers) in the interaction which stimulated the patient's trauma-based behavior? You help the patient pinpoint this. And just what is the relevant trauma history at play? You discuss this, too, briefly or at more length depending upon whether it has already been elaborated in the therapy. For advice about how to proceed in this manner, read carefully through Chapter 10.

And next, assuming you have located a trigger, there may be more work worth undertaking. This is to use exposure techniques with the video trigger. Such techniques can substantially reduce a trigger's stimulus power. For the details here, see Chapter 10.

Work of this nature with trauma triggers can be extremely valuable. It is intricate, but once you have gone through it with several patients you will likely feel pleased to have added it to your repertoire.

This concludes the third stage. If you have arrived all the way to here, congratulations – well, triple congratulations!

I turn next to two more topics. One is a short chapter describing several other video intervention methods I find of value. The second is fine-grained observation, covered in the final three chapters.

13 Other video intervention methods

If you have been reading this book it is surely obvious to you, by now, that there could be many possible forms of video intervention. And indeed there are. A good number currently exist.

In this chapter, I will briefly describe several approaches. They are all ones with which I have had a direct acquaintance. I personally know the persons who developed the approaches, or I have seen them present them in a training or similar.[1]

I mention these methods because I have a suggestion. If the present book stimulates you to begin with video intervention, then it makes sense to keep your eyes open, too, with respect to other approaches. There always is something to learn from how someone else scans and analyzes a clinical video. There always is something learn from how they intervene with video, and from how they conceptualize that.

So should it happen that method X is going to be presented in a conference you will be attending, or two days of method Y will be taught somewhere within reach, consider taking advantage. For sure you will find it interesting.

Recommended, as well, is to have a look at relevant publications. I cite several here.

Some Historical Background

What set the stage, historically speaking, for the emergence of therapeutic video intervention? The answer seems clear. It was chiefly the growing use, during the sixties and seventies, of video for child development research.

We find it in approach after approach. The majority were inspired by one or another video research method. Indeed in some cases, as we will see, it was the researcher themselves who turned to putting video to work in a mental health context. In a moment I will give examples.

But first let me make an aside comment. What about the systemic family therapy tradition? Hasn't video long been used by some family therapists?

Yes it has been, no it hasn't been. The question is in fact interesting. Yes it has been, in this sense: since the very beginning of family therapy, video, and/ or film, has been used for supervision.

DOI: 10.4324/9781003621669-13

In the earliest period it was of course film which served such a function, as video technology had not yet been developed. Therapists in training would film themselves working with a family or couple and then bring the film to supervision. This permitted detailed commentary by a supervisor.

Nevertheless, this rich tradition, over the years, has led to rather little such intervention with patients. A few systemic therapists have tried. Some useful observations have been shared.[2] But a more thorough framework has so far not emerged.

What could have been another precedent, one would think, is the use of video for sports coaching. Today it is a widespread tactic. A video is made of the athlete performing, and then coach and athlete regard it together.

Sports coaching professionals began developing such procedures quite a bit earlier than psychotherapists began developing their equivalent. Patrick Dowrick (1991), for example, particularly influential in this field, was already publishing about it in the seventies.

Dowrick's writings are even cited by some video intervention practitioners. As far as I know, however, neither his work nor any other in the sports coaching field seems to have served as the initial stimulus for a specific mental health video approach.

So let's return to mental health intervention, and to specific methods. By a "method" I mean, here, an approach which has an explicit procedure, and about which at least a small amount of literature has been published.

Worth remarking of course is that video now serves as one small tool among others in a good many treatment contexts. One common use is in group therapy settings where role-plays are done, for example, as a part of social skills training. A role-play is filmed and then looked at in the group immediately afterwards (e.g., Malekoff, 2015). Another is when a video is one component of initial assessment. After being filmed it might then be used for a single intervention (e.g., Dishion & Kavanagh, 2003).

Some uses are more unusual. For instance, one program for anxiety patients includes video-filmed practice behaviors – for example, the patient with a public speaking phobia now speaks before a group. Later, they can observe the video in order to challenge negative expectations (McEvoy et al., 2018). "Oh, I'm not as terrible as I thought, I see."

Typically however, in the literature about such programs, the use of video is mentioned only in passing, and almost nothing is said about what is done with it on a practical level. My comments here will be confined, instead, to approaches where intervention with video has a more central role, and where at least a minimal account of technical procedures can be found.

Concerning any such formal method, what are some of the most relevant questions we might ask about it? Useful can be the following, certainly:

- Who are the target patients?
- What is the range of scenarios which are filmed?
- What techniques are used for intervention?
- Is the video work stand-alone (i.e., with only sessions with video primarily taking place)? Or is it integrated within the wider treatment context?

I begin with several methods whose target patients are limited to parent-infant and parent-toddler dyads.

The Intervention Approach of Beatrice Beebe

This method has been mentioned previously in the book. Beatrice Beebe is of course best known as a parent-infant video microanalytic researcher. However, she is also a psychotherapist, psychoanalytically-oriented (Beebe & Lachmann, 2014).

Originally, as a psychotherapist, she was only doing individual therapy with adults. But eventually, after seeing countless research videos of parent-infant interaction, a new inspiration came (Beebe, 2003, 2006). She was regularly encountering some parents who seemed in need of therapeutic assistance concerning their relationship with the infant. Why not use video to help them?

Beebe's target patients were, and still are (almost entirely), mothers with young infants. The scenarios she films are (almost exclusively) face-to-face interaction. The parent sits in a chair, the infant in an infant chair – that is, like a car seat – each quite close to the other. The parent is told simply to interact with the child. Two to 3 minutes are filmed.

As for techniques when intervening, Beebe shows the parent, and discusses, a number of fine-grained details. Relevant psychoeducation is brought in when appropriate. Some brief exploration of the parent's childhood past may take place.

Typically her video work is stand-alone. It is not coupled with any wider treatment. Only video sessions take place, with no or few non-video sessions.

However, two kinds of exception must be mentioned. First, Beebe and several of her colleagues have explored an intervention variation designed especially for highly traumatized mothers. Here video sessions are mixed with non-video sessions, the latter being focused on trauma work (Beebe et al., 2012).

Second, Beebe has experimented, as well, with something radically unusual. Occasionally, in her adult psychotherapy, she arranges that a part of a session is filmed, and then she and the patient look at the video together. She has written about this venture with respect to a couple of patients. (For one account see Sandberg & Beebe, 2020, and for a commentary on my part, Downing, 2020.[3])

The Intervention Approach of Mechthild Papoušek

Mechthild Papoušek's journey was akin to that of Beebe's. She was one of the earliest important video microanalytic researchers. For years she collaborated with her husband, Hans Papoušek, in creating innovative paradigms for early developmental research.

At a certain point she turned, as well, to intervention using video. This led her to create a treatment center for parent-infant and parent-toddler dyads.

Video intervention was here only one part of a wider program. It was designed as a central part, however (Papoušek & Wollwerth de Chuquisengo, 2006).

As for scenarios, Papoušek liked using face-to-face, akin to Beebe. But she experimented, as well, with several others. One, for instance, was a scenario long popular in child therapy: play with toys, on the floor or at a table. For a video intervention this means, of course, that the parent plays too.

Another was an ingenious idea of her own creation. It was done with parents who had a child between 2 and 4 years old.

The parent was instructed to sit in a chair while the child played on the floor. They (the parent) were given a magazine, and were told to inform the child that now for several minutes they (the parent) were going to read the magazine, and that the child was just to play and not bother them.

The resulting videos were often quite fascinating. In most cases a struggle over boundaries ensued, often subtle, sometimes far from subtle. Exploration of the video with the parent would then normally lead to a discussion about how the parent might more successfully set clear boundaries at home.[4]

The Group Attachment-Based Intervention Approach

This rich method was developed by the attachment researchers Howard Steele and Miriam Steele together with Anne Murphy, psychologist. It is designed especially for parents living in difficult socioeconomic conditions – for example, poverty, nearby urban crime, and so on (Steele et al., 2014). Most have experienced multiple traumas, both during childhood and in present-day circumstances. The children are aged 0–3 years.

The sessions in Group Attachment-Based Intervention (GABI) take place three times a week. The sessions are 3 hours long. They are conducted by one or two lead therapists together with anywhere from two to six apprentice therapists (typically psychology graduate students). The parents come with their children.

For a portion of each session the parents have group therapy alone with the lead therapists. In a separate room, at the same time, the children receive play therapy from the apprentice therapists. Video intervention is a frequent part of the group therapy. A video of one of the parents and their child is shown, and reflected upon by the therapists and group members. Attachment as well as other issues are thematized.[5]

The Video Intervention for Positive Parenting Approach

This method was developed jointly by Marian van Ijzendoorn and Marinus van Ijzendoorn, prominent attachment researchers, together with Femmie Juffer, a clinical psychologist (van Ijzedoorn, van Ijzedoorn & Juffer, 2013). Especially to admire is its elegant sparseness.

Five (or occasionally six) video sessions are done, typically in a home visiting context. The techniques used are few. However, they have been especially well-chosen, I find. Extensively employed, for instance, is the mentalizing technique of "speaking for the baby," as described here in Chapter 9.

The target patients are parents of infants or toddlers. Normally the approach is stand-alone, not part of any wider program.[6]

The Circle of Security Approach

This method was created by Robert Marvin, another prominent attachment researcher, together with Kent Hoffmann, Glen Cooper, and Bert Powell, therapists. Marvin, along with his research colleague Jude Cassidy, has been responsible for developing research coding for the important area of Strange Situation behaviors of children 2 to 4 years old (Cassidy & Marvin, 2002). So here, once again, we find a video intervention approach which first emerged from a video research background.

As for theoretical orientation, apart from attachment theory the approach draws heavily on the thinking of the psychoanalyst James Masterson (e.g., 1976).

The Circle of Security (COS) is delivered in a group setting, over a fixed number of sessions (Powell et al., 2014). The patients are parents of children between 1 and 4 years of age.

Extensive psychoeducation is given. Each patient also works with two videos. The scenario filmed both times is Strange Situation, with 5 minutes of parent-child reading and 5 minutes of a put away toys task also added.

With the first video, the intervention focus is on helping the patient to reflect on how what is seen in the interaction might be tied to the patient's childhood past, and especially to early attachment issues. A negative behavior is identified and a replacement behavior recommended. Often a change of underlying attitude is recommended too.

With the second video the emphasis is upon any visible implementation of the new behavior, with praise given for it.

The method is largely implemented as self-standing. Marvin himself, however, has developed an alternative possibility too, one integrating the same intervention mode into a family therapy context (Marvin et al., 2002).[7]

I turn now to two other methods, both of a nature quite different from the ones described so far.

These two methods initially were one method. I will explain.

The Marte Meo Approach

In the mid-1980s, in the Netherlands, Maria Aarts, a social worker, and Harry Biemans, a psychologist, were both working at a center for disturbed school-age children. The center's program included consultation with parents.

At a certain point they decided to film parent-child interactions, and then look at the video together with a parent. Having heard about the microanalytic research of Daniel Stern and Colin Trevarthen, they wished to work out some analogous use of video as an aid for coaching parents.

Eventually the two of them separated as colleagues, each going their own way. Each, however, continued to develop video intervention strategies. Aarts came to call her version "Marte Meo" ("My Strength"). It is an approach widely practiced today, and in a number of different countries. (About Biemans and his version I will say more shortly.)

Perhaps most distinctive is Aarts' much broadened range of target patients. The method is now used for intervention with parent-infant, parent-child, parent-adolescent, and even sibling-sibling relationships. Here is a major difference from the other methods I have previously described.

A second major difference is the intervention style. The sessions are largely instructional. Psychoeducation takes center stage. Positive behaviors in the video are first praised, and then counseling is given about new behaviors to add.

Typical video-filmed scenarios are play, family meals, and family discussions. With infants and toddlers, feeding, a bath, or a clothes change are sometimes used.

The approach is often done as stand-alone. Some practitioners, however, integrate it into wider treatment contexts.[8]

The Video Intervention Guidance Approach

As mentioned above, Harry Biemans and Maria Aarts were originally working together in the 1980s and then separated as colleagues. Biemans, too, continued developing his own intervention version. For some years he called it Video Home Training. Later the name was changed to Video Interaction Guidance (VIG).[9]

It is widely practiced today throughout the Netherlands, and elsewhere too, especially in England and Scotland.[10]

In many basic respects VIG parallels Aarts' approach. It can be practiced with children of all ages, not just with infants and small children. Similar filmed scenarios are used. Intervention is conducted in an instructional mode. Positive behaviors are shown, and positive exception behaviors (Chapter 5) highlighted. One difference, however, is that VIG puts a stronger emphasis on stimulating the patient themselves to conclude what might be new behaviors to try, rather than the therapist simply informing them about this.[11]

Although the method can be used as stand-alone it is frequently integrated into wider treatment programs.[12]

Additional Approaches

Finally, let me more briefly mention several other methods, ones with which I have had little or no direct contact. I refer to them, first, because of having heard positive recommendations from other professionals, and second, because what I have seen of the literature about each makes good sense to me.

Each method employs video intervention. Each is intended for assistance with parent-infant or with both parent-infant and parent-small child relationships.

Two methods which have been quite influential in the United States are the Interaction Guidance (IG) approach of Susan McDonough and the Steps Toward Effective Enjoyable Parenting (STEEP) approach of Martha Farrell Erickson and Byron Egeland. Both employ short interaction videos. Both emphasize a pointing out of positive behaviors. IG has been incorporated into a variety of different treatment settings (McDonough, 1995). STEEP is designed specifically as a home visiting coaching program (Erickson & Egeland, 2004).

Attachment and Biobehavioral Catch-Up (ABC), created by Mary Dozier and her colleagues, is a more tightly structured approach. A ten-session format is followed. Predetermined themes are elaborated in each session. In eight of the sessions video intervention is done during part of the session (Dozier et al., 2005; Dozier et al., 2018).

The approach of Daniel Schechter, called Clinical Assisted Videofeedback Exposure Session (CAVES), is designed for aiding traumatized mothers having difficulties with their infants. CAVES is a single session intervention. The mother's trauma background is already known beforehand. When the video is explored with the mother a trauma trigger (e.g., an infant loudly crying) is found. A specific video image then provides a focus for exposure techniques. (In this respect the method has parallels with video intervention therapy [VIT] work with traumatized patients [see Chapter 10].)

The Future

What shall we expect about future developments? For myself, I am confident that video intervention is still much in its beginning moment.

Personal sharing of short videos has become a part of daily life. Out come the phones and we video our pet in the garden or a friend dancing or a sports event which excites us.

Such habits have become so ubiquitous that the fact that video is now sometimes used in therapy contexts seems hardly a surprise. And a good guess would seem that such use will proliferate in the coming years. How could it not, one wonders.

Notes

1 For some descriptions of still other methods, see Steele & Steele, 2018.
2 See, for example, Alger, 1976; and Ray, 2007. Of interest, too, is Hawellek (2005), an anthology of writings about the use of Maria Aart's video approach in combination with systemic therapy. Aart's method is discussed later in this chapter.
3 As I have already mentioned earlier in the book, Beebe, a close friend, and I have exchanged ideas for many years about how to scan clinical videos and how to intervene with them.
4 It was during the years when I had first started in with video intervention that I got to know Papoušek's work well. She and I traded ideas and looked at videos together. Several times, I supervised her treatment group. On a couple of occasions

she and I also collaborated with helping psychiatric teams integrate parent-infant work into their treatment programs. I learned a lot from her.

5 As already mentioned, Howard and Miriam Steele are also close friends and we have shared exchanges over many years. I assisted them and Anne Murphy with working out how to use video intervention in the GABI context.

6 I am acquainted with Video Intervention for Positive Parenting (VIPP) through having attended a training seminar which was offered at a conference, as well as having had several useful discussions with Femmie Juffer. I quite appreciate the method, period.

But in addition, getting to know it has helped me with a particular issue. Sometimes I am asked to assist one or another professional group who wish to make use of VIT, but who require a pruned-down version. Perhaps their intervening coaches or therapists have only limited clinical training, for instance. I find VIPP an instructive model for how such a program can be conceived.

7 Over the years, a large number of COS practitioners have participated in my own trainings and supervision. I have had plenty of opportunity to see the useful work they do.

Apart from that, Bob Marvin is another person with whom I have had numerous exchanges, including looking at videos together. What I most appreciate about the COS approach are Marvin's sophisticated, original ways to scan both research and clinical videos.

8 At the time I first met Maria Aarts I had just started with my own version of video work. She graciously permitted me to attend several supervision seminars she was leading. What was, for me, especially appealing was to see how video intervention can be used effectively with children of all ages, and that there was no need to limit it to parent-infant and parent-toddler treatment.

Over the years many Marte Meo practitioners also have been in my own trainings and supervision. This has given me additional opportunity to witness this mode of parental coaching in its details.

9 Biemans and Aarts called their original joint approach "the Orion project." When they separated, each dropped this name.

10 See Kennedy et al. (2011) for an anthology of articles on VIG as practiced in England and Scotland.

11 Between VIG and Marte Meo some differences also exist in how videos are scanned. I will not go into that here.

12 My acquaintance with the method comes in part from having VIG practitioners attend my own trainings and supervision. In addition, at the request of the Holland organization I have done a small amount of teaching for some of their teachers and supervisors, concerning how video intervention can be done in psychiatric settings.

14 Observing videos: The body alone

Throughout this book I have emphasized that you can start with video inter-vention without having any specialized lens for the videos themselves. In fact I find it a better way to start. Just zero in on obvious events which stand out.

But there is another side of the coin. Over time, to learn to observe on a more fine-grained level is a worthwhile project. It will give a lot. It will make doing video intervention still more interesting. And when you analyze a video, pondering about what to work with in a session, you will discover more options.

How can one go about learning new observation skills? There is a good way, a fairly sure way. In this and the following two chapters I describe a large number of items – ones about the body, and ones about what is said – which can be of interest in a clinical video. What I recommend, if this idea appeals to you, is, gradually, over time, to make yourself familiar with them.

But let me explain. Here is what I don't mean: that you ought to strive consciously to notice all these things, all these items, while scanning a video. On the contrary, that would be impossible. There are too many items here. It would be absurd to try to give conscious attention to every one of them. No one could, nor should they.

Instead, the goal is to sharpen up your implicit awareness. The goal is to train your eyes and ears to take in more details. Most of what they take in on this level will not become conscious. But some will, here and there, and this will add to your overall feel for and evaluation of the video you are observing.[1]

So what to do with this three-chapter list is to poke around in it, and ac-quaint yourself gradually with what it talks about. Do this bit by bit. Don't pressure yourself. And above all, when you are pondering a specific video, relax. Let your eyes and ears simply see what they see and hear what they hear and then note what has settled into your conscious awareness after you have looked though the video, or through a selected part of it.

Before starting in I have a few more comments about the list itself.

As it stands it is arbitrary. It could have been shorter. It could have been longer. It does include many of the items I point out when I teach.

Each item will be discussed only briefly – all too briefly. At times I cite relevant research, but just in passing.

I now and then suggest normative perspectives – "It is better, in the inter-action, when action X looks like this and this, not that and that." But keep in

DOI: 10.4324/9781003621669-14

mind that these perspectives are only my guesses. Occasionally there is modest research support, but mostly not.

Regretfully left out in these chapters is one quite significant topic, cultural diversity. The problem is that the topic is large. I have plenty of experience doing and supervising intervention with different cultural groups, and know some of the relevant research, but there simply is not space here to give these issues the discussion they merit. So many interaction habits and, importantly, interaction norms can vary from one cultural group to another. And then there are plenty of variations within any group.

I do encourage you to think about diversity, anytime you work with a video where it is a potential factor. See if the session helps you learn something new. Some videos can prove highly effective for educating about cultural tendencies, and especially (but not just) with regard to the nonverbal level.

Here is an overview of the material now to be presented. I begin, in this chapter, with just the body, looking at it and listening to it. After that, in the subsequent two chapters, I turn to what gets added when we pay attention to language content too.

And concerning the body, I cover two distinct aspects. First, what should we notice with regard to a single body? Second, what else is there to notice when we shift our gaze to how the two (or more) bodies in the interaction coordinate with each other (or one another)?

So, let's consider first the single body alone.

A Single Body

Facial expression in clinical videos is sometimes more visible and sometimes less. A father and a child are playing together on the floor. Perhaps, for a while, one turns his head and we can't see his face at all.

This is not dire. We can still see and hear plenty of other aspects. But obviously the face, when visible, is an important indicator. It gives us clues about what the person is feeling. In addition, we know the other person in the interaction may be responding to the same clues.

Giving attention to someone's face, notice how flat or lively it seems. Notice, too, what emotion quality, or qualities, it has – playfulness, sadness, and so on. As the interaction progresses, notice if the emotion quality shifts. Does playfulness at some point morph into frustration, for example?

Notice contradictions too. Be careful here, however. Better said be tolerant. Mild, fleeting contradictions – the lips are smiling but the brow frowns now and then – are typically not of clinical interest. They come and go in almost any interaction.[2]

Be more on the alert for something like warm, playful eyes (i.e., the region surrounding the eyes) contradicted by a patently angry mouth, with all of this lasting a good many seconds or more. Why is anger making so clear an appearance in this part of the video? It could be one thing to consider exploring in the session.

Ekman's research can guide us here. If you want to get more really more familiar with the complexities of facial signaling then give attention to three different zones. There is the forehead, for example, an angry frown, a puzzled frown. There is the region around the eyes, for example, a hard squinting, a warm softening. There is the mouth and jaw region, for example, a smile, a jaw thrusting aggressively forward. In each region there are things to notice. Moreover, how do the three regions fit together – coherently? With contractions? This is also something to notice.

A good exercise can be to take a video where facial activity can be seen and watch a few minutes, focusing only on the face of one person. Track moment by moment when the expression shifts, and how. If a lot seems to be going on, you might want to look through these minutes several times more, each time focusing on one of the three regions.

The *extended body* is the rest of what is visible on the screen – head, neck, torso, arms, hands, legs, feet. Posture and gesture are included here. Any other shaping of this extended whole is included here. (About gesture, however, I say a little more in Chapter 15.)

An arm might fold itself inwards, for example. Or it might extend itself outwards. It might move with slowness or rapidity, with steadiness or jerkiness, with tenseness or a relaxed quality. It might go in a straight line or wavy winding one. It might move in conjunction with other body parts or it might move alone.

Videos vary immensely with respect to the amount of extended body movement. Often it depends on context. A video of a 2-year-old and his parent playing on the floor probably will have a lot of extended body movement. A video of a couple sitting in chairs, talking to each other, probably will have a lot less. A video of a teenage daughter and her mother preparing food in the kitchen will likely have something in between.

Expect it to take plenty of time to get more familiar with extended body movement. If facial expression is complex, extended body shaping is arguably even more so. On top of that, we are less used to giving detailed attention to extended body movement. It is right there in front of us, happening all the time in interactions, yet we seldom notice the particulars apart from a prominent gesture or posture shift. Do get to know it, I recommend, but don't be in a hurry.[3]

The *voice* is a universe in itself. It is especially useful to go through a portion of video focusing on the voice alone. To this day, when preparing for a session, I do it fairly often.

Listen to pitch. Listen to rhythm. Listen to variability. Listen, above all, to emotional quality. It is amazing how many nuances can be transmitted by the voice channel.[4]

Gestures as movement are a special form of bodily action. Of course, gestures are equally a form of speech, akin to a word or a phrase. Here I will comment about the movement dimension, and in Chapter 15, a little more about the speech dimension.

Most gestures are done with the hands and arms. It might be with the right hand (and arm) or the left hand or both together. A hand might move vertically or horizontally or both, and/or more towards the torso or away from it. The movement might be steady or changing, slow or fast. A hand might or might not take on a special shape (e.g., a fist).

A gesture can also be done with, or include, a movement of the head, a postural shift, or even an exaggerated facial expression.

Note the shaping and size of gestures, note their frequency, note their clarity. An interesting aspect, too, concerns the back and forth of an interaction. Do the two (or more) persons begin, at times, to match and repeat each other's gestures? This can indicate a good rapport is developing, at least for the moment.

Of course, especially important from a clinical perspective is how the speaker fits all this together with the words they are saying. This side I will take up in Chapter 15. But it is worth training your eyes to see the movement aspect in its own right. The better you can track it, the better you will be able, also, to evaluate how it fits with the spoken words.[5]

Body clarity concerns the overall coherence of the body organizing flow. How well do the face, voice and extended body fit together, or perhaps fail to?

Do significant contradictions occur? Does the face suddenly break into liveliness and playfulness just as the torso collapses inwardly? Does the voice coo warmly while the eye zone flashes hostile anger? Phenomena like these, if prevalent in the video, may well be important from a clinical point of view.[6]

Another aspect of body clarity is what we might call readability. To what extent is the body as a whole transmitting useful information? How present does the person seem? How easy is it to track and follow their body organizing flow?

Contradictions will, of course, reduce readability. But something more is involved too, something, admittedly, a little elusive to define. For example, someone in the video might fall often into a dissociated state. Their body looks flat and lifeless in these moments. It, their body, shows no contradictions, yet its readability is minimal.

Two or More Bodies

So far, I have been talking about a single body regarded alone. Let's turn now to mutual body organizing. What newly becomes significant when we look at two or more bodies interacting?

To start with, let me introduce a distinction. It is one I recommend to keep in mind. We can focus on *emotion coordination* but we can also focus on *instrumental coordination*.

Emotion coordination is the exchange of visible and audible emotion signals. We can notice (1) when does person A with their face, and/or voice, and/or extended body show signs of affective feeling? We can notice too (2) when does person B show such signs? But what we can and should notice as well is (3) how are the signals of each coordinated with the signals of the other? In what ways does A impact on B? In what ways does B impact on A?[7]

A lot of good research exists here. Most parent-infant video microanalytic research, for example, is about precisely this area.[8] Invaluable adult-adult interaction findings exist as well (e.g., Heller, 2012).

To precisely what should you give your attention? Would that I had a nice neat answer to this question. The best I can do is to sketch out several hints.

First, be ready to pay attention to short time intervals. Sometimes, plenty of times, person A does something with their body and person B seems to respond a half second or a second later. The succession of events can go quickly.

Second, if person B does respond, they may do so by mobilizing the same or a different body aspect. What I mean is, A might make a facial scowl and then B might react with only a vocal grunt, for example. Or A might laugh, a vocal signal, and B might just smile, a facial signal. Be ready for different possible couplings of face, voice, and extended body use.

Third, give attention to signal intensity. Perhaps persons A and B are exchanging positive signals. Suppose, however, A's signals are only slightly expressive, whereas person B's are much stronger – she, person B, is using a louder voice, and/or much fuller facial expressions, and/or much fuller overall body movements.

This may work okay between them. Or it may not. Follow the process closely and you may discover person A giving more mixed signals, for example, smiling but frowning at the same time. Or you may see A break off contact completely.

Fourth, I have been talking about person A and person B. But what if there is a person C? What if there is a person D?

Suppose three persons are present. Then you may want to give separate attention to the A-B exchange, the A-C exchange, and the B-C exchange. But keep in mind too that the triadic A-B-C exchange may have its own properties worth noticing.

To take just one example, suppose A and B are in the middle of a good dyadic episode, with a nice back and forth flow. How, then, does C relate to this? Does C stay on the sidelines, giving room to A and B? And then suppose B turns to C, giving a quick brief smile? Does then C give a smile back, but without trying further to engage B in a way which might break up the A-B exchange? These and the like are new things to watch when you have three or more individuals in the video.[9]

Instrumental coordination has to do with practical action. What are persons A and B trying to accomplish together? What practical task, or succession of tasks, appears to be their shared goal?

Of course multiple goals, some shared, some unshared, may be at play. Imagine the 15-minute video is of a mother helping her 11-year-old son with school homework. Here a major goal, getting the homework done, is clear and shared. At the same time each may have other agendas too, openly or not. Mother, for instance, may have as a goal that the homework gets done, but also that the son learns more generally how to concentrate and sit still.

Emotion coordination and instrumental coordination will, plenty of times, overlap. Even then however they are usually (though not always) easy to distinguish.

You are preparing for a session. The case is of an infant feeding disorder. The video is 10 minutes of spoon feeding, mother with her infant girl.

How does the mother coordinate her spoon movements with the infant's behavior? This is instrumental. The infant opens her mouth. How soon, and with what clarity, does the mother bring the spoon near the infant's face? Does she then hesitate a moment (a good idea) before slipping spoon into mouth? And what actions does the infant do – reject the spoon, accept the spoon but then spit out the food, accept the spoon and swallow the food?

But perhaps this will be an interaction fraught with emotion signals too. As she spits the infant scowls. In response the mother's voice turns sharp. Two seconds after that the infant starts to cry.

So we need to distinguish the practical actions stream and the emotion signals stream. And when we intervene in the session we might work with the one or the other or both.[10]

I turn now to several interaction aspects which can have importance with respect to either emotion or instrumental coordination.

Body location creates a framework for both emotion and instrumental co-ordination. It sets the stage.

Body location means simply where in the room (or in the physical setting, e.g., in a video filmed outdoors) each person places her or his body. Where do they sit, or stand, or lie down? To put it even more exactly, where does the weight of their body press against the floor or chair or whatever?

Body location merits attention because of how it facilitates, or fails to facilitate, the body-body exchange. Father walks over to where the child is about to begin playing and then sits on the floor directly behind her. Here he can quite well watch what she does. But potential eye contact and a sharing of facial signals have been rendered next to impossible.

In some videos body location will have been dictated ahead of time, by the therapist or the person filming. "Please sit in these two chairs and face each other while we film the video." Naturally, as each person lands in his chair there is plenty of other body organizing to notice. Just how does each arrange his body, pelvis facing where and head facing where and so on? But this is separate from body location. Once a person has landed at point X, there are literally hundreds of ways they could shape their face and extended body, yet the body location would remain the same.

The more the interaction participants are free to move around the room, the more body location becomes clinically interesting. Three siblings are playing on the floor. As any one of them changes where they sit or lie or stand, where do they next land? Does something strike us about their choice? Perhaps this positioning could now better facilitate contact with both the other siblings? Or could it perhaps better facilitate contact with sibling B while at the same time blocking contact with sibling C? Or does it perhaps look more like a withdrawal from both the others?

Body location is the easiest of the categories to get to know, by far. It is informative, nonetheless.

Interestingly, you will find that to notice it can also help how you observe a video. "Ah, now I see person X moving himself over to ... to ... yes, right there. Good, there they are, installed in their new place, ready for new inter-action episodes. Let's see what they and person Y start in with now.... " The stage has been set anew.

Physical contact occurs in only some videos. When it does, here is another element worth close attention.

We see it most in parent-child interactions, naturally. The younger the child, the more likely its occurrence. But it can happen between a parent and an older child also, or between two adults.

One aspect to notice is the timing. In the video, does the moment of touch-ing seem like an appropriate moment? For instance, during a joint attention episode a child turns to her father and laughs. He laughs too and simultane-ously touches her shoulder lightly. This all fits together well.

Sometimes, however, you will observe touching which is interruptive and distracting, particularly when the child is focused on something else.

Note, as well, the quality of the touching. Is it executed with a nicely timed movement? Is it too quick and sudden?

And then there is the degree of pressure as person A touches person B's body. Does the touch pressure look right, or does it look invasive, overly forceful?[11]

Moving a child, physically moving them, is another form of physical con-tact. An adult or older sibling picks up a child, transports them to another spot, puts them down. There are all kinds of potential manners, positive and negative, in which this can be done.

Holding a child is yet another form. Would that we could see here more than we can see, typically. Just what is happening on a more subtle level? In what ways is the one body making minute adjustments and the other making corresponding ones? So little of this is visible from the outside.

Take in, nevertheless, whether any obvious things stand out. One evident negative indicator, for instance, can be when a child's body obviously is being held at a poor angle, for example such that their head leans too much to one side, clearly causing discomfort.

Much physical contact is instrumental in nature. But accompanying the practical acts stream may well be an emotion signals stream. Notice the voice tones and face of both persons. You may pick up a kind of commentary.

Nonverbal repair is an element of particular importance. We can speak of both nonverbal repair and verbal repair, the latter being a sister element I will discuss in Chapter 15.

A background point is significant here. As Tronick (2007) puts it, almost all interaction is "sloppy." It is "messy." Most of us have an overly idealized picture of how interaction works, or anyway, of how it should work. Once you get down to a micro level you find that even an interaction which is, on the whole, positive is full of intermittent confusions, misreadings, mismatches (emotion X expressed in response to emotion Y is a poor fit with emotion Y), and erratic timing.

What then distinguishes interactions which function well from those which function poorly? As Tronick underlines, the critical question becomes the frequency of repair. In an interaction which functions well we will see not only plenty of misalignments but also plenty of repairs. One person or both will be making successful shifts, successful readjustments.[12]

Tronick's research is about emotion exchange, and the examples of repair he gives take place in emotion exchange contexts. In videos the concept appears to be just as important with respect to instrumental coordination, however, or so I would suggest.[13]

Notes

1 Coan and Gottman (2007) have a good discussion of this issue. Although their remarks concern research coding, what they recommend is fully applicable to clinical video observation.

2 Ekman's research has shown how perversive and frequent such momentary contractions are. Ekman's writings (e.g., 1975, 1978, 2007) are eminently readable, by the way, and much recommended should you be tempted to immerse yourself even more deeply in analysis of facial expression.

3 Helpful literature on the extended body is remarkably sparse. The most useful comes from the Laban tradition. Back in the first half of the 20th century Rudolf Laban developed a system of categories for looking at (what I call) extended body movement. His own book (Laban, 1966) is of interest, and discussions by Lamb & Watson (1987) and Sossin (1999) are helpful. Dana Shia (e.g., Shia & Belsky, 2011; Shia & Fonagy, 2014) has creatively applied the Laban perspective to observation of parent-infant interaction. A superb book on extended body research, regretfully (at the time of writing of the present book) only available in German, is Frey (2000).

4 For more information about the voice I can recommend Arbitbo (2016) and Colapinto (2021). Did you know the tongue has 17 muscles?

5 For an excellent account of gesture research, including her own important studies, see Lausberg (2022).

6 The family therapy literature has long pointed out the potential perniciousness of such nonverbal "double messages" (e.g., Bateson, 2000). Keep in mind I am speaking here of contradictions within the body organizing itself. We will come shortly to contradictions between body organizing and spoken verbal content, another form of "double message."

7 I should mention that when I here say "impact," I am referring to visible impact. A signals, B responds, and we can outwardly see B's response. But naturally we should think, too, of another, wider sense of impact, one which takes into account that A might have an inward effect on B, yet B might not visibly show this.

8 For example, Beebe, 2006; Stern, 1985. Shia (Shia & Fonagy, 2014) also looks at how what I have been calling the extended body functions with respect to parent-infant emotion coordination.

9 The writings of Elizabeth Fivaz-Depeursinge and her colleagues (Fivaz-Depeursinge & Corboz-Warnery, 1999; Fivaz-Depeursinge & Philippe, 2014) are full of insight about so-called triadic exchange. Her research findings in this area are significant too.

10 What about helpful research concerning instrumental coordination? Regretfully, here, in contrast to emotional coordination, there exists little to draw upon. The most useful I know is the work of Tomasello (2008).

11 As discussed in Chapter 10, once in a while, in a video you may see oversexualized touching, a different form of intrusiveness. Obviously, this is a red flag. It may or may not be correlated with anything still more serious. But you will need to decide when and how to address this issue in the therapy.

12 Tronick (2007) found clear research support for this idea. Looking at mothers with young infants, he compared mothers with postpartum depression and nondepressed mothers. Both groups showed high quantities of "ruptures" and "misalignments." The difference was that the nondepressed mothers far more frequently followed up a misalignment with a repair.

13 This is a guess. The research of Tronick and others about nonverbal repair has been limited to emotion coordination.

15 Observing videos: The language exchange

In this and in Chapter 16 I go to language use, to what is said. Language is, of course, used differently depending on the ages and developmental levels of the persons in the video.

Most of the categories listed here can be applied when observing adult-adult, adult-child, or child-child interactions. Later in the chapter I describe a small number of categories specific to parent-child exchanges only.

Some Basic Language Use Categories

Contact initiatives are attempts to start a conversation or to break into one. "Bids" is another name. Notice carefully what happens when one is made.

Is the bid phrased and shaped (the body dimension) appropriately? Does the other person notice? Does the other person respond?

There can be purely nonverbal initiatives as well: a look, a vocal sound. In an interaction between an adult and a child or infant these bids can be of particular importance. The autistic 3-year-old in the video seemingly has no interest in contact, she is in her own world – but not entirely, as here in the video she looks for a short moment at her mother's face. A key aid for this parent will be to learn to give much more attention to such fleeting bids.

Verbal turn-taking tends to happen rapidly. Once you start watching it and listening to it you may be surprised by its quickness. Typically once person A stops speaking, person B begins in well under a second.[1] This is usual not only between adults but also between an adult and a language-fluent child, or between two children.

Keep your ears open for two types of exception. One is interruptions. How often do one or both parties break in before the other has finished?

Occasional interruptions are of course typical, and of little clinical interest. But does one person (or both) cut the other off time and again, to a degree which strikes you as excessive? If yes, it could be a negative pattern perhaps worth exploring. What lies behind it – a refusal to listen to the other person, a desire to control them, a more primitive lack of focus on the other, and so

DOI: 10.4324/9781003621669-15

on – might deserve investigation. And whatever the cause, on a behavioral level it is worth shifting.

Watch, too, for response delays. One person ends his turn, the other pauses for several seconds or more.

Sometimes this can be quite appropriate. He is thinking about what to say. Even, for example, a tilt of the head and a concentrated look on his face might signal this.

But at other times, something else might be at play. It might a dissociative fading, for example. Or it might be a hostile withdrawal, what Gottman (2018) calls stonewalling.

Naturally, turn-taking tends to look quite different when multiple persons (three or more) are present in the interaction. For one thing, the nice neat pattern, first you and then me and then you and then me, is gone. More hesitation and uncertainly become likely, which will at times produce longer pauses.

For another thing, normally how the turn progression unfolds, with who is coming in when, and how often, is open. An exception of course is when person A asks person C a question. In that case person C is expected to respond. More often a degree of uncertainty exists.

Usually there is also little reason to expect an "equal" sharing of turns. Pay attention, nevertheless, to whether one person seems to overly dominate the exchange, and/or whether one person, despite opportunities, seems to come in all too seldom.

Turn length concerns how long a person speaks. Here is something enormously variable. Everything depends on the conversation context.

You have just asked how my vacation went. I start recounting, with you in your turns replying with, "Really?," "That sounds fun," "What did you do next?" and the like. Here my turns will be long and yours brief, as fits.

One potential negative pattern to pinpoint, however, is when a speaker frequently goes on and on, in a monologue which appears inappropriate. Another can be when someone's replies become excessively brief. This may reflect an unwillingness to engage further in the exchange. It may even be another form of hostile withdrawal.

Turn clarity concerns the understandability of a turn, the clearness of the spoken message and its accompanying body dimension. How coherent is what is communicated? Does it have any striking contradictions, for example?

One kind of contradiction can be purely verbal. Something said later in the turn contradicts something said earlier. Another kind can be between verbal content and nonverbal shaping. Someone says she feels fine but her face looks obviously upset.

Be aware that in many interactions a degree of unclarity is par for the course. You and I are talking. As I speak I may know what I want to say but choose my words poorly, or fail to complete a sentence. Or, and this is common, I may not quite know what I wanted to say in the first place. It is by engaging in our give-and-take that I try to think through what I mean.

For such reasons, expect a lack of spoken clarity to be of low clinical interest. But there are exceptions, naturally.

To take one example, consider assertions, in the sense of asserting what one wants or desires. Some patients have serious difficulties with this. Perhaps in the video, for instance, they try, but they choose words which are so vague that their statement has minimal impact. More will be said about assertions later in the chapter.

Turn follow-up is something which once you learn to track will teach you a lot. Person A says something, person B responds. How does what person B says fit in with (1) what person B just said, as well as (2) the overall conversation so far in general? How relevant does the new turn seem to what has come before?

Maybe it confirms what the other said. "Right." "Sure, I agree." Maybe it picks up and continues. "That's a good idea, and it makes me think about something else about the problem." Maybe it challenges. "I see what you mean, but I see the matter differently. My opinion is more that...." Any of these examples are, in their way, likely supportive of the conversation flow.

Keep clear that turn follow-up is quite separate from turn internal organization. A turn can be short and impeccably clear yet it might poorly serve the progression of the conversation. Person B might abruptly change the topic, for example, and in a moment when the original topic needed more elaboration.

Or, the opposite case, perhaps what person B says is only partly clear, it is ambiguous, fuzzy. Yet their half-formulated idea proves useful, and helps the exchange move forward.

Of course, that person B's follow-up is relevant does not in the least mean that it is a positive contribution, everything considered. It could be positive, it could be negative. Perhaps it is a put-down of what person A said, for example. The insult is relevant for the conversation sequence but harmful to the exchange on another level.

As you might imagine, turn follow-up often has clinical significance. It merits careful attention.

Respectfulness is about the atmosphere of the exchange. Does the back-and-forth stay respectful on both sides? This doesn't mean warm, friendly, playful. It means just an absence of disrespectful language use and/or nonverbal signals.

A subdued, neutral manner, with plain phrases and a flat tone, is quite all right, at least as far as respectfulness is concerned. For a good many patients, in fact, to learn how, in conflict situations, to stay with plain and flat can be a good therapy goal.[2]

Scorn, contempt and disgust, conveyed with words or body, are red flags to watch for especially.

Keep in mind, too, that to be respectful does not mean one has to agree with the other person. The question, instead, is how disagreement, when it occurs, is expressed. What we want to hear is disagreement communicated in a nonjudgmental manner.

Humor is also an element not to underrate. Delivered rightly, it can enliven and even enrich many types of interaction. It can also soften a more difficult exchange.

Consider Gottman's research, for example. He and his colleagues compared couples who stayed together 7 years with couples who split (Gottman, 1979). The stay-together couples, filmed discussing a contentious conflict, often interspersed short humorous comments and expressions. Perhaps anger dominated the exchange, but the humorous moments were there.

Humor can, of course, impede a conversation. Too much of it might be distracting when the topic is a serious one. Or humor might be used to avoid emotion disclosure. Especially negative can be nasty, wounding humor, as just mentioned with regard to respectfulness.

Humor also counts for a lot in parent-child and parent-infant play. Perhaps "playfulness" is a better word to use here, with explicit humor messages, jokes and the like, considered a part of playfulness. In a video what is good to see is when the parent manages to create a playful atmosphere. A warm face, laughs, and playful voice tones will contribute, as will moments of humor in the more explicit sense.

Co-thinking is the ability of two or more persons to think together in a collaborative manner. It concerns the ability of each to influence, and be influenced by, the thoughts and questions of the other. Ideally, each scaffolds the other, and each stimulates the creativity of the other.

Co-thinking is important in some videos only. Perhaps at a family dinner there is a lively exchange about the food as well as some sharing about events which have happened during the day. But any co-thinking exchanges are brief, and this seems fitting.

On the other hand, perhaps 14-year-old Bertha brings up some difficulties she is having with a teacher. Bertha clearly wants help, both with understanding the situation and with what she should do about it. Here a longer co-thinking process, with Bertha and one or both parents taking part, would be good to see.

Notice, when you are observing a video, are there moments in the exchange when co-thinking might add a positive element? Do the participants move at such a moment to co-thinking? If not, is an absence of co-thinking a typical pattern for them?

And if you do see a co-thinking event, how does it go? And who is stimulating and guiding who?

Co-deciding takes place, or should take place, when some kind of mutual agreement is needed. Some co-deciding events are quick and easy, and some require a more extensive, prior co-thinking process.

I will be saying more in Chapter 16 about verbal negotiations. But worth remarking here is that one of the things which can fall short in a negotiation is the co-deciding element. The video participants talk, have ideas, discuss the advantages of this and the disadvantages of that, but they never get to co-deciding. Or perhaps they get there, but you have the sense that one of them is really making the decision and the other is just submitting.

Verbal Repairs

I conclude this chapter with the topic of verbal repairs, a form of metacom-munication. Verbal repairs are as if to say, "something here is wrong with our communication, so let's fix it."

As Tronick says, human interaction is "messy," it is "sloppy," and this is true (I will add) of not only nonverbal but also verbal behavior. Ongoing mainte-nance is required, and often quite a bit. As a result, verbal repairs in interac-tions are surprisingly frequent.

The therapy literature has long focused on one important kind, what below I call attitude repairs. But there are other kinds too, as will be described.[3]

Clarification repairs are about making sense of something just said. Person A speaks. Person B, in their turn, replies with, for example, "Huh?" or "What do you mean exactly?" or "I'm not quite understanding." Person B has initi-ated a repair attempt. They need some clarification in order to maintain the exchange.

Clarification repairs are extremely common. Typically this type of repair attempt is immediately followed by an adequate response. Helen asks, "What do you mean exactly?" Carl answers, "When I said the trip seemed long I meant, just, that after a while I wanted to be back home."

Sometimes one person makes a repair initiative and then goes on to ac-complish the repair themselves. "Wait a minute, I see I'm not being clear. What I meant to say was...." We can call this a solo repair.

Most clarification repairs are of little interest clinically. But there are ex-ceptions. Someone might have persistent difficulty communicating in an understandable way. Or one person might hound the other with basically unnecessary clarification repairs.

Or, a particularly unhelpful response: someone might initiate a repair with an aggressive tone. Normally, "What do you mean exactly?" will be said in a friendly or neutral way. But expressed in a sarcastic manner it can function as an attack. For some adult couples and adult-adolescent dyads the attack mode is all too common.

Before I continue, let me profit from these examples with a more gen-eral comment. With respect to all types of repair, look for a coupling of two events. Initially comes the repair attempt, with its message of, "we need to fix something here." And then, typically, comes the repair response immediately after, that is, the other person's reply.

This second person might agree with the need to fix something. Or they might disagree. Or they might take a step to try to make things better, or might take a step which makes things worse, and so on. And once in a while a specific response might not even happen. The other person might talk on as if nothing on a meta-level had been said.

Of course, as illustrated above, occasionally one person will take both steps. They will verbalize the need for a repair and then themselves make the repair. This can happen too.

Word-meaning repairs are a kind of mini-negotiation. A discussion is launched about exactly how a particular word should be defined.

Betty might speak about a recent event as having been "unfair." Jack might respond with, for example, "That was not *unfair*. Maybe it made you uncomfortable, but to call it 'unfair' is going too far." Now the exchange has jumped to a metacommunication level. A dispute is underway about when and when not to apply the word "unfair."

Critical to realize is that such word-meaning negotiations are almost inevitable.[4] This is because of how language works and functions. Many of the words we draw on lack clear definitions. Their meanings are underdetermined. To forget this, and it is so easy, is to fall into a kind of trap.

So when you hear a word-meaning negotiation emerge in a video, don't automatically assume it is undesirable in itself. But do look, nevertheless, for other potential implications.

Sometimes there will be other implications. Is the dispute quickly resolved, or does it keep going, consuming a number of turns? What is the tone and manner on each side? Do you perhaps get the sense that underneath the word dispute lies a more serious dispute? It can easily happen. If you do suspect that some more serious theme is at play, to inquire about this can be one option when working with the video.

Topic repairs have to do with the direction of the exchange. Does one person think the exchange, topic-wise, is getting off the path? They might suggest, for example, "Let's get back to the subject of our monthly budget."

Typically where topic repairs become of clinical interest is when the video participants are involved in negotiation or problem solving. In these exchanges a common difficulty can be a losing of the thread of what needs to be discussed. More attention to this, and more use of topic repairs, may be a skill one or both persons could usefully develop.

Notice, as well, the tone of a topic repair. Normally the tone is neutral. But once in a while a patient needs to learn how to propose such repairs without a criticizing or hostile voice.

Attitude repairs have to do with the emotional attitude one or both persons are manifesting. This is the form of repair which has long been discussed in the therapy literature.

Gottman (e.g., 1979) was one of the first to talk about it. His research showed that, when discussing a conflictual theme, couples who more generally do well together tend more often to initiate and successfully execute attitude repairs.[5]

Such findings underline the significance of this repair type. Of the various types, it is patently the most important from a clinical perspective.

When you are analyzing a video and you observe an attitude repair initiative, notice, first, how well or poorly the initiative is made. And then track carefully what follows next.

There can be solo versions. "Oh oh, I'm getting heated up here, I need to calm down," remarks one speaker.[6] And hopefully they follow up by calming down.

There can be request versions. "You seem to be getting heated up here. I want to hear what you are saying, but could you drop calling me a dodo and things like that?" A request version, of course, is hard to do well, as it requires a somewhat precarious balance of the "want to hear you" element and the "but please say it differently" element.

There can be joint repair versions. These are common too. Often they will be phrased in "we" language. "We seem to be getting heated up here. I think we both need to calm down a little." "We seem to be getting heated up here. Let's take a short time-out, okay?"

When you observe an attitude repair initiative, keep in mind that the fine-grained details count for a lot. Notice, first, how well or poorly the initiative itself is made. And then track carefully how the other person responds, and how the exchange continues. Does each acknowledge what the other has said? Do their responses to each other stay respectful, at least in a neutral sense? And, most importantly, are one or both able to shift, if even a little? And do they thereby manage to improve the interaction atmosphere?

I will now summarize. In this chapter, a first series of verbal scanning categories have been covered. These include the following:

- verbal turn-taking
- turn length
- turn clarity
- turn follow-up
- respectfulness
- humor
- co-thinking
- co-deciding
- clarification repairs
- word-meaning repairs
- topic repairs
- attitude repairs

In Chapter 16, I continue with additional verbal categories. Ones involving or related to mentalization will be discussed.

Notes

1 Extensive research, for example de Ruiter, Peter, Mitterer & Enfield (2006), confirms this. Note too that, remarkably, the average switching pause in adult conversation is just as brief as the switching pause in adult-infant nonverbal vocal exchange (Beebe & Lachmann, 2016).
2 See Gottman (1979) and Gottman & Gottman (2018).
3 A range of diverse forms of verbal repair have been studied in conversation analysis research. See, for example, Enfield (2013) and Hayashi et al. (2013).
4 For a fine overview of this issue see Ludlow (2014).
5 "Attitude repairs" is my language. Gottman just calls them "repairs." He doesn't distinguish between different forms of repair, as is typical in the clinical literature.
6 To note is that here the statement, "I'm getting heated up here," is a form of mentalization disclosure. The speaker is sharing something about their mental state. This topic will be further discussed in Chapter 16.

16 Observing videos: Spoken mentalization

Also to notice in videos is what we can call spoken mentalization. As previously explained (Chapter 9), it is useful to distinguish between inner and spoken mentalization. The first, inner mentalization, is a noticing of one's own mental state, or else a thinking about someone else's. The second, spoken mentalization, is when, with language, one directly shares such observations or thoughts.

Conversations are full of spoken mentalization. Most instances are of no clinical interest, but some very much are. I will first give an overview of spoken mentalization types. After that I will discuss several more complex kinds of exchange where spoken mentalization has only a part, yet can have a significant role.

Consider first what I will call "disclosures."

Emotion disclosure is a verbal sharing about the speaker's emotional state. Body expressions, of course, reveal a lot, and indeed often more, about inner feelings. But verbal communications about emotion have their own importance. Often enough in videos they have clinical relevance.

Notice, for instance, if a patient can openly speak about their emotions, at appropriate moments. How wide a range of emotion can they speak about? How differentiated is their language for what they feel? And are their body signals congruent with what they verbalize?

Emotion disclosure can be just about the emotion itself, for example, "I'm feeling sad." Or it can be about the emotion together with what it is about, for example, "I'm feeling sad about what happened with Henry yesterday."[1]

Thought disclosure occurs when I share what I am thinking. It is a conversation staple. Ordinary interactions are full of thought disclosure. I might say, "I think it might rain today." Or I might just say, "It might rain today."

Obviously, such messages have no clinical significance, typically.

However, there are obvious exceptions. "Here's what I think about that fight we had yesterday," one couple partner says to the other. The shared thoughts which then follow will likely be of strong significance.

Notice, when a sharing like "What I think now about that fight" occurs, if the moment for it seems appropriate. Notice, too, if the manner of delivery seems fitting.

Wish disclosure is often of interest. One's personal wishes, wants, desires – can a patient freely communicate them when the interaction context is right? Can they openly state what it is they want?

DOI: 10.4324/9781003621669-16

Preference disclosure is next door to wish disclosure. A particular preference is shared. "This is the kind of soup I enjoy." "Movies like that one are not something I care for."

Preference disclosures, like these examples, show up fairly frequently in everyday interactions. Perhaps one fundamental purpose of conversational exchange, perhaps more than we realize, is that you get to know my preferences better and I yours.

Note the difference between wish disclosure and preference disclosure. A wish disclosure speaks about a current wanting. A preference disclosure speaks (usually) only about a tendency, a leaning. While eating a bowl of soup, I comment, "This is the kind of soup I enjoy." I am not asking for a second serving. I am not asking to have the same soup tomorrow. I am just sharing that, concerning the topic of soups, this is one type I find appealing.[2]

But if I share a wish for X doesn't this also imply a preference for X? Certainly, it does. Nevertheless, the distinction is useful for scanning clinical videos, because wish disclosures are much more often relevant than preference disclosures.

Intention disclosure is a stating of what one intends to do. For example, it might concern a present action already underway. "What I am trying to do here is just to give everyone coffee."[3]

Be attentive to intention disclosures, and to whether the speaker is adept at expressing them. In a good many interactions they play a helpful role. Used appropriately, they can create more clarity. They make one person more transparent to another.[4] Our decisions about how to act in the world are a significant part of our inner life.

Perceptual disclosure is about what a person sees, hears, smells or otherwise experiences with the body (separate from emotion). "I don't see my phone anywhere, have you seen it?" "My legs felt really strong today when I did my run." "My shoulder is sore again."

Here, again, is a kind of sharing that is much more frequent in everyday interactions than in clinical videos. Nevertheless, in certain types of video they are likely to show up.

Mealtime videos are one example. You may hear a lot of comments about food taste, for instance.

Some parent-child videos are another, especially if the child is quite young. Talk about perceptual experience happens often. Mother is helping 4-year-old Katie to get ready to go out. "Mom, this sweater is too tight," says Katie. Father is reading to 5-year-old Jack. "A goose," says Jack, pointing to the page (i.e., communicating, "Visually, I am seeing a goose.")

Videos filmed in a Theraplay context (Buckwater & Downing, 2017) can be quite interesting in this regard, I might add. In a Theraplay video a parent and child undertake a series of planned tasks. Often, one task will be several minutes of the parent rubbing cream into the child's hand or arm, and then the child doing the same with the parent. Remarks about body experience are almost sure to emerge, and the quality of how they are made and received can be clinically informative.

More generally, when you see perceptual disclosure exchanges, or see what could have been opportunities for them, keep in mind certain questions. How well is the child learning to give conscious attention to their perceptual world, body sensations included? How well are they learning to finding appropriate language for these experiences?

How effectively does the parent encourage and support their sharing about them? How effectively does the parent model such sharing? And with regard to tactile and kinesthetic experience, is the parent helping the child to learn how to become at home in their body?

In the therapy literature about mentalization, sensory awareness and perceptual experience are seldom mentioned. Yet this is surely also a basic component of our inner lives.[5]

So far we have been looking at mentalization disclosure. Consider, now, what we might call mentalization inquiry. This occurs when person A asks person B something about their, person B's, inner world. A's question reflects a concern with other-mentalization, in other words.

Emotion inquiry is questioning about feelings. "How do you feel about this?" "How are you reacting to what happened this morning?"

Thought inquiry occurs when person A asks person B about his thoughts or opinion or point of view. It might be as simple as, "What do you think about it," where the "it" refers to something person A has just said. It might be a wider probing, for example, "Tell me something about your perspective on [subject X]."

Wish inquiry is questioning about desires and wants. "What would you like to do after school tomorrow?" "Which dessert do you prefer?" "What solution would fit best for you?"

Intention inquiry is questioning about what someone else has been doing, or has decided to do. Suppose father sees Tom carrying a chair. Then, in a certain sense, father already knows what the behavior is – Tom is crossing the room with this heavy object. Still perhaps he, father, doesn't know what Tom is up to, so he asks, "What are you doing now?"

Plenty of times someone's intention is not apparent from the outside. One reason is actions as experienced by the actor can have different levels of description.[6] Tom might reply that he is preparing the dining room table for dinner. Or he might reply that he is showing his little sister that he is strong enough to carry the chair. Or he might reply that the chair has something broken and he is taking it to the basement to fix it.

Perceptual inquiry is similar. "Are these pants too tight on you?" a parent might ask a child.

Next, let's look at mentalization hypothesizing. This, too, is spoken mentalization. But here, instead of asking about the other's inner world, the speaker proposes a guess, a hypothesis about it.

Give close attention to these communications. They often are delicate. The intentions driving them can be quite diverse. Their effects on the other can be quite diverse.

Emotion hypothesizing is saying what you suppose the other person is now feeling.

Such a message might be quite positive. One helpful version, for example, can be a "Perhaps you are also feeling [emotion X]." Jerry has been telling his partner Lois that he is angry that his brother just called to cancel a planned visit. Lois, reading his nonverbal signs, proposes, "Maybe you are feeling sad about it too, Jerry," and he then admits it is so.

The exchange is productive. Jerry has more clarity now about his inner state. He also feels supported by Lois.

But emotion hypothesizing can also be negative. Perhaps a child, hesitantly mentioning they are feeling sad or down or something of the like, hears in response that no, they don't feel that way, they actually feel okay. This would be seriously invalidating. If it happens often enough it would cause the child to experience considerable confusion about their inner world.

Thought hypothesizing is the advancing of a guess about what the other person is thinking.

A majority of the time it amounts to a simple attempt at clarification. "I suppose that what you think about this is more or less that ...," one speaker might say, with a respectful tone. Here the statement is just a checking out. They, the speaker, are making sure they understand the other's opinion. This would be a positive purpose.

Some thought hypothesizing can be hostile, and even demeaning, however. "I know what's going on here, you just think you have a right to do whatever you want," remarks person A in an angry manner.

Concerning this last example, by the way, note two possibilities. One is that in reality the thoughts going on in person B are far from what A said. In that case, there are two problems. First, person A's beliefs about person B's inner experience are mistaken. Second, he is delivering his message in an inappropriate manner.

The other possibility is that person B is, in fact, operating at the moment with an exaggerated sense of entitlement. In this instance A's statement is not so off target with regard to B's inside state. All the same, person A's word choices and nonverbal style remain unproductive, and likely disruptive.

Wish hypothesizing is similar. It is a proposing about what the other person wants or wishes or desires. "I'm wondering if maybe what you really want is .... " Just as with thought hypothesizing there can be positive or negative versions.

Intention hypothesizing is a suggesting about why it is that the other person is doing something, has done something, or is planning to do something. "Am I right, that you're putting those books on the table because you're going to do your homework now?" Although akin to wish hypothesizing, intention hypothesizing is more frequently seen in interactions.

Intention hypothesizing, too, can have positive or negative functions. Perhaps the speaker just wants to be up to date about the other's actions. The "books on the table" example above might be this. Sometimes a speaker even desires to help the other person better understand some of the intentions driving their (the other person's) behavior. Arguably such co-thinking is frequent in psychotherapy.

In clinical videos, however, plenty of instances of intention hypothesizing appear obviously negative in quality. "The real reason you are doing that is …. " "The real reason you are saying that is …." A reaction of this kind can be both an inappropriate critique as well as a refusal to take seriously the other person's perspective.

Perceptual hypothesizing communicates a guess about the other's perceptual and sensory world. Two-year-old Linda is lying on her belly on the rug and mother is nicely massaging her back. "This feels good, huh?" remarks mother. Hopefully her tone and manner implicitly encourage Linda to give attention to the "good" and enjoy it as much as possible.

To complete our overview of spoken mentalization something more needs to be mentioned. All the examples so far have been of mentalizing concerning the present. Jim tells Doris about what he, Jim, is feeling right now. Or Jim asks Doris about what she is feeling now, or he is hypothesizes about what she is feeling now.

But reference to other time periods can be made. This, as well, you will hear in videos, and often enough.

Reference might be made to the past, for instance.[7] "What I was feeling when that happened was overwhelmed and sad, desperate almost," Jim remarks. Or he asks Susan, "When you first moved to New York, what was that like for you?" Or, hypothesizing, he tells Susan, "I'm imagining that when your sister first left home it must have been sad for you."

Reference might be made to the future. Jim comments, "When we visit Cathy and Tomosso in Italy I'm going to be so glad to see them." Inquiry or hypothesizing statements will be sometimes about the future too.

Reference might be made, also, to what we can call the counterfactual past. This is not what really happened then, but what might have happened – it is "counter" to the "facts." Counterfactual mentalizing is a kind of speculation. "If your mother could have come for a shorter period that would have worked better for me," says Jim. Inquiry or hypothesizing statements can be made about the counterfactual past too.

Finally, reference might be made to the counterfactual present. This is the present as it could have been if something about it were otherwise. "If only my inbox didn't have so many new e-mails I would be more relaxed this afternoon," says Jim. Inquiry or hypothesizing statements invoking a counterfactual present are also, at times, made.

Notice that these last examples I have given have been just about emotion disclosure, emotion inquiry, and emotion hypothesizing. But obviously, equivalent communications can be made about thoughts, wishes, intentions, and perceptual experience. For instance, "If that chair only had a pillow you would probably be more comfortable," to take a perceptual experience example.

Let me quickly summarize the mentalization categories just seen. Proposed has been that mentalizing can be about any of the following:

- emotions
- thoughts
- wishes and desires
- preferences
- intentions
- sensory experience

Spoken mentalizing can then occur in any of these forms:

- disclosure
- inquiry
- hypothesizing

Moreover, spoken mentalizing can make reference to any of these time periods:

- the present
- the past
- the future
- the contrafactual past
- the contrafactual present

This might seem an excessively detailed grid (90 categories in all). But to get to know it is surprising easy, and you will find it helpful when analyzing videos.

I turn next to a series of closely related categories. These will either include mentalization as a component or will stand next door to it.

Some Mentalization-Related Categories

Preconditions awareness is very relevant in certain exchanges. Do there exist any special factors which might limit the other person's ability to comprehend what is being said? If yes, then the speaker needs to take them into account. To be aware of these factors can be considered a form of other-mentalization.

Developmental factors are an obvious example.[8] An adult speaking with a child has to choose words and phrase length which correspond to the child's current level of comprehension.

It is a frequent issue in video work, actually. Most often the problem is the adult speaks at too high a level. Occasionally the level is too low, which means opportunities to stimulate the child's language development are being passed by.

Neurological conditions can be relevant in an analogous way. Suppose the listener is an adult with an intellectual disability. Here, too, the speaker needs to give careful attention to word choice and perhaps phrase length.

Or, another example, suppose the listener is an adolescent with serious attention-deficit/hyperactivity disorder problems. Suppose, too, that this child's language development is average or higher. The problem, however, is that her attention span may be severely limited. This will produce its own kind of conversation constraints, ones the speaker needs to be aware of.

Attachment transactions are a complex type of interaction. I use this special term to highlight their significance. You will see them sometimes in videos.

An attachment transaction has three parts. Watch each carefully.

First, one person in the interaction, child or adult, displays an attachment need. They have become sad or fearful, for example, a state of neediness meriting coregulation from the other. They need soothing, consoling.

They make this emotion disclosure verbally or nonverbally or both. Notice the disclosure's form and manner. To what extent is it open, congruent, direct?

Second comes the other's response. Observe the level of competence here. Is it a confirming response, or a dismissing one? Is a response even given? How usefully does this second person soothe, console, and so on? To take just one example, a negative one, in a Strange Situation video we might see the parent immediately respond, and in an initially confirming manner. But then their actions become, for example, hectic or even frantic. The child's overaroused state stays the same or even worsens.[9]

The third piece, equally important, is what happens next on the part of the first person. Track this too, as it represents still another set of abilities. Suppose the second person has, in fact, managed to provide some minimum of competent soothing. How well can the first person, the one who expressed the need, take it in? How well can they use the coregulation help? Can they let themselves be comforted, be regulated down?

The same three steps are required when an attachment transaction occurs between two adults.[10] To take one example, you might observe that the need is communicated well enough, and the soothing support provided well enough, but then, during the third step, the need state person seems unable to make use of the support. They can't let themselves be regulated down.

Each step requires its own skills. Video intervention can be an excellent way to help an adult or older child with any of these. And, of course, when a small child is concerned, then the adult can be assisted with how to help the child develop the needed skills.[11]

Validation is a special form of mentalization hypothesizing which, deservedly, has been much discussed in the clinical literature.[12]

Validation normally consists of a response to another person's communication. This other person has just expressed an opinion, feeling, wish, or intention – a mentalizing disclosure, in other words.

The speaker who now validates conveys back a message with two parts. First, they, the speaker, indicate that they have conceptually understood the other's thought, feeling, wish or intention.

Second, they also indicate that they understand why it is that such a thought, feeling, wish or intention is present in the other person. "You're so stupid, so stupid!" insists a furious teenage daughter, protesting against her mother's stand that she, the daughter, cannot leave for the weekend with a certain friend group. "I know you really want to go, these are friends you like a lot," replies mother, validating the daughter's standpoint.

A key point, of course, is that for me to validate what you just said need not imply I agree with what you said. My own opinion, feeling, and so on, might be quite different. What I am communicating is just that I now grasp what you mean, and to a certain extent I can sympathize with it.

Validation, as frequently pointed out, can help keep disputes and disagreements from escalating into excessive anger. It is not certain to prevent this, but it can help. I would also suggest that validation can add economy to the exchange. Once person A takes in that person B has understood them, there will be less need for them to keep repeating the message. They can move on to next steps in the discourse.

Be aware, by the way, that there can also be very short versions of validations. "Sure, I see," murmurs Jack, during a conflictual discussion with Rachael. The examples given in the clinical literature are usually more complex. But sometimes even a minimal validation can effectively convey understanding. If you were watching the Jack and Rachael video, a good indicator of the effectiveness of Jack's statement would be Rachael's next response, and especially its bodily quality. Moreover, at times a short turn can seem better in terms of keeping up the conversation flow.

Assertions are a mentalizing variant which also deserve discussion. I am using the word in its familiar clinical sense.[13] A person expresses, openly and perhaps forcefully, something they desire, for example, "I really want to spend a couple of hours by myself tomorrow." At other times the assertion, coming as a response to something the other has just said, might be a simple refusal, for example, "No, not now," or "Sorry, no."

This is a form of spoken wish disclosure, clearly enough. But often there is something more too. I am saying my wish, but I am also expressing, implicitly or explicitly, that I think I have a right to it. The clinical literature sometimes speaks of a person "asserting themselves," for instance, which of course makes no sense grammatically but which nicely conveys this "having a right" aspect.

Many therapy approaches concern themselves with the capacity to make assertions. If a patient, in their life, holds back too much from openly stating wishes and needs, change in this area will commonly become a theme in the therapy. It is a frequent goal in VIT as well.

In a clinical video, any moments when one would expect an interaction participant to make an assertion are therefore of strong interest. Does the patient use the opportunity, actually making an assertion? If yes, is their statement sufficiently clear? How is the manner? Does the patient's nonverbal style render the assertion halfhearted, wishy-washy? Or, the opposite, is the assertion overdone, excessively dramatic?

Some patients, of course, swing back and forth, at times failing to assert themselves and at other times doing so in too pushy a form.[14] With such a patient you may well see in today's video either just the one mode or just the other. Or you may see both.

Another point to keep in mind is this. As I have already mentioned, in many kinds of interaction excessive repetition is a negative factor, as it keeps the dialogue from moving forward. Repetition of an assertion, however, can sometimes function otherwise.

Suppose the video is of a volatile, hostile exchange. Suppose you observe one person expressing her wish repeatedly, using more or less the same wording. This may represent a constructive choice. She thereby maintains her position, despite attacks and criticisms. In addition, the very act of repeating the same thing can be a way to avoid slipping into a counterattack mode.

Negotiations are another complex interaction phenomenon. Some videos are filmed specifically to put a negotiation center stage. Another name often used for this type of exchange is problem-solving.

Spoken wish disclosure, or assertions, in other words, are obviously central to negotiations. Validations can play an important role too.

At times, other types of spoken mentalizing can aid as well. "It sounds like a good movie, but I'm tired. Well, I don't know …," says Harry, who is having trouble clarifying what he would like. "Maybe for you it would be better we see it this weekend instead of tonight," comments Sandra, stimulating Harry to answer, "Yes, good, during the weekend." Sandra here uses wish hypothesizing. Wish inquiry, wish hypothesizing, emotion inquiry, and emotion hypothesizing can all be productive in such moments.

Simple emotion disclosure can put information on the table too. "That idea for a solution makes me anxious right away." "I think if we went there for our vacation a lot of the time I would feel bored."

In the therapy literature one can find an assortment of theories about how a negotiation should proceed – three stages, five stages, and so on. Certainly, these theories have useful ideas but do they perhaps set the bar quite high? I wonder, because I have seen a lot of negotiation videos which had decent outcomes but poorly fitted a stages model.[15]

Possibly a simpler criterion of a satisfactory negotiation might have two parts. First, the atmosphere stays reasonably respectful (including the possibility of "neutral," that is, emotionally flat respectfulness). And second, a co-decision moment is successfully arrived at, with clear acknowledging statements from both (or more) sides about what has now been decided.

I turn now to some categories which are useful specifically for scanning parent-infant or parent-child videos.

To start with, consider what is often called "descriptive language," a concept favored by a number of useful parent-infant and parent-child treatment approaches.[16] How does this notion map onto the mentalization perspective discussed here so far?

Basically, the forms of descriptive language typically advocated are forms of mentalization hypothesizing. I will explain.

Parent descriptive language for feelings is one form. For instance, a child is playing. Her mother, perhaps following psychoeducation advice she has learned, comments, "You like that bear a lot." Patently this is mentalization emotion hypothesizing.

Parent descriptive language for wishes is another. "Ah, you want the other doll." Here we have mentalization wish hypothesizing.

Parent descriptive language for what the child is doing is another. "You are putting the train on the track." In most instances this can be regarded as intention hypothesizing.

Parent descriptive language for what the child sees or hears is yet another. "It's a big red ball," says a father to his 3-year-old daughter, who is holding and looking at the ball. Such comments are sensory hypothesizing.

These are the standard recommendations. Almost all VIT therapists use them also. In addition, I aim for two more variants, as follows.

Parent self-description for feelings is one.[17] The mother might say to the child, "I like that bear too." This is mentalization emotion disclosure.

Needless to say, a parent should be careful about what feelings to mention to a child, and when, and spoken about how.

Parent self-description for intentions is similar. "I am putting the engine on the track." "I'm going to go in the kitchen for just a minute, I will be right back." The first example is of present and the second of future intention disclosure.

What might be the importance in these parent-child spoken mentalizing variants? McNeil and Hembree-Kigin, writing about their use in Parent-Child Interaction Therapy (2010), offer some good reflections.

For one thing, the child is being made aware that they have the parent's full attention, and are being held in mind. Second, what the parent says likely stimulates language development. These are words which correspond to objects and actions the child is immediately focused upon. Third, they probably aid the child in concentrating better, and perhaps structuring their activity better.

I would add that the parent self-descriptions suggested above, for feelings and intentions, likely have their own advantages. For one thing, they help the child to learn how to mentalize about the parent.

Second, the parent is doing good modeling. Over time the child can better learn how, on his own part, to do appropriate mentalizing disclosure to others, a valuable interaction skill.

So for all these reasons, when observing videos of parent-infant and parent-small child interaction, be on the lookout for opportunities for descriptive language statements, and for actual occurrences of them. It is an area that is definitely worth thematizing.

Praise is another speaking behavior which has received much attention in the therapy world, and for good reason. Especially in parent-child interactions it is seen as productive. It gives positive reinforcement for wished-for behaviors.[18] It also can help create a nice tone to the interaction.

I would suggest that praise has a significant mentalization component embedded in it. The reason has to do with what I will call action awareness.

As someone executes an action there will be an internal following, a tracking and evaluating, of the action.[19] It may be largely nonconscious, but bits and pieces are likely to be conscious, at least marginally. Now I am bringing the cup of coffee to the table …. I need to move a little more slowly, I might spill it … now as I put it on the table I better move my arm even more slowly … there, no problem, I did it just fine.

Often such inner monitoring will finish up with a concluding evaluation, a last commentary on the action as a whole. Of course, this evaluation will now and then continue afterwards: for example, I should have organized those boxes more carefully, I should have taken more time for it, and so on.

What, then, might be the effect of praise from someone else? The praise message likely functions as a kind of suggestion, a kind of proposal, for the action person's inner evaluating. The parent says overtly, "Hey, you cleaned your room really well." But this is also as if to say, "In your inner state right now, as you evaluate what you did, notice in fact how good it was." The parent is making a suggestion for how the child mentalizes about the action, in other words.[20]

Naturally a second message is implied as well. This is, more or less, "Be aware too that I, your parent, appreciate what you did." This second message is a form of emotion disclosure on the parent's part.

Praise, of course, is not confined to parent-child interactions. An adult can praise another adult, or one child can praise another.

Nevertheless, I will add a few more comments about parent-child praise. First, if we look at praise from the angle I am suggesting, it seems apparent that by giving the praise the parent is doing two kinds of teaching at the time. On the one hand, they are reinforcing the child's behavior, and thereby aiding the child in learning to do that behavior regularly. On the other hand, they are also aiding the child in learning a more precise and fitting type of action monitoring. It could even be that this second lesson is, in the long run, the more important of the two.

Returning, then, to practical observation, let me add three details worth noticing when you hear praise being given in a parent-child video. First, how is it worded? A general consensus in the therapy literature is that short and simple is preferable.

Second, how explicit is the message? Here clinicians are divided. Some hold that praise should always be so-called labeled praise, with what is being praised specifically named. "Good work, how you helped your sister find her blanket," is an example. Others, myself included, are fine with some praise being labeled and some being minimally brief. "Nice going!," "Well done", and "Okay!" are examples of minimally brief.[21]

Third, how frequently are praise messages being given? Here, too, clinicians are divided. Consider a parent and small child play context. Some clinicians are for a steady stream of praises. At least one praise every 30 seconds is one recommendation, for example.[22] Others, myself too, finding this excessive, prefer a more dosed use, with the exact frequency dependent upon the concrete occurring events.

Limit setting is a critical area in some videos. Usually the interaction will be an adult-child one. Perhaps the filmed task was even designed so that a need to set limits would be likely.

Most therapists are well versed in what to look for here. One significant part is how the instruction – the command – is stated. We want to hear an instruction that is simple, short, and phrased in words appropriate for the child's language capacity.

In addition, the message, ideally, will have no ambiguity. "Come sit down at the table now," not, "Would you like to come sit down at the table now?"

A reference to a positive behavior rather than a negative one is also helpful: not, "Don't throw the toys into the box," but, "Put the toys carefully into the box." The idea underlying all these word choices is that we want the child cognitively to focus as sharply as possible on the wished-for behavior.

Apart from that, we hope to hear an absence of criticisms and negative labeling. We want, also, to hear praise if the child does the requested behavior, however partially, or a repeat of the command if the child does not. Consequences may need to be mentioned too. All this is standard, from one influential point of view.[23]

Videos can be an invaluable help with every bit of this. You can give careful attention to the instruction itself, and then you can track exactly how the interaction continues. On the child's side, what are the nuances of their behavior? Do they appear simply stubborn, or simply out of control, or do they seem to seek to provoke? On the adult's side, what is the ongoing body shaping, the nonverbal manner? And, of course, how effective are their, the adult's, continuing messages – their repetitions of the instruction, and perhaps an implementation of a consequence?

Interestingly enough, there can be a place in all this, in some limit-setting interactions, for spoken mentalization. First, in some contexts, when the instruction is initially given it can be appropriate to add a mentalizing hypothesis about wishes. Father might first say, "Put down the iPad and come now to the lunch table." But he might then add, "I know you want to keep playing the video game, but we going to eat so you have to come to the table." The idea is to offer the child workable language for the complexity of their experience. They now have words for their inner dilemma, the conflict between what they have to do as opposed to what they would prefer to do.

Second, if the situation escalates and the child goes into meltdown mode, a possible way for the parent to continue is to stay fairly close to the child, physically, and to continue with additional spoken mentalizing. Comments can be offered such as, "It's hard, I know," "It's hard for you, you're all upset," or "It's upsetting, I understand, you can't do what you want and you have to come to the table."

Here again opinions are divided, needless to say. Some therapists, myself too, see a value in this second type of accompanying.[24] Others prefer that the parent simply withdraw. I will not enter into this dispute here. The point is that if you do recommend the "staying close" option to parents, to be able, with a video, to observe how they actually try to implement it is invaluable.

What about when an adult sets a limit with another adult? Usually this has a quite different structure.

Most of the time what we hear is simply a variant of assertiveness. Whether or not the message is effective then depends on the interaction context, on who the other person happens to be, and the like.

Sally may say to Grant, "No, I definitely don't want to do that," clear and simple. Or she may say, "I think I don't want to do that, what I am thinking is …," and continue with a slightly meandering further disclosure. But usually this second version will also work well enough, as long as the embedded boundary message is clearly stated.

The critical questions then of course are, first, how does Grant respond. And second, if he doesn't agree on his side, or even continues his discourse without even referring to what she said, then what does Sally say and do in order to maintain her position. You will need carefully to evaluate subsequent turn-takings in that case.

This concludes our three chapters of observation suggestions. Naturally more categories could be added, but the list is already long.

A summary of the spoken mentalization categories was given earlier in this chapter. Let me now add a second summary. This will be of the additional categories covered, the more complex ones which include spoken mentalization as a component.

- preconditions awareness
- validation
- assertions
- negotiations
- parent descriptive language for feelings
- parent descriptive language for wishes
- parent descriptive language for what the child is doing
- parent descriptive language for what the child sees or hears
- parent self-description for intentions
- praise
- limit-setting

Notes

1 What the feeling is about is called the "intentional object" in emotion theory (Downing, 2000).

2 But if I share a wish for X doesn't this also imply a preference for X? Indeed it does. One could in fact argue that wishes are just a subtype of preferences. Nevertheless

on a practical level the wish/preference distinction is quite practical to keep in mind when scanning clinical videos. Wish disclosures are often quite more relevant than preference disclosures.

3 I am leaving out another possible category: what we might call action awareness. As I execute an action I am often aware, to a degree, of how the action is going and what it is like to do it. For example, I might say, "I'm having trouble here giving everyone a coffee." Note the difference in this statement from the intention disclosure example just given. The reason I am leaving it out is that action awareness as spoken mentalization rarely shows up in clinical videos. (One exception, however, I will be mentioning shortly, in the discussion below of praise.)

4 A nice point, emphasized by Aarts (2008).

5 In the background, here, there are some interesting theoretical issues which I will not pursue now. For a well-argued wider perspective on mentalization contents see Kriegel (2015).

6 See Davidson (2001).

7 It is interesting to note that when first developed, the concept of mentalization had mostly to do with past mentalizing. Fonagy et al. (1998) worked out the Reflective Function coding system as an alternative perspective to use with Adult Attachment Interview (AAI) transcripts. AAI transcripts are almost entirely about the interviewee's childhood past.

8 Reflective Function research coding (Fonagy et al., 1991) emphasizes this, one entire scale being devoted to it.

9 This is one pattern typical with an ambivalent attachment (Ainsworth et al., 1978).

10 Bodenmann's research of what he calls Dyadic Coping (one adult helps another with a stress state) is of considerable interest here (e.g., Bodenmann, 2000; Falconier, Randall & Bodenmann, 2016). Sue Johnson has also discussed what I am here calling attachment transactions between adults (e.g., 2002, 2019).

11 Naturally, in the case of a small child the new skills needed will usually have to do with either the first step (giving a clear needs signal) or the third (taking in and using the provided consoling). But does this mean a small child never takes on the role of the consoling person, that is, never engages in Step 2? A fascinating result from attachment research is that a small minority of children aged 1–3 years indeed acquire this capacity. They use it, and in a sense overuse it, to console the adult. These are children who at 12 months, if tested with Strange Situation, display a disorganized attachment. During the subsequent months they then develop what has been called "compulsive caregiving" strategies, probably as a means of gaining more control in the context of their relationship to the adult (Marvin & Britner, 1999).

12 See, for example, Gottman (1999), Hughes (2010), and Lineham (1993).

13 In most theoretical frameworks about language, for example speech act theory, an assertion is merely a direct statement of some supposed fact (e.g., Searle, 1969).

14 Lineham (1993) has well described this phenomenon.

15 Typically, with these videos, the therapist's corrective intervention had to do with specific language use and/or expressive style, not "stages."

16 Eyberg's Parent-Child Interaction Therapy is one such well-known approach (e.g., McNeil & Hembree-Kigin, 2010).

17 The usefulness of parental descriptive language for the parent themselves has been nicely elaborated by Aarts (2008).

18 Naturally, a few forms of praise are not for behaviors. "What a handsome boy," exclaims a father as his son is looking at himself in the mirror.

19 As mentioned in Endnote 3, action awareness is another component of unspoken, inner mentalization, one not included here in the spoken mentalization categories since interactional talk about actions almost always speaks about intentions.

20 Interestingly, Meins and Fernyhough (2015), in their coding of "mind-mindedness," include praise as a positive indicator, albeit without explaining why.
21 In this regard, I would suggest it is easy to underrate the extent to which even small children are aware of the contextual implications of spoken messages (cf. Sperber and Wilson, 1995).
22 This is the standard proposal in Parent-Child Interaction Therapy (McNeil & Hembree-Kigin 2010).
23 This approach has been elaborated by Gerald Patterson (1975), Webster-Stratton (2005) and numerous others.
24 Some therapists who appreciate the "stay close" option advocate it for all families. Others, myself included, see it rather as a plan B approach, for cases where the standard procedure simply doesn't bring about change.

References

Aarts, M. (2008). *Marte Meo: Basic manual* (2nd ed.). Eindhoven, Netherlands: Aarts Productions.

Alger, I. (1976). Integrating immediate video-playback in family therapy. In P. Guerin (Ed.), *Family therapy: Theory and practice* (pp. 530–547). New York: Gardner Press.

Asen, E., & Fonagy, P. (2021). *Mentalization-based treatment with families*. New York: Guilford Press.

Bateman, A., & Fonagy, P. (2004). *Psychotherapy for borderline personality disorder: Mentalization-based treatment*. New York: Oxford University Press.

Bateson, G. (2000). *Steps to an ecology of mind*. Chicago: University of Chicago Press.

Beck, A., Rush, J., Shaw, B., & Emery, G. (1979). *Cognitive therapy of depression*. New York: Guilford Press.

Beebe, B. (2003). Brief mother-infant treatment: Psychoanalytically-informed video feedback. *Infant Mental Health Journal, 24*(1), 24–52.

Beebe, B. (2006). Co-constructing mother-infant distress in face-to-face interactions: Psychoanalytically-informed video feedback. *Infant Observation, 9*(2), 151–164.

Beebe, B., Cohen, P., Sossin, M., & Markese, S. (2012). *Mothers, infants, and young children of September 11, 2001: A primary prevention project*. New York: Routledge.

Beebe, B., & Lachmann, F. (2014). *The origins of attachment: Infant research and adult treatment*. London: Routledge.

Berg, I. K. (1994). *Family-based services: A solution-based approach*. New York: W. W. Norton.

Bowlby, J. (1979). *The making and breaking of affectional bonds*. London: Tavistock.

Buckwater, K., & Downing, G. (2017). Slowing down the dance: Use of video intervention therapy with parents and children. In K. Buckwater & D. Reed (Eds.), *Attachment-based interventions with children & adolescents* (pp. 441–466). Lanham, MD: Rowman & Littlefield.

Carter, S., Osofsky, J., & Hann, I. (1991). Speaking for the baby: A therapeutic invention with adolescent mothers and their infants. *Infant Mental Health Journal, 12*(4), 291–301.

Coan, J., & Gottman, J. (2007). The specific affect coding system. In J. Coan & J. Allen (Eds.), *Handbook of emotion and assessment* (pp. 267–285). Oxford, England: Oxford University Press.

de Shazer, S. (1984). The death of resistance. *Family Process, 23*(1), 11–17.

Dishion, T., & Kavanagh, K. (2003). *Intervening in adolescent problem behavior: A family-centered approach*. New York: Guilford Press.

Downing, G. (2000). Emotion theory reconsidered. In: M. Wrathall & J. Malpas (Eds.), *Heidegger, coping and cognitive science: Essays in honor of Hubert L. Dreyfus* (pp. 245–270). Cambridge, MA: MIT Press.

Downing, G. (2008). A different way to help. In A. Fogel, B. King, & S. Shanker (Eds.), *Human development in the 21st century: Visionary ideas from systems scientists* (pp. 200–205). Cambridge, England: Cambridge University Press.

Downing, G. (2010). La video microanalisi nella terapie della coppia madre-bambino [The use of video microanalysis in the therapy of mother-infant dyads]. *Ricerca Psichoanalitica: Revista della Relazione in Psichoanalisi, 21*(1), 9–18.

Downing, G. (2015a). Early interaction and the body: Clinical implications. In G. Marlock, H. Weiss, C. Young, & M. Soth (Eds.), *The handbook of body psychotherapy and somatic psychology*. Berkeley, CA: North Atlantic Books.

Downing, G. (2015b). Work with mentalization in video intervention therapy: Help for children, adolescents, and their parents. Published in Italian translation in F. Lambruschi, & F. Lionetti (Eds.), *Strumenti de valutazione e interventi de sostengo alla genitorialita* (pp. 211–232). Rome: Carocci.

Downing, G. (2020). An unusual window: Commentary on paper by Larry Sandberg and Beatrice Beebe. *Psychoanalytic Dialogues, 30*(4), 499–505.

Dowrick, P. (1991). *Practical guide to using video in the behavioral sciences*. New York: Wiley & Sons.

Dozier, M., Lindhiem, O., & Ackerman, J. (2005). Attachment and biobehavioral catch-up: An intervention targeting empirically identified foster infants. In L. Berloin, Y. Ziv, L. Amaya-Jackson, & M. Greenberg (Eds.), *Enhancing early attachments: Theory, research, intervention, and policy interview* (pp. 178–194). New York: Guilford Press.

Dozier, M., Roben, C., Caron, E., Hoye, J., & Bernard, K. (2018). Attachment and biobehavioral catch-up: An evidence-based intervention for vulnerable infants and their families. *Psychotherapy Research, 28*(1), 18–29.

Erickson, M., & Egeland, B. (2004). Linking theory and research to practice: The Minnesota Longitudinal Study of Parents and Children and the STEEP Program. *Clinical Psychologist, 8*(1): 5–9.

Facchini, S., Martin, V., & Downing, G. (2016). Pediatricians, well-baby visits, and video intervention therapy: Feasibility and acceptability of a video-feedback infant mental health support intervention in a pediatric primary health care setting. *Frontiers in Psychology, 7*, Article e179.

Foa, E., Hembree, E., & Rothbaum, B. (2007). *Prolonged exposure therapy for PSTD: Emotional processing of traumatic experiences (treatments that work)*. Oxford, England: Oxford University Press.

Fonagy, P. (1991). Thinking about thinking: Some clinical and theoretical considerations in the treatment of a borderline patient. *International Journal of Psychoanalysis, 72*, 639–656.

Fonagy, P. (2008). The mentalization-focused approach to social development. In F. Busch (Ed.), *Mentalization: Theoretical considerations, research findings, and clinical applications*. Mahwah, NJ: Analytic Press.

Fonagy, P., Steele, M., Steele, H., Moran, G. & Higgitt, A. (1991). The capacity for understanding mental states: The reflective self in parent and child and its significance for security of attachment. *Infant Mental Health Journal, 12*(3), 201–218.

Fraiberg, S., Adelson, E. & Shapiro, V. (1975). Ghosts in the nursery: A psychoanalytic approach to problems of impaired infant-mother relationships. *Journal of American Academy of Child Psychiatry, 14*(3), 347–421.

Greenberger, D., & Padesky, C. (1995). *Mind over mood: Change how you feel by changing the way you think*. New York: Guilford Press.

Gottman, J. (1979). *Martial interaction: Experimental investigations*. New York: Academic Press.

Hackmann, A., Bennett-Levy, J., & Holmes, E. (2011). *Oxford guide to imagery in cognitive therapy*. Oxford, England: Oxford University Press.

Heller, M. (2012). *Body psychotherapy: History, concepts, methods*. New York: W. W. Norton.

Hunter, M. (2007). *Healing scripts: Using hypnosis to treat trauma and stress*. New York: Barnes & Noble.

Juffer, F., Bakermans-Kranenburg, M., & van Ijzendoorn, M. (Eds.). (2007). *Promoting positive parenting: An attachment-based intervention*. New York: Routledge.

Kennedy, H, Landor, M., & Todd, L. (Eds.) (2011). *Video Interaction Guidance: A relationship-based intervention to promote attunement, empathy & wellbeing*. London: Jessica Kingsley.

Lamb, W., & Watson, E. (1987). *Body code: The meaning in movement*. London: Routledge.

Leahy, R., Tirch, D. & Napolitano, L. (2011). *Emotion regulation in psychotherapy: A practitioner's guide*. New York: Guilford Press.

Levine, P. (1997). *Waking the tiger*. Berkeley, CA: North Atlantic Books.

Lillas, C., & Turnbull J. (2009). *Infant/child mental health, early intervention, and relationship-based therapies: A neurorelational framework for interdisciplinary practice*. New York: W. W. Norton.

Lyons-Ruth, K., Bronfman, E., & Parsons, E. (1999). Managing frightened, frightening, or atypical behavior and disorganized infant attachment patterns. *Monographs of the Society for Research in Child Development*, 64(3), 67–96.

Malekoff, A. (2015). *Group work with adolescents*. New York: Guilford Press.

Marvin, R., Cooper, G., Hoffman, K., & Powell, B. (2002). The Circle of Security project: Attachment-based intervention with caregiver-preschool child dyads. *Attachment & Human Development*, 4(1), 107–124.

McEvoy, P., Saulsman, L., & Rapee, R. (2018). *Image-enhanced CBT for social anxiety disorder*. New York: Guilford Press.

McDonough, S. (1995). Promoting positive early parent-infant relationships through interaction guidance. *Child and Adolescent Psychiatric Clinics of North America*, 4(3), 661–672.

McNally, R. (1987). Preparedness and phobias: A review. *Psychological Bulletin*, 101(2), 283–303.

McNeil, C., & Hembree-Kigin, T. (2010). *Parent-child interaction therapy*. New York: Springer.

Morlinghaus, K. (2012). Korperorientierte Psychotherapie und Tanztherapie auf der Mutter-Kind-Einheit in Heidelberg. In S. Wortmann-Fleischer, C. Hornstein, & G. Downing (Eds.), *Stationaere Eltern-Kind-Behandlung: Ein interdisziplinaerer Praxisleitfaden* (pp. 157–161). Stuttgart: Kohlhammer.

Murphy, C., & Eckhardt, C. (2005). *Treating the abusive partner: An individualized cognitive-behavioral approach*. New York: Guilford Press.

Ogden, P., Minton, K., & Pain, C. (2006). *Trauma and the body: A sensimotor approach to psychotherapy*. New York: W. W. Norton.

Oppenheim, D., & Koren-Karie, N. (2002). Mothers' insightfulness regarding their children's internal worlds: The capacity underlying secure child-mother relationships. *Infant Mental Health Journal*, 23(6), 593–605.

Papoušek, M., & Wollwerth de Chuquisengo, R. (2006). Integrative kommunikationszentriete Eltern-Kindkind-Psychottherapie bei frühkindlichen Regulationsstörungen. *Praxis der Kinderpsychologie und Kinderpsychiatrie*, 55(4), 235–254.

Persons, J. (1989). *Cognitive therapy in practice: A case formulation approach*. New York: W. W. Norton.

Porges, S. (2011). *The polyvagal theory: Neurophysiological foundations of emotions, attachment, communication, and self-regulation*. New York: W.W. Norton.

Powell, B., Cooper, G., Hoffman, K., & Marvin, R. (2014). *The Circle of Security intervention: Enhancing attachment in early parent-child relationships*. New York: Guilford Press.

Riva Crugnola, C., Ieradi, E., Albizzati, A., & Downing, G. (2018). Promoting responsiveness, emotion regulation and attachment in young mothers and infants: An implementation of video intervention therapy and psychological support. In H. Steele & M. Steele (Eds.), *Handbook of attachment-based interventions* (pp. 441–465). New York: Guilford Press.

Rothstein, A. & Arnold, R. (1976). Bridging the gap: Application of research on videotape feedback and bowling. *Motor Skills: Theory Into Practice, 1*, 35–64.

Sandberg, L., & Beebe, B. (2020). A patient who does not look: A collaborative treatment with video feedback. *Psychoanalytic Dialogues, 30*(4), 479–498.

Shapiro, F. (2018). *Eye movement desensitization and reprocessing (EMDR) therapy*. New York: Guilford Press. Levine

Shia, D., & Fonagy, P. (2014). Beyond words: Parent embodied mentalizing and the parent- infant dance. In M. Mikulincer & P. R. Shaver (Eds.), *Mechanisms of social connection: From brain to group* (pp. 185–203). Washington, DC: American Psychological Association.

Sperber, D., & Wilson, D. (1995). *Relevance: Communication and cognition* (2nd ed.). Oxford, England: Blackwell.

Sroufe, L. & Ward, J. (1980). Seductive behavior of mothers of toddlers: Occurrences, correlates, and family origins. *Child Development, 51*(4), 1222–1229.

Slade, A., Sadler, L. S., & Mayes, L. (2005.) Minding the baby: Enhancing parental reflective functioning in a nursing/mental health home visiting program. In L. Berlin, Y. Zi, L. Amaya-Jackson & M. Greenberg (Eds.), *Enhancing early attachments: Theory, research, intervention and policy*, (pp. 152–177). New York: Guilford Press.

Steele, H. & Steele, M. (2008). On the origins of reflective functioning. In F. Busch (Ed.), *Mentalization: Theoretical considerations, research findings, and clinical implications* (pp. 133–158). New York: Analytic Press.

Steele, H. & Steele, M. (Eds.) (2018). *Handbook of attachment-based interventions*. New York: Guilford Press.

Steele, M., Steele, H., Bate, J., Knafo, H., Kinsy, M., Bonuck, K., Meisner, P., & Murphy, A. (2014). Looking from the outside in: The use of video in attachment-based interventions. *Attachment & Human Development, 16*(4), 402–415.

Stern, D. (1985). *The interpersonal world of the infant: A view from psychoanalysis and developmental psychology*. New York: Routledge.

Thoma, N. C., & Greenberg, L. S. (2015). Integrating emotion-focused therapy into cognitive-behavioral therapy. In N. C. Thoma & D. McKay (Eds.), *Working with emotion in cognitive-behavioral therapy: Techniques for clinical practice* (pp. 239–262). New York: Guilford Press.

Tomasello, M. (2008). Origins of Human Communication. Cambridge, MA: MIT Press.

Tompkins, M. (2004). *Using homework in psychotherapy: Strategies, guidelines, and forms*. New York: Guilford Press.

Tronick, E. (2007). *The neurobehavioral and social-emotional development of infants and children*. New York: W. W. Norton.

von der Kolk, B. (2014). *The body keeps the score: Brain, mind, & body in the healing of trauma*. New York: Viking Press.

Zayfert, C., & Becker, C. (2007). *Cognitive-behavioral therapy for PSTD: A case formulation approach*. New York: Guilford Press.

Index

For Product Safety Concerns and Information please contact our EU
representative GPSR@taylorandfrancis.com
Taylor & Francis Verlag GmbH, Kaufingerstraße 24, 80331 München, Germany

www.ingramcontent.com/pod-product-compliance
Lightning Source LLC
Chambersburg PA
CBHW050649280326
41932CB00015B/2845

9 781041 024477